OKINAWAN RELIGION

OKINAWAN RELIGION

Belief, Ritual, and Social Structure

▲▼▲ *William P. Lebra*

UNIVERSITY OF HAWAII PRESS

COPYRIGHT 1966 BY THE UNIVERSITY OF HAWAII PRESS
DESIGNED BY JAMES C. WAGEMAN △ MANUFACTURED IN
THE UNITED STATES OF AMERICA BY THE MISSION PRESS
LIBRARY OF CONGRESS CATALOG CARD NUMBER 66-16506

PREFACE

My study of Okinawan religion commenced in 1953–54 (September to June) during nine months of field research under the auspices of the Pacific Science Board of the National Research Council. From October of 1955 through August of 1957 I divided my time between Japan and the Ryukyu Islands, continuing field studies in the latter area and studying relevant literature available in Japan. In January of 1960 I returned to Okinawa and remained until August under a research grant (M-3084) from the National Institute of Mental Health. Finally, a brief trip was made in September and October, 1961, for the purpose of following up certain aspects of the 1960 research. Aside from minor changes, this manuscript was completed by the end of 1961.

The primary intent of this study has been to present a systematic, descriptive account of the indigenous religion of Okinawa. By "indigenous religion" I mean those beliefs, practices, and organizations constituting the autochthonous system rather than such religions as Buddhism and sectarian Shinto which have developed elsewhere and have remained coherent, recognizably foreign imports. This does not imply that Okinawan religion has evolved independently of any external influences, for quite the contrary can be shown to be the case. Numerous Buddhist concepts and practices, elements of Chinese folk religion, and resemblances to Shinto are easily detected; furthermore, this borrowing has been a long and cumulative process, one that continues to this day. There remain, nonetheless, many traits which appear to be purely local, and these as well as those of foreign origin have been integrated into a configuration unique to Okinawa and its neighbor islands. It is with this system that we shall be concerned.

A secondary focus relates to the process of change within a given historic context. Utilizing elderly informants and written sources, I have attempted to reconstruct the system as it was in the last quarter of the nineteenth century and to use this material for comparative purposes when describing the contemporary religion. During the lifetime of the oldest generation, Okinawa has been subject to extensive cultural, social, and physical changes of such magnitude that virtually no aspect of life or scene has escaped unaltered. Three governments—those of the Ryukyuan Kingdom, Japan, and the United States military occupation—have successively administered the area during the past eighty years; each has been the product of a different culture and marked by radically different programs and administrative objectives. World War II culminated in a catastrophic invasion which served to accelerate the process of change. Traditionally, Okinawan religion has been characterized by a collectivity focus; its main foci have been the state, community, kin group, and family-household. The advent of Japanese administration effected the collapse of the Ryukyuan state and state religion, but the community, kin group, and family have managed to preserve their ritual integrity with varying degrees of success until the present time. A marked decline in religious activities has occurred during the past fifty years, accompanied by the gradual emergence of individualism in contrast to the traditional emphasis on communalism and familialism. In the light of these changes, the persistence of certain aspects of the religious system and the rapid disappearance of others warrant our attention.

An ideal-type analysis has been followed throughout. Several factors necessitated selection of this method, the principal one being that it best served the objective of treating Okinawan religion as a total system while allowing variations to be gauged against the total construct. The process of change has not been uniform throughout the islands. Therefore, an attempt to amplify the religion of any given community, kin group, or household as representative of the whole would be misleading. For example, the presence or absence, support or nonsupport, of religious ceremonies within a given community has been determined by a variety of factors. Rural settlements of gentry origin have always been without formalized community ritual, while in many commoner villages that formerly had an active religious life, the death of the hereditary priestess(es) in the war brought an abrupt end to all communal rites. In other villages, though the priestess may still be alive, want of support by acculturated political leaders often precludes her enjoying any significant, active role. Fishing villages have retained a stronger emphasis on community religion than farming villages, while both decidedly exceed the towns and cities in this respect. One further reason has been that I have drawn heavily on written sources to supplement field data; these materials have been obtained from widely scattered areas of the island, still older unpublished manuscripts, and a variety of informants and observers. Here, any approach other than the ideal-type would simply have been impracticable.

Field data were gathered in all parts of Okinawa, from informants in more than one hundred communities ranging in size from Naha, the capital, down to small hamlets.[1] The major approach in field research was the interview, although the usual corollary techniques of observation, copying records, photographing, recording, mapping, etc., were also employed. I found that Okinawans tended to respond unfavorably to persistent direct questioning, as in following a rigid interview schedule or questionnaire. Consequently, most interviews were of the open-end type—when a given subject had been introduced, the informant was not unduly pressured by a barrage of predetermined questions but was allowed considerable freedom in discourse. No professional informants were employed, and no informants were paid for their services, although small gifts of food or tobacco were sometimes made. During the 1960 and 1961 field trips virtually all interviews were recorded.

Japanese and Okinawan were the languages of interviewing, and the services of an interpreter were employed. Most Okinawans today are bilingual, speaking Japanese and Okinawan, but the very old use the native language almost exclusively, while most country women appear to do so by preference. Not infrequently, discussion initiated in Japanese would lapse into Okinawan, for the simple reason that many informants were more articulate in the latter. In this study, Okinawan terms have been preserved wherever a given concept, practice, status, or item has proved sufficiently important to warrant distinction and/or defy accurate translation. The system of orthography followed is described in the Note on Foreign Words appearing on page xiv.

Source material on Okinawan religion in Western literature tends to be meager and superficial. Turning to Japanese sources, one is confronted not by a lack of material but rather by an absence of systemic approach.

For the most part, Japanese researchers have been of the folklorist (or more properly *Volkskunde*) school—usually students or disciples of Yanagita Kunio. The Okinawan contributors have been largely amateur folkhistorians. Commonly, the writings of these individuals have been based on very brief periods of field research (more in the nature of tours than protracted field studies), on personal reminiscences, or on the interpretation of old Okinawan literature. Japanese scholars early recognized many similarities between Okinawan religion and ancient Shinto; thus, for not a few the sole attraction of the former has been its significance with regard to the latter. In most studies the frame of reference has been Okinawan religion and culture vis-à-vis Japanese religion and culture. Use of comparative material from Taiwan, China, and Korea has been conspicuously absent. Excessive reliance on old literature and a lack of extensive field research have tended to produce studies which are either highly subjective and speculative or simply catalogues of the more obvious facets of this culture. The usefulness of such research has been further impaired by a steadfast refusal or inability to record Okinawan words as spoken. In virtually all studies save those of the linguists Hattori and Kinjō, Okinawan terms have been persistently Japanized; one must decode 'okode' into *ukudii*, 'noro' into *nuru*, 'nebito' into *niitchu*, and so on. Failure to check written data against the knowledge and speech of living informants not infrequently has produced ludicrous results. For example, the title of the chief priestess is regularly rendered as 'kikoe o gimi' in Japanese, but use of this title invariably elicits a blank response from informants, who are accustomed to the Okinawan *chifijing ganashii mee*. Much of the usual vocabulary of "native terms" is, consequently, without meaning in Japanese or Okinawan. If the nonspecialist reader feels inundated by native terms in my study, it should be remembered that I have tried to compensate for errors of the past and to ease the task of field workers to follow. No aspect of Okinawan research, however, can be undertaken without recourse to Japanese sources; I have merely sought here to indicate some of their limitations. Their usefulness will be attested by the frequency of citation.

During the past few years I have been amused by certain seemingly astute observers who have commented on the lack of religion among Okinawans. Basil Hall Chamberlain noted, "No country that I have ever visited shows scantier evidence of active religious influence than Loochoo,"[2] and not too long ago an American official on Okinawa remarked to me that, insofar as religion is concerned, "They haven't got any!" These points of view, at least, should be dispelled by this study. But an opposite situation may arise when one immerses himself in the religion of a particular people, as I have attempted, and that is the tendency to discern evidences of religion almost everywhere. Lest the reader unfamiliar with Okinawa gain the impression that these people are decidedly "otherwordly," I would like to repeat Allport's comment that, chronologically, viscerogenic or "bodily" values take precedence over psychogenic or "spiritual" values.[3]

My indebtedness extends to many people and institutions. The Pacific Science Board, the National Institute of Mental Health, and my parents have sustained me while in the field. The University of Pittsburgh twice granted a release from all teaching duties, and the East-West Center of the University of Hawaii provided me with support while writing. Further benefit was gained from colleagues of the first field trip, Drs. Forrest R. Pitts of the University of Hawaii and Wayne P. Suttles of the University of Nevada, with whom the exchange of ideas often provided insights which widened the scope of my research. Special appreciation must be accorded Mr. Kiyoshi Yogi of Naha, who functioned as field assistant, interpreter, and companion, and who did much to facilitate the progress of my research. Mr. Teruo Tanonaka of the United States Civil Administration gave freely of his hospitality and broad knowledge of the area on occasions too frequent to enumerate, and Mr. Dale Lock of Canada Dry of Okinawa frequently solved my transportation problems by loaning me his car. Lastly, my sincerest gratitude extends to innumerable Okinawans whose keen interest and kindly patience with the often trying questions of an outsider contributed so much to make the periods of field study both enjoyable and rewarding. Responsibility for the accuracy of data and conclusions derived therefrom, however, rests solely upon myself.

WILLIAM P. LEBRA
Honolulu

CONTENTS

FIGURES

TABLE

PLATES

Cover photograph courtesy F. R. Pitts

NOTE ON FOREIGN WORDS

With some modifications, the orthography developed by Chamberlain (1895*b*) has been employed in transcribing Okinawan speech, but use of the macron has been omitted and the vowel has been repeated to indicate length. His attempt at handling the glottal has been eschewed altogether without, I believe, any gross injustice to later attempts at replication. With the exception of proper nouns, Okinawan words have been italicized throughout. Japanese (and occasionally Chinese) terms, set off by single quotation marks, have been included where actual cognates or reasonable synonymity might bring greater clarity. Unless otherwise noted, Okinawan terms are rendered in the dialect of Naha, the largest population center. Each term has been defined at first appearance, and a glossary has been provided following the text. The Japanese and Okinawan practice of giving the surname first has been followed in the text.

OKINAWAN RELIGION

I

INTRODUCTION

Habitat and Population

Okinawa lies midway astride the Ryukyu archipelago, which stretches over the eight hundred miles separating Kyushu from Taiwan. Figures 1 and 2 show the Ryukyu chain and Island of Okinawa, respectively. The largest of the 140 islands in the chain, Okinawa has an area of 485 square miles, but a ruggedness and marked variation in terrain serve to belie its small size, a length of 65 miles north to south and a width varying from 3 to 15 miles. Although this island falls well within the temperate zone, warm currents of the Kuroshio produce a humid, subtropical, marine climate best described as benign were it not for the frequent devastation by typhoons brought by the summer monsoons. Normally, there is an adequate supply of rainfall evenly distributed throughout the year, and a luxuriant plant cover, somewhat stunted in appearance, wreathes the land. In the hilly northern area—heavily wooded with pines, cycads, bamboo, pandanus, and tree ferns—farming remains confined to the coastal strips and small river valleys, while terraced fields gird surrounding slopes. The central and southern areas, marked by low-rolling hills and flat tablelands, lack extensive forestation, having been denuded by war and by intensive agricultural exploitation. Soils in the central and southern areas are largely coral limestone in origin, but in the north, shale and schist predominate. Extensive offshore coral reefs afford a peaceful shoreline to much of the coast. In certain localities the porous nature of the soil frequently contributes to water shortages if several weeks pass without rain. There are few fauna aside from wild boar, mongoose, bats, mice, rats, birds, and several varieties of snakes, including a deadly venomous species which took a heavy toll prior to the introduction of an effective antitoxin. The seas surrounding the island contain an abundance of marine life which provides a supplement to the diet.

In 1960 approximately 50 per cent of the households were dependent on full-time farming for their livelihood; by contrast, in 1939, 75 per cent of the households were engaged in agriculture. While the population has risen from 475,766 in 1940 to 758,126 in 1960, there has been only a slight change in the total number of farming households. The over-all increase in the labor force has been siphoned off by direct and indirect military employment, construction, new industries, commerce, and government. Despite these significant developments, agriculture remains the backbone of the economy, and many families still depend on part-time farming to supplement outside employment. In 1960 the average farm household contained five members and worked less than an acre of arable land subdivided into a number of small and scattered plots. Sweet potatoes, rice, sugar, pineapple, and vegetables are the major crops, with rice, potatoes, and vegetables forming the mainstay of the diet. Pigs make up the bulk of the livestock population with an average of two per farm household; cattle and horses are kept primarily for work purposes rather than for food. The favorable climate permits double-cropping, but only grains and sugar are planted with seasonal regularity, as most of the vegetables may be planted and harvested throughout the year. Although machinery has been used increasingly in food processing, the highly fragmented land-tenure system precludes extensive utilization of machinery in cultivation. High yields have been attained only by an inordinate expenditure of human labor which, in turn, necessitates a large rural population. Population densities in excess of 1,000 per square mile are typical in the farming areas of the central and southern regions, which include more than 80 per cent of the total population. The land is not excessively poor, but the cultivators are, due to their numbers. Unlike their counterparts in adjacent areas of East Asia, however, they have not been further handicapped by the blight of landlordism.

Despite a four- to fivefold increase in the population and extensive urban growth during the past eighty years, the rural/urban ratios have narrowed slowly, and approximately 60 per cent of the people still reside in rural areas. Naha, the capital and major urban center, attained a population of 222,799 in the 1960 census and has assumed the general charac-

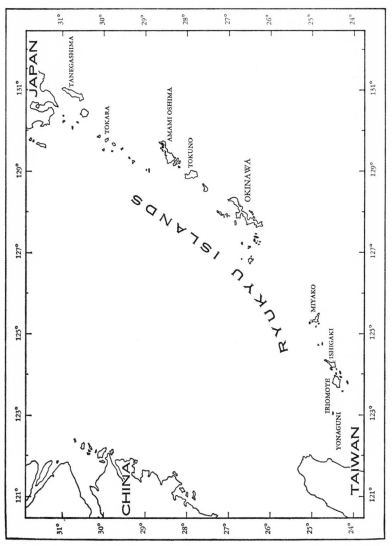

FIG. 1. Map of Ryukyu Islands.

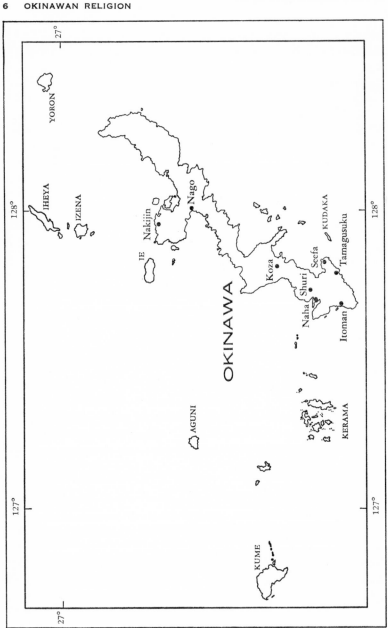

Fig. 2. Map of Okinawa and outlying islands.

teristics of Japanese cities comparable in size. The only other city worthy of the name is Koza, a postwar development which derives its livelihood from surrounding military bases. Aside from these, there are five regional market centers—towns ranging from 8,000 to 18,000 in population—but even here large segments are engaged in agricultural pursuits.

Settlement patterns in the rural areas display considerable uniformity. A typical village occupies high ground and consists of a tightly nucleated cluster of dwellings surrounded by fields. Two or three variant patterns may be found. In the north, villages cling to the beaches on narrow coastal strips or are situated on low ground at the mouth of small streams. In contrast to the usual pattern, the *yaadui* or *haru yaadui* (field settlements) are non-nucleated, with houses more widely dispersed, often in the midst of the best agricultural land. A postwar phenomenon following the construction of modern, surfaced highways has been the appearance of elongate roadside settlements. Expansion of transportation facilities concomitant with highway development has been a potent factor in shattering former isolation and in providing greater mobility for rural villagers.

Racial Characteristics

Studies on the physical anthropology of Okinawans have been few and techniques rather limited by contemporary standards. Although no large-scale ethnic intrusions have occurred in historic times (accurate records on Okinawa begin in the early fifteenth century), there are legendary accounts of Japanese refugees entering the area during the late Heian period. Suda[1] declares that Ryukyuans are not outside the Japanese racial stock, but his statement would carry greater weight if buttressed by comparative data from aboriginal Taiwan, North and South China, the Philippines, and Korea, as well as Japan. Relative to the Japanese, Okinawans are characterized by shorter stature, broader shoulders, darker skin, greater nasal breadth, wider eye opening, and less prognathism. The most notable phenotypic difference between the two peoples is in the relative degree of hairiness. Anyone who has used public baths in Okinawa is aware that a heavy mat of hair covering the back and buttocks of males is by no means a rarity. Matsumura and Baelz[2] found heavy quantities of hair on the lower legs of 25–30 per cent of the Ryukyuan males surveyed as compared to 1 per cent of the Japanese (in Tokyo and Hiroshima). Unfortunately, this trait has been seized upon by those addicted to single-trait racial classification and has been attributed to an Ainoid intrusion. This point of view ignores the Ainu's light skin color, deeply socketed eyes, and protruding brow ridges, traits which the Okinawans lack. Moreover, Smith[3] has shown in his study of dactyloglyphic characteristics that the Japanese fall between the Ainu and Ryukyuans. Serological studies also fail to support the Ainu argument; in passing southward through Japan and the Ryukyus into the Philippines, blood type O increases while type A decreases. If the basis of comparison must be Japanese versus Okinawan, I am inclined to regard the latter as exhibiting a stronger Southern Mongoloid component.

Language

An indisputably close relationship exists between the Japanese and Okinawan languages. The degree of their relationship has been likened to that of French and Italian. While the two are not mutually intelligible, their morphological, phonological, and lexical correspondences indicate a not too remote common origin. In 1955 Hattori[4] estimated the time of separation of Shuri (Okinawa) and Kyoto (Japan) to be 1,453 years previous, or approximately A.D. 500, although he modified the standard Swadesh formula, which yielded 1,029 years (*ca*. A.D. 920). The language of Okinawa may be classified as a member of the Ryukyuan group of languages in the Japanese-Ryukyuan family. This family extends from Hokkaido in the north to Yonaguni (forty-five miles off the Taiwan coast) in the south. The Ryukyuan group occupies the area from Amami Oshima to Yonaguni. At least four major languages, coinciding with the four main island complexes (Amami Oshima, Okinawa, Miyako, and Yaeyama), have been distinguished in the Ryukyuan area. Despite decided similarities, these are not mutually intelligible.

The Okinawan language comprises many dialects and subdialects which are mutually intelligible with varying degrees of ease. Nakasone[5] distinguished five major dialects and an additional eighteen speech islands, generally corresponding with *yaadui* settlements, in the northern Kunigami area alone. Although it would be an exaggeration to claim a distinct dialect for each community, the diversity and variety of local speech constantly impresses one. To a certain extent this diversity can be attributed to geographical factors, but basically it reflects the old social system wherein peasants were bound to the land in a state of serfdom and a rigid practice of village endogamy further reduced mobility and communication. Naha, Shuri, and certain other of the larger population centers such as Itoman, Oroku, and Yonabaru possess dialects sufficiently distinct to be readily recognized by most Okinawans. Currently, Naha dialect enjoys the greatest number of speakers and most widespread usage throughout the islands, although nearby Shuri, now incorporated in the greater Naha area, formerly claimed this position, as the administrative capital of the old kingdom and as the place of residence for most of the gentry and nobility.

As a result of Japanese control, most Okinawans have become bilingual; but in spite of assiduous efforts by Japanese educators, use of the indigenous language remains widespread. Okinawan persists as the language of most homes and villages and is used almost exclusively in religion and the folk-theater, while in government, education, the press, cinema, radio, television, and in nearly all phases of public and professional life, Japanese has virtually displaced Okinawan.[6] Generally, old people and children speak only Okinawan, and country people, especially women, appear to be more articulate in the native tongue. The limited education in Japanese of two generations has been insufficient to displace Okinawan, although a decided drift toward Japanese phonology is occurring in the speech, while an increasing number of Japanese words is appearing in the vocabulary. The new generation, the third since the establishment of universal education, is receiving considerably more exposure to Japanese than its parents or grandparents, and the use of Okinawan may be expected to decline rapidly in the next two decades.

Prehistory

Many evidences of prehistoric occupation remain on Okinawa, but few intensive scientific studies have been made, so that dating remains highly conjectural. Aside from a Pleistocene deer bone bearing questionable evidence of human workmanship, the earliest positive cultural remains date from the Holocene and have been found in numerous shell middens in widely scattered coastal areas of the island. To date, the pre-pottery layers, if present, have not been isolated in the middens, which contain pottery, shells, stone and bone tools, and some objects of iron. Attempts at dating have relied on comparisons of pottery styles with the established stylistic sequence in Japan. This approach has decided limitations, for the late Jomon culture of Japan (*ca.* 1000–250 B.C.) extended only as far south as Okinawa and is not found in the southern Ryukyus, while the later Yayoi culture (250 B.C.–A.D. 250) can be found in the northern Ryukyus but not at all on Okinawa or the southern islands. For the Japanese Tomb Culture period (A.D. 250–650), evidences are also lacking on Okinawa. Only in recent years have Japanese archaeologists come to accept the possibility that the diffusion of culture into the Ryukyus has not been exclusively from the north. Recent excavations on Amami Oshima of the northern Ryukyus reveal an ill-defined "southern culture" which apparently predates the Jomon evidence.[7] Kanaseki[8] suggests that at least two distinct waves of culture passed northwards through the Ryukyus; he believes that as late as the Sui dynasty of China (A.D. 581–618) the Ryukyus were culturally similar to Taiwan, and that in the southern Ryukyus, especially Yaeyama, this condition prevailed until perhaps as late as the Ming dynasty (A.D. 1368).

Although no adequate prehistoric sequence has been determined for the Ryukyus, for our purposes the significant aspect of these cultural remains is the evidence they provide of prehistoric contacts paralleling those of historic times. Southern elements include pig raising, cylindrical axes, teeth deformation by extraction of incisors or canines, and patu-like objects. Prehistoric evidences of contacts with China include knife-shaped coins dating from the late Chou and the Chin (*ca.* third century B.C.) and pottery of later periods. With Japan, as noted, there are indications of contact dating back to at least the late Jomon. The location of Okinawa—approximately three hundred miles equidistant from China to the west, Taiwan to the south, and Japan to the north—provided a crossroads where three cultural traditions met and merged to form a unique local configuration.

Taiwan and Okinawa

Systematic treatment of the traits shared by Okinawa and the extant aborigines of Taiwan poses several problems. Not only do the tribes in Taiwan differ one from another, but the peoples who once occupied the fertile plains of the west and who may have been the most advanced in technology and social organization have been displaced or absorbed by Chinese immigrants. Moreover, the whole of the Indonesian culture area lacks a major focal point which might be delineated for comparative purposes. Further handicaps are imposed by insufficient historical accounts or archaeological studies which might bolster ethnographic data. Lastly, throughout much of South China, Southeast Asia, Indonesia, the Philippines, Taiwan, the Ryukyus, and to a lesser extent Japan may be found a basic culture stratum with respect to technology and certain patterns of living, which obfuscates efforts at isolating specifically shared traits between any two contiguous cultures within the larger area.

A few of the specific traits shared by Okinawa and Taiwan are sibling creator deities, dugout canoes (without outriggers), tattooing, red fingernail coloring, postnatal "roasting" of mother and child, fermentation of ceremonial wine by chewing grain, banana cloth, ikat textiles, special houses for young unmarried adults, cockfighting, and bullfighting. Some of these are rare or moribund on Okinawa today but can be readily recalled by older informants.

A basic agricultural complex of terraced wet and dry fields predominates in both areas and occurs in association with pig raising. Although rice, sugar, sweet potatoes, and pineapple constitute the major crops of contemporary Okinawa, sugar and sweet potatoes were introduced in the seventeenth century, and pineapple in the present century, while rice has assumed a greater importance in the past fifty years following the Japanese development of rapid-maturing varieties which permit double-cropping. The older food complex appears to have consisted of millet, taro, wheat, and rice, as among the Taiwan tribes. It is not my intention to argue here for an Indonesian substratum in Okinawa but merely to indicate that the instances of shared traits are too numerous to be ignored and that these suggest lengthy contiguity and mutual influence.

China and Okinawa

The earliest Chinese references to the Ryukyus occur in the Sui dynasty annals, which tell of exploration and warring raids in the country of Liu Chiu, but considerable disagreement exists over the location of

"Liu Chiu" among contemporary scholars. Later annalists followed contradictory practices—referring to Taiwan and the Ryukyus collectively as Liu Chiu, designating Okinawa as Great Liu Chiu and Taiwan as Little Liu Chiu, and eventually applying the name exclusively to Okinawa. The descriptive accounts of Liu Chiu found in the Sui annals mention some of the traits previously cited as jointly shared by Okinawa and Taiwan; so ethnography cannot aid appreciably in resolving this problem. The presence of Chinese coins dating from the third century B.C., however, suggests at least the possibility of contact prior to the Christian Era.

The historic record shows that the Yuan dynasty tried and failed to conquer Okinawa during the last decade of the thirteenth century, and a formal relationship commenced in 1372, when the central state of Chuzan on Okinawa voluntarily recognized the suzerainty of China. From this date until 1874 regular tribute payments were made to China—an arrangement which proved beneficial to the small nation by providing advantageous trade opportunities. No administrative control was exercised over the islands, and China's sovereignty remained purely nominal. A permanent Okinawan factory was established in Fukien Province, and a small Chinese colony was founded in Kume (now part of Naha) for purposes of trade and teaching. The calendar was introduced and the Chinese system of writing adopted. Students from Okinawa periodically went to the mainland for study, and among the upper classes things Chinese came to be greatly admired. Confucian ideology, in particular, played a significant role in altering the politico-economic character of the state, ultimately transforming its feudal structure into a civil bureaucracy based on the classical Chinese model.

Diplomatic and trade access to China provided ample opportunities for borrowing traits of Chinese culture. Sugar, sweet potatoes, and certain vegetables were introduced from China and bolstered a declining economy and food supply, a situation created in the seventeenth century by the imposition of heavy tribute demands from the daimiate of Satsuma in southern Japan. Roof tiles were adopted from China, and the large omega-shaped tombs, so characteristic of Okinawa today, are unquestionably patterned after those of Fukien Province. Selected aspects of Chinese folk-religion were incorporated—the techniques of geomancy and fortunetelling in particular—and certain of the hearth rites indicate Taoist influences. Chinese cultural influences had their greatest impact upon the upper classes residing in the Shuri-Naha area of southern Okinawa; in the northern areas and on the offshore islands, Chinese traits had weaker effect. In the sixteenth century the upper classes adopted Chinese styles of dress and subsequently were organized into a hierarchy based upon the Chinese model. Although the rigidity of the Okinawan social system tended to restrict Chinese influences to the upper classes and the urban areas where they resided, five hundred years of continuous contact as a tribute state permitted assimilation of many traits which ultimately affected all levels of society.

Japan and Okinawa

The cultural relationship of Okinawa to Japan, though more intensively studied than its relationship to either China or Taiwan, has been confounded by the implicit assumption on the part of many Japanese scholars that Okinawan culture is essentially Japanese and represents an isolated provincial development. However, to any foreign observer reasonably familiar with Japan, Okinawa does not suggest a mere provincial entity but rather a distinct culture evincing varying degrees of affiliation with neighboring cultures. Haring[9] makes the analogy that Okinawa differs more from Japan than Ireland from England or Quebec from Ontario. Not only the readily apparent material differences—large tombs, massive stone walls surrounding house lots, red tile roofs, clothing and hair styles, and food—but basic differences in personality and values soon impress the observer. A significant distinction may be cited in the higher status accorded women in Okinawan society, which may stem partially from the absence of militarism during the past five hundred years, although female domination of religion suggests a more deeply embedded trait. Nearly all Western visitors since the time of Captain Hall have commented on the mildness and lack of overt aggression in Okinawan behavior. The absence of any martial spirit save where infrequently inculcated by the Japanese was particularly apparent in the battle for Okinawa during World War II, when virtually every Japanese fought until killed or committed suicide while Okinawans were not averse to surrender when they could. It should also be noted in this connection that prior to the war the incidence of crimes of violence and suicide on Okinawa was the lowest in the Japanese nation. Overt aggression and violence simply have not characterized the Okinawan ethos. Those in doubt might try boarding a bus in Naha during the evening rush hour and then try the same thing in any city of comparable size in Japan.

These observations are presented not to refute or depreciate obvious linguistic ties, similarities in religion, and parallels in social organization, but to emphasize that certain marked disparities may be found between the two cultures. Taking a long-range view, on the basis of such evidence as is now available it is apparent that there has been an ebb and flow of contacts through the centuries, not a continuous and unilateral interaction. The archaeological record, as noted, suggests contact during the terminal phases of the Japanese Jomon (1000–250 B.C.), but for the succeeding Yayoi (250 B.C.–A.D. 250) and Tomb Culture (A.D. 250–650) periods there has been little evidence to date. This appears to accord with Hattori's computation giving 1,453 years for the separation of Shuri and Kyoto speech, perhaps even better with the uncorrected date of 1,029 years, and with legends of Japanese refugees entering the area in the late Heian (ca. A.D. 866–1185). What language, it may be asked, did the Okinawans—who had agriculture, raised pigs, and obtained Chinese coins—speak prior to this time? This question cannot be answered scientifically at present. But I agree in substance with Dr. Kanaseki[10] that evidences of southern cultural influences are extensive, and I would add that the seafaring Malayo-Polynesians, who spread their language across the world to points as far removed as Madagascar and Easter Island, could not have been seriously hindered by the forty-five miles of open sea separating Taiwan from the westernmost of the Ryukyu Islands. Undoubtedly, the subsequent penetration of the Japanese language during the last thousand or so years was accompanied by the diffusion of other elements of Japanese culture, and I am inclined to regard the gradual emergence of a feudal society on Okinawa as due to Japanese influence and perhaps even movement into the area. This would not necessarily imply that the spread of Japanese language and culture into the Ryukyus was accomplished by large-scale migration or the establishment of political domination. History shows that it was not until the twelfth century that the daimiate of Satsuma first extended its political control over the most northerly Ryukyu Islands of Tanega Shima, Yaku Shima, and parts of Tokara Rettō. Regular trading contacts are known to have existed in the fourteenth century, but by this time Okinawan shipping was plying the whole of the China Seas—southward to Cambodia, Thailand, and Java, as well as northward to Korea and Japan. Japanese influence increased markedly after the disastrous war with Satsuma in 1609, which reduced the small kingdom to the status of a tributary vassal. Following direct annexation by Japan in 1879, the process of Japanization proceeded at an accelerated rate, but the extent of acculturation has not been sufficient to make present-day evidences of Japanese culture more than a veneer on an Okinawan base.

Okinawan Kingdom

The emergence of what might be termed the protohistoric period occurs in the late twelfth century with the appearance of a ruler called Shunten (*ca.* A.D. 1187–1237). According to historical legend, his reign was preceded by a dynasty of twenty-five generations called the Age of Tenson, after its founder, who reputedly was descended from the gods, as the characters for his name suggest, and who, as the tale goes, ruled for more than seventeen thousand years. Tenson aside, little is actually known about Shunten and his immediate descendants, for the oldest extant annals date from 1403, and the most often cited histories date from the seventeenth century. Moreover, later annalists and historians generously added pure fabrication to legend and fact, perhaps in an effort to confer upon the royal family respectable antecedents and a lengthy history of royal succession with hegemony from mythical times. Thus, for example, we are treated to the patently spurious account of Shunten being sired by the famous Japanese warrior, Minamoto Tametomo, while Shunten's name suggests that it may have been copied from that of the legendary Chinese emperor Shun, renowned for his sagacity. Similarly, in the case of Tenson the same characters and reading are employed as for the grandson of the sun goddess in Japanese mythology. The usual presentation of Okinawan history creates the impression that, except for the period 1315–1429, a unified state had existed from the time of the Tenson dynasty. This can only be regarded as conjecture. It does appear reasonably certain, if the belief in a weakly centralized state is accepted, that during this protohistoric period the island was divided among a number of independent chieftains or feudal lords, called *aji* (also *anji*), each of whom ruled a small territory with a group of armed followers. By the early fourteenth century these territories had coalesced into three petty feudal states—Hokuzan, Chuzan, and Nanzan—roughly coinciding with the present northern (Kunigami), central (Nakagami), and southern (Shimajiri) regions. There is no evidence from archaeology, ethnography, or history to sustain Iha's contention[11] that the northern people were hunters, the central people farmers, and the southern fisherfolk.

Political unification of the entire island was accomplished by Shō Hashi in 1429 and brought an end to all further internal conflict. At this time, the local *aji* pledged their loyalty to the king at Shuri; however, as each possessed an armed retinue within his fief, they posed a constant threat to the central government. There emerged shortly a strong ruler, Shō Shin (1477–1526), who abruptly ended feudalism and established a Confucian state. Private possession of arms was forbidden, and the *aji*, their families, and chief retainers were required to take up permanent residence in the capital of Shuri. Although the *aji* were permitted to retain a portion of the income from their fiefs, henceforth the majority of the upper classes subsisted on rice stipends controlled by the government. Class distinctions were rigidly prescribed in matters of dress, housing, justice, occupation, and mobility. Commoners were prohibited from wearing all but the rudest of clothing; even the use of sandals and umbrellas was denied them, though unlike the Japanese peasant they were not enjoined from riding.

The upper classes were ordered into a hereditary social system of nine ranks and eighteen grades seemingly modeled on that of Tang China. Rank in the political bureaucracy theoretically was based on achievement in competitive examinations, but in fact only the upper classes received educations or were given the opportunity to compete. Moreover, the highest positions in the bureaucracy tended to be held by the nobility, usually close relatives of the ruler. The peasants were relegated to a status of perpetual serfdom, forbidden to move or to alter their occupations without official sanction. Internal peace, an industrious peasantry, and extensive overseas trade contributed to the growth of the small state. In the period 1500–1879 a sizable proliferation of the upper classes seems to have occurred; and in an effort to alleviate overcrowding in the capital and to improve economic opportunities for the upper classes, the government permitted them in 1724 to engage in trade, develop handicrafts, or migrate to the country and take up farming. Restrictions on the peasantry were never relaxed, however, and such changes as were instituted were under-taken for the benefit of the ruling elite. The strength of their control was remarked upon by a member of the Perry Expedition who noted that "all resistance has ceased and a motion of a fan or a wink is as effectual as a blow."[12]

The Satsuma daimiate in southern Kyushu long asserted claim to all of the Ryukyus, and on occasion the Okinawan kingdom had paid tribute through Satsuma to the shogunate for the purpose of currying favor and gaining trade privileges. Like the Chinese, the Japanese exercised no direct control over Okinawa. When Hideyoshi planned the invasion of Korea in 1592, the Satsuma leaders called upon Okinawa for assistance, but this request was rejected and China was promptly notified of Japan's intentions. By way of punishment, Satsuma launched a punitive action against the kingdom in 1609 which led to defeat and capture of the king, who was taken prisoner to Kagoshima. Although Okinawa's refusal and betrayal furnished the ostensible reasons for the war, the enviable trading position of the small nation undoubtedly provided a further inducement. Moreover, the gradual political expansion of the kingdom into the northern Ryukyus secured control over areas regarded by Satsuma as part of its domain.

The release of the king after two years' captivity was contingent upon recognition of Satsuma overlordship and agreement to pay an annual rice tribute. The islands of the Amami group, north of Okinawa, were annexed by Satsuma, but direct administration of the Shuri government was not undertaken, although spies and inspectors were stationed in the island. Hence, a semblance of independence was preserved by the kingdom; in fact, Satsuma appeared anxious to preserve this fiction, and tribute payments continued to China as before. By this means Satsuma was able to profit from Okinawa's trading position, a situation which became of even greater value after 1637 when the Shogun's exclusion policy officially closed Japan to outside trade relationships. Throughout the period from 1637 down to the Meiji Restoration, Satsuma engaged in a profitable smuggling trade through Okinawa; the rewards of this activity reportedly exceeded those obtained from rice revenues, the usual income of daimyo. For Okinawa, the loss of trade profits, heavy tribute payments, and a reduced area produced general impoverishment and economic stagnation. The Satsuma policy of maintaining the status quo served to buttress an already rigid social system, and gradually the nation drifted into a dormant state which lasted until annexation.

Japanese Prefecture, 1879–1945

In 1872 the post-Restoration government of Japan proclaimed its intention to annex Okinawa and the southern Ryukyus on the grounds that control over the territories of all former feudatories had passed to it. With considerable adroitness the last Okinawan ruler, Shō Tai, managed to frustrate Japanese efforts to dethrone him until 1879, when he was forcibly removed to permanent exile in Tokyo. During the first two decades, the most significant changes imposed by the new administration were the abolishment of the old class system and the curtailment of upper-class pensions. The latter had the effect of producing a mass exodus of lower-ranking gentry to the farming areas in search of a livelihood, and many new villages were established at this time.

The land reforms of 1899–1903 abolished communal land tenure and introduced the Japanese system of private property and inheritance; this single act ushered in a series of changes which altered the whole fabric of village life. Official policy aimed directly at the eradication of Okinawan culture and the transformation of Okinawans into Japanese nationals. The most effective institution for attaining this objective was the new educational system. Schools were first introduced in the Naha-Shuri area and ultimately, by World War I, extended over the entire countryside, providing the first educational opportunities the peasantry had known. Where necessary, repressive laws and police measures were also resorted to by the government, and things Okinawan were generally discredited. Initially, there was considerable reaction against the policy of Japanization and discrimination, but in time this feeling subsided and a sense of inferiority replaced it. Ultimately, the government succeeded in creating a favorable response to Japanese culture, and Okinawans came to regard that culture as superior and worthy of emulation. This achievement may be attributed in part to the linguistic and cultural affinities of the two peoples, since sufficient resemblances existed to make their differences bridgeable; a wider gulf might have produced lasting antipathy, as in the case of Korea. While the Japanese repeatedly discriminated against Okinawan culture, full and equal participation in their culture was proffered as an alternative. Equally significant was the official policy which treated Okinawa as one of the home prefectures and not as a colonial dependency. Many Okinawans, though often resentful over slights against themselves and their culture, came to acknowledge the Japanese as providers of modern, enlightened government, for the new administration had abolished class divisions, freed the peasants from a serflike status, equalized justice, greatly reduced taxes on arable land, and granted some voice in government to the common man. Even members of the former upper classes were not wholly alienated, for as the best educated and most wealthy they were often the first to obtain positions in the new bureaucracy or to invest in new economic opportunities. Sixty-six years of Japanese administration witnessed the progressive integration of Okinawa into the Japanese nation. However, the span of time was too brief and Okinawa's physical isolation too remote to eradicate the indigenous culture, although it had been severely altered.

United States Military Occupation

The battle for Okinawa during World War II brought widespread destruction to all areas and resulted in death or injury to 20 per cent of the population. The effects of destruction, loss of life, and displacement were far reaching: families were shattered, virtually all homes and buildings destroyed, and the records of government destroyed. The people were rendered impoverished and apathetic; for several years the land lay gutted.

Since July 1945 the United States Army (except for eight months of Navy control) has administered the government of Okinawa and the southern Ryukyus, constructed large military bases, and maintained a sizable garrison of troops. Currently, an estimated 55,000 Americans live on the island. Relief and reconstruction measures instituted by the military government and employment of a considerable segment of the labor force in military and subsidiary occupations have contributed to a gradual recovery and, more recently, to an accelerated rate of economic growth. Okinawa's small size and high population density have served to place Americans and Okinawans in close proximity. Their relationship has tended to become symbiotic, at least in the economic sphere. The importance of this physical nearness, however, might be easily exaggerated in considering its influence on culture change. The social distance separating the two peoples precludes significant interaction. Despite some changes in the higher echelons of government, the same political and educational system operates at the local level as before the war, and the postwar extension of the period of compulsory schooling by an additional three years has served to further the process of Japanization. Moreover, the prestige of Japanese culture remains undiminished and perhaps actually enhanced by this new association. There is neither the opportunity nor the urge to identify with America, and virtually all segments of society regard reunification with Japan as desirable, although some may temporize in fear of the possible repercussions in the economy.

The most dramatic socio-cultural changes in contemporary Okinawa have occurred in the technology and the economy. At the present time, Okinawa enjoys an unprecedented economic expansion, and commercial development is proceeding apace. Nearly all Okinawans acknowledge being better fed and clothed than ever before, and the scars of war have been largely erased. To one who observed Okinawa in 1945, the external changes are startling. The new university situated on the ruins of the royal castle symbolizes an intent to modernize intellectually as well as materially; but some Okinawans must find the present confusing, for old and new are juxtaposed in bewildering fashion. In a decade they have experienced changes that have transpired over several generations elsewhere. With respect to technology and economic organization, they have largely caught up with the twentieth century, but beliefs and patterns of living have not altered so rapidly, leaving much to suggest the heritage of the Forgotten Kingdom.

II

CONCEPTS OF
THE SUPERNATURAL

The Spirit World

KAMI. For the Okinawan, the whole of the universe, animate and inanimate, is occupied by myriads of indwelling spirits, the most important being the *kami*. These appear markedly similar to the Japanese 'kami' in most respects, although the Okinawan *kami* seem less personalized and even more vague than those of the Japanese pantheon. In a sense, the *kami* are deities, but I prefer to preserve the term untranslated. They are possessed of superhuman and supernatural powers, sanctity is attached to them, and rituals are performed in their behalf. They bear little resemblance to the Western—Graeco-Roman or Judaeo-Christian—concept of God. While not distinctly anthropomorphized, they are discrete entities or spirits capable of independent action; consequently, I do not view them as being predominantly animatistic, mana-like forces.[1] If arranged on a continuum, with animatism (represented by the Polynesian concept of mana) at one end, and animism (represented by the Greek concept of God) at the other, the Okinawan concept of *kami* might be centrally located yet definitely exhibiting an animistic bias. It is true that myths relating to the lives of the *kami* are notably few and simple, even when compared with the Japanese system, in which a similarly elaborate pantheon shows marked underdevelopment with regard to the functions, powers, abodes, and activities of the 'kami.' Certainly, the lack of any accounts of lives of the gods as exist in Greek mythology is striking; yet, while lacking in these respects, the Okinawan *kami* can speak, be seen, and mete out punishments and rewards—quite unlike impersonal, mana-like forces.

For the purpose of systematic presentation, the *kami* may be grouped in five general categories. While Okinawans do not conceptualize them this way, a vague sense of hierarchical gradations and powers does exist. The first category may be designated as the heaven and natural phenomena group. These, to mention but a few, are exemplified by *ting nu kami* (heaven *kami*—often vaguely regarded as supreme), *unjami* (sea *kami*), *tiida-gami* (sun *kami*), *miji-gami* (water *kami*), etc. In the second category are the place or location *kami: kaa nu kami* (well *kami*), *fii nu kami* (hearth or fire *kami*), *fuuru-gami* (pigpen or toilet *kami*), *taa nu kami* (paddy *kami*), *yashichi-gami* (house-lot *kami*), etc. Occupational or status *kami* comprise the third category: *fuuchi nu kami* (bellows *kami*, patron of the blacksmith), *funi nu kami* (boat *kami*, associated with the boatbuilder), *sheeku nu kami* (carpenter or woodworker *kami*), *nuru-gami* (the special *kami* of the village priestess, *nuru*), etc. This category apparently has undergone considerable reduction, for the influx of manufactured goods in recent decades diminished substantially the number of native crafts. For example, Shimabukuro[2] mentions a *kami* for the net-maker; but according to informants in the fishing community of Itoman, this specialist has disappeared, and Japanese-manufactured nets have replaced those made locally. The fourth category contains the ancestral spirits, *futuki*, who are viewed as *kami* of low rank. The *futuki* provide an important link between their living descendants and the supernatural. The fifth category includes the *kaminchu* (*kami* person or persons), living person(s) regarded as possessed of *kami* spirit. *Kaminchu* include the priestesses of the community and kin group as well as those males who function as ceremonial aides or servants to the priestesses. There is some difference of opinion as to whether the shamans are *kaminchu;* certainly they regard themselves as such and decidedly resent the term *yuta* usually applied to them. Some informants felt that shamans, by their association with sickness, disease, and misfortune, are unclean and hence contrary to what is *kami*, for, in contrast, the priestesses must assiduously avoid these "pollutions." There is also a more widespread conviction that not all shamans speak the truth and that not a few pretend to hear and see the *kami* in order to make money; but for those who conscientiously follow their *kami* and who utilize their powers to help others, the title would be regarded as deserved. *Kaminchu*, therefore, denotes one who has *kami* spirit and who actively measures up to the obligations imposed by the *kami*. It implies a moral quality and the presence of charisma.

The *kami* are neither omniscient nor omnipotent; but, possessed of powers not enjoyed by man, they have the capacity to supervise, influence, and alter the events of life. Basically, the *kami* are affectively neutral, neither inherently good nor bad. Man bears an obligation to maintain reciprocity with the *kami* through proper ritual procedure, and the *kami* may become harmful if this relationship is not preserved. Through ritual, their powers may be harnessed and they may be manipulated or even deceived into following man's bidding. The basic attitude of the layman, however, seems to be aimed at avoiding trouble with them rather than positively enlisting their support.

FII NU KANG (FII NU KAMI). In the course of ordinary affairs, the single most important *kami* is that of the hearth or fire, *fii nu kami* (usually pronounced *fii nu kang*). This concept and its associated ritual have received considerable attention from scholars. Generally, the function of the *fii nu kang* appears to have been grossly misunderstood by these scholars. Spencer,[3] for one, has regarded it as the central focus of Okinawan religion, suggesting that in ancient times fire was considered a sacred gift. This misunderstanding has been occasioned in part by the fact that the major priestesses and, indeed, the senior female member in every household devote considerable attention to the hearth. Actually, the *fii nu kang* provides a link between the household or community and the higher *kami*; it functions as the messenger and observer of the group, not as a primary end of ritual action.

To what specific higher *kami* does the *fii nu kang* link? Such a question occasions pause and reflection from informants, who usually reply *ukami* (the *kami* or great *kami*) or *ting nu kami* (the heaven *kami*). The implication seems to be that the *fii nu kang* links man simply to more remote, higher *kami* of the first category rather than to any specific *kami*. Torigoe,[4] among others, flatly contends that *fii nu kang* and *tiida-gami* (sun *kami*) are one and the same; but I have found no field evidence corroborating this. Okinawan explicitly distinguishes *fii* (fire) from *tiida* (sun), which is contrary to the case in Japanese, where both fire and sun are designated by 'hi.' Furthermore, informants did not regard the *fii nu kang* as representing the sun or directly linking to it. I would acknowledge that early literature and documents show the rulers and high priestesses in the past to have borne in their divine names (*kaminaa*) the word *tiida*, suggesting perhaps a symbolic identity of supreme political and religious leaders with the sun.

This does not *ipso facto* relate sun and hearth, and strong likelihood exists, on the basis of field research and linguistic evidences, that these have never been related.

The *fii nu kang* symbolizes the continuity of the household and its relationship to the higher *kami*, just as the ancestral tablets symbolize continuity in the male line and the family's relationship to familial spirits. Though recognized as a female deity and prayed to almost exclusively by females, *fii nu kang* is invoked for the benefit of the group, not for female members alone. The communal hearth, believed to be that of the founder, is considered of higher rank than those of individual households.

UMINAI-GAMI—UMIKII-GAMI. Oral traditions hold that two sibling deities, *uminai-gami* (sister *kami*) and *umikii-gami* (brother *kami*), descended from heaven to create the first land and produce the first human beings. During the period of the Okinawan kingdom, major political positions were paired with religious positions; the female priestess and the corresponding male political leader were likened in their relationship to *uminai-gami* and *umikii-gami*. Today, certain religious roles within the community and kin group are still paired in this manner. Although these two *kami* were the creator deities and their mortal counterparts were to be found in key roles within the religious and political structure of society, they do not appear to play any significant function in ordinary life or even to serve as objects of ritual. They may possibly symbolize the female-male principle in the universe, but I do not see this as analogous to the Chinese concept of 'yin' and 'yang,' particularly since in the Ryukyus the female is regarded as spiritually superior to the male. Quite clearly, this theme fits into an Island Asia pattern, and these deities can be likened to the sibling deities 'izanami'—'izanagi' in Japan, 'baibai'—'lalaki' ('sibabay'—'silalaki') in the Philippines, and those of the Taiwan aborigines.

FUTUKI. The ancestral spirits are called *futuki*, a word obviously of Japanese-Buddhist origin representing the Okinawan pronunciation of the Japanese term 'hotoke.' The older Okinawan term for ancestors is *fafuji* or *uya fafuji*, but whereas this term implies all ancestors, *futuki* specifically denotes those in the male line and their wives. According to historical accounts, Buddhist temples supposedly date as far back as the fourteenth century on Okinawa; but the major impact of Buddhism, particularly in the rural areas, dates from only the seventeenth century, when Satsuma control brought an upsurge of Japanese missionary activities. According to one Buddhist priest, the adoption of household altars was stimulated by the zeal with which Satsuma inspectors sought to locate Christians; the presence of an altar gave assurance that the family was not Christian. Whatever may have been the factors prompting their adoption, they are unquestionably in virtually universal use today. The Buddhist altar, *buchidang* ('butsudan') or *guriijing* ('goreizen'), containing the ancestral tablets, *iifee* ('ihai'), constitutes the second major focal point of household ritual after the *fii nu kang*.

The concept of *futuki* shows indication of mixture with earlier indigenous concepts. In fact, it may be said that Buddhism has been only partially assimilated. The Buddhist concepts of heaven and hell are well known, but Okinawans speak of these in a remote and abstract fashion, and many do not believe that the dead go to heaven or hell. Most feel that their ancestors remain in the tomb close to their worldly abode and that they are near at hand observing the life of their descendants. All agree that the ancestors may cause endless misfortune for the living if proper ritual ties are not maintained, and nearly everyone believes that it is obligatory to produce many offspring, especially males, so that one will be properly worshiped after death. Conversely, it is also recognized that maintaining this tie with the ancestors is a burdensome task. The compensating factor is that the relationship is reciprocal—the *futuki* will work positively for the benefit of their descendants if ritual obligations are observed.

MABUI. Every person possesses a vital, life-sustaining spirit called *mabui*. This spirit is called *ichi mabui* when present in a living person and *shini mabui* after death. The location of *mabui* is in the chest, and a sudden shock, surprise, sneeze, or fright (such as from seeing a ghost) may dislodge it from the body, effecting *mabui uti* (dropping the *mabui*). Since loss of *mabui* will cause death, a ritual practice called *mabui-gumi* (putting in *mabui*) should be resorted to whenever loss of *mabui* is presumed to have occurred. When a person has a lengthy illness or lingers near death, *mabui nugi* (withdrawal of *mabui*) is said to be taking place, with the implication that it is responding to an external agency. Once separated from the body, the *mabui* usually heads for the tomb, and, once it is inside, not even the most skilled shaman can retrieve it. According to some informants, *mabui* remains in the tomb for a period of forty-nine days, the traditional period of Buddhist mourning; it then journeys to *gukuraku* ('gokuraku'), the Buddhist paradise. Others stated that *mabui* remains in the ancestral

tomb forever; this latter seems the most commonly found point of view.
Although Yanagita[5] categorically states, "The *mabui* never causes harm to anyone; it has no connection with ghosts," I found that this was decidedly not the case. *Shini mabui* resulting from violent or unnatural deaths do not enter their tombs but instead become ghosts which may plague the living. Some difference of opinion exists among informants as to whether animals (especially pigs, cows, and horses) possess *mabui*, although the majority regarded *mabui* as being limited to man alone.

SAA. Humans have a spiritual rank or value called *saa*. For ordinary persons this appears to be conceived of as being determined by one's birth year in the Chinese calendrical cycle and by one's inheritance. Certain individuals, however, are *saadakachu* (high-*saa* person) and are destined to become *kaminchu* (*kami* person; i.e., occupying a role primarily oriented toward serving the *kami*). Such persons must eventually become priestesses, priests, or shamans. The *saadakachu* are said to be *saadaka nmari* (of high-*saa* birth or born with high *saa*). They are selected by the *kami* from the time of birth. *Saadaka* is not something that one can acquire, nor can one reject it. The nature of one's *saa* may be determined by a shaman or a fortuneteller, but since certain major religious offices are inherited, many *saadaka* persons are recognized from the time of birth in a certain kinship status. In the case of prospective shamans and kin group priestesses, however, the *kami* must usually give notification in order to make them aware of their special *saa*.

SHIJI. The concept of *shiji* appears to have undergone considerable revision in recent centuries and to persist in a modified form today. Many people are vague or utterly confused as to its meaning, and leading Okinawan scholars disagree as to its interpretation. Shimabukuro[6] describes it as *kami* spirit, 'shinrei' in Japanese, while Nakahara[7] regards it as a spirit force or power, 'reiriki' in Japanese. The distinction hinges essentially on whether *shiji* is construed as *kami* spirit or as a force or power emanating and detachable from the *kami* and hence mana-like. In his study of the *Omoro Sōshi* (a collection of 1,553 songs, largely of a religious nature, dating from prior to the seventeenth century), Nakahara[8] has amassed impressive evidence showing that the high status of female religious functionaries in ancient times rested on their power to invoke and attach *shiji*. Those things and persons possessing *shiji* had great power. *Shiji* present in the water of a well was beneficial to the users; a ship with *shiji* enjoyed safety at sea; a ruler with *shiji* was superhuman. *Shiji* was inherently beneficent, working for the good of those who possessed it. Nakahara states that this supernatural power was impersonal, lacking a will of its own, and he likens it to the South Seas concept of mana.[9]

Shimabukuro's study[10] of religion in the old[11] Okinawan village gives a different interpretation: Ordinary people could bring down the *kami* spirit, *shiji*, through offerings made in their households, but only the chief priestess of the village had the power to bring *shiji* into the shrines or fields. Here, *shiji* is construed as *kami* spirit, the deity itself.

In contemporary usage the highest-ranking village priestess, *nuru*, is said to be *shijidakasang* (high *shiji*); other *kaminchu* also may be said to have *shiji*. Although the highest priestess can be referred to as *shijidaka nmari* (born to high *shiji*), *shiji* does not appear to be acquired at birth. When the new priestess succeeds to office, she performs a ceremony, *shiji kamiing* (placing *shiji* on the head), which signifies her taking over the *shiji* of her predecessor. When used in this sense, *shiji* and *kami* are said to be the same; *shiji* here implies *kami* spirit and power.

A less common usage of *shiji* applies to the *utaki* or sacred grove, which is said to be *shijidakadukuru* (high-*shiji* place). Such areas are regarded as sacrosanct even today, and in the recent past, during the lifetime of the oldest generation, they were taboo to ordinary villagers, especially the males. *Shijidakadukuru* implies a high order of sanctity and close association with the *kami*.

Currently, the concept of *shiji* does not appear to be one of an impersonal supernatural power as some have suggested. When applied to *kaminchu* or to sacred places, a considerable degree of vagueness surrounds its meaning. The commonest meaning of *shiji*, which some informants contend is actually a homonym, is "male line"; thus, one may speak of a son's child as *shiji nu nmaga* (male-side grandchild) or of a father's side of the family as *shiji nu kata*. As one informant explained: "*Shiji* does not mean 'blood' when referring to male ancestors; it means that you have their spirit. Your parent (father) gives his *shiji* to you and your siblings in the sense that his spirit is divided among you."

CHIJI. Shamans and priestesses frequently speak of their *chiji*, meaning the particular *kami* or remote ancestor whom they serve and who guides them. Prospective shamans spend much of their time trying to find and identify their *chiji*. For the established shaman, *chiji* is highly personalized and ever present; "My *chiji* tells me what to say" is frequently heard. A prospective shaman or kin group priestess who died without having found her *chiji* was described as having been drowned by her *chiji* (*chiji-nburi*).

The concept of *chiji* also includes the meaning of being heir to a spirit entity. A village priestess, when asked how she had obtained office, replied that she was *yumi chiji* (daughter-in-law *chiji*), indicating that she had married into the house which traditionally retains the office. This could be contrasted with *winagungwa chiji* (daughter *chiji*), used for a woman who attains office by birth in such a house. Similarly, the first son in any household falls heir to the family ancestral tablets on the death of his father and may be spoken of as the *gwansu chiji* (ancestor *chiji*).

Informants sometimes confuse *shiji* and *chiji*, often perhaps as a mere slip of the tongue, but the distinction is fairly clear. *Chiji* carries no connotations of being divisible or being an impersonal force or power as is the case with *shiji*. *Chiji* denotes a specific spirit entity or an heir to one, and these are not mutually exclusive alternatives. They are, in fact, reciprocals of one another. In attempting to explain the meaning of *chiji*, informants emphasize the words "connection" and "connecting"; *chiji* implies a specific spirit (or a specific category of spirits, as in the case of household ancestors) as well as the person who assumes the specific role obligations attendant upon serving that spirit.

SHII. The concept of *shii* has a number of interpretations in contemporary usage. The younger generations generally equate it with the Japanese 'tamashii' (soul or spirit), but older informants reject this. One Okinawan scholar[12] has equated *shii* with 'rei' (spirit or essence) in Japanese, but again knowledgeable informants declare that the two are not equivalent. Okinawans generally believe, as Shimabukuro[13] has written, that all things are possessed of spirit. The most usual interpretation seems to regard *shii* as a common term for all manifestations of spirit—*kami* spirit, human spirit, animal spirit, tree spirit, and so on.

Some informants, however, conceive of *shii* somewhat differently. They hold that *shii* is an animistic spirit inhabiting only objects of stone (including metal) and wood (including plants). Man, they say, does not possess *shii*, nor do such natural phenomena as fire, water, earth, the sun, etc., which have only *kami*. They believe that *shii* enjoys plaguing man by teasing, tormenting, and practical joking, but the annoyance or danger from *shii* can be nullified by proper ritual. Therefore, when a new house is constructed, it is imperative to perform necessary rites to ensure that the *shii* in the stone or wood are properly placated or negated. If this is not done, the *shii* in the new house will be bad, bringing misfortune to the occupants. A few who subscribe to this narrower interpretation of *shii* believe *shii* to be those spirits of the dead who have become ghosts and that this accounts for *shii* being a source of trouble and annoyance to man.

Virtually all interpretations of *shii* agree that it is detachable from whatever it occupies and that its strength may be increased or decreased by external agencies. As in the case of *shiji*, the current confusion over the meaning of *shii* suggests considerable change in meaning in recent time.

CHII. There is a general term meaning "spirit," *chii*, which does not figure too importantly in religion at the present time. Its most common use, for example, would occur in saying that so-and-so is in high spirits— *chii nu tatchoong*. It is sometimes used by shamans and their clients to describe or identify an individual according to his birth year in the calendrical cycle, as in *nma nu chii* (horse-year spirit) or *tura nu chii* (tiger-year spirit). Another instance of its use is less certain to me and should be regarded as conjectural. People usually say *jii nu kami* when referring to the earth *kami*, but some will say *jiitchi nu kami* and occasionally simply *jiitchi*. One shaman stated that *jiitchi* alone has the meaning of "earth spirit" or *kami*, and another informant suggested that the terminal *chi* in *jiitchi* derives from *chii*. I cite this merely as a possible indication of an earlier and more widespread use of *chii*.

YANAMUNG. Those spirits or forces which are consistently malevolent are termed *yanamung* (evil or malevolent thing). Ghosts are prime examples of what may be designated *yanamung*, although the term covers all other types of malevolent spirits as well. Often, man cannot determine the specific spirit which has attacked or plagued him, so he speaks of *yanamung*. A youth returning to a village late at night got lost in a thicket and was somewhat frightened by the experience. His family described this as *yanamung kai maiasariing* (to be led astray by *yanamung*). When pressed for clarification of this concept, informants seem to believe that most *yanamung* are in reality ghosts; thus, in the case of the youth led astray by *yanamung*, it was deemed likely that this was probably a ghost. Certain winds believed to cause disease are called *yanakaji* (evil wind).

MAJIMUNG. The world is filled with many ghosts, *majimung* (or *maji-*

munaa), that can cause trouble for the living. Those who die violent or unnatural deaths or who die away from home and are not treated to proper death rites become ghosts. In fact, anyone who dies and does not receive interment in the family or kin group tomb may become *majimung*. They are capable of transforming themselves into human, animal, or other forms and can appear or disappear at will. Since *majimung* have no tomb or resting place, their unhappiness and restlessness impel them to work harm upon the more fortunate who are still alive. Some believe that each ghost must steal the spirit from a living human in order to find rest. For example, the ghost of a person who accidentally drowned in a river will hover near the place until such time as it can cause another swimmer to drown. Seeing a ghost while walking alone at night may cause the loss of *mabui* and subsequent death if measures are not taken to restore it. Ordinarily, ghosts cannot be seen unless they wish to be. However, a young woman who has died without having had intercourse may appear as a beautiful woman to men whose spirits she endeavors to steal, but to women she is clearly visible as a *majimung*. The shaman has the ability to discern *majimung* in any guise, and certain people termed *kanabui* (this is a condition or state of being rather than a social role) see ghosts easily; such individuals are usually afraid to go outdoors at night. The shaman, however, can negate or ward off the actions of ghosts, whereas the *kanabui* can only see them.

For the living, *majimung* are troublesome and potentially very dangerous; yet I would not regard the Okinawans as ghost-ridden in the light of ethnographic accounts from other parts of the world. The majority of problems believed to be of supernatural origin do not stem from ghosts and their activities. Moreover, the fact that an individual may encounter a ghost or suffer from the action of ghosts is usually taken to indicate more serious difficulties with the *kami* or ancestors.

KIJIMUNG. A male tree spirit called *kijimung* (or *kijimunaa*) dwells in the Indian banyan trees common in the rural settlements. Shimabukuro[14] suggests that it is possibly the same spirit as the *shii* in wood. *Kijimung* (possibly, *ki* + *shii* + *munu* = tree spirit thing) has a reputation for mischief and enjoys bedeviling people; his favorite trick is to molest sleepers by pouncing on their chests. To awake startled from a dream or suffer momentary shortness of breath on awakening is said to be *kijimunaa kai usariing* (attacked by *kijimung*). People will frequently drive nails into the banyan trees within their house lots to keep him away.

Sometimes a *kijimung* will arbitrarily befriend a person and endeavor to help him. Fishermen who have his friendship are said to be especially successful. He may, however, be a potential source of trouble for fishermen, for he has the ability to walk on the water and may follow boats to sea. Those who break wind at sea infuriate him, and he may retaliate by trying to upset the boat. He is said to be very small and entirely red in color. Every child has heard of *kijimung*, but he does not appear to be regarded seriously. An encounter with him does not justify a visit to the shaman, whereas an involvement with a ghost decidedly would.

FIIDAMA. A fireball or meteor, called *fiidama*, can be interpreted as an ominous sign of spirit activity. When it appears shortly before a birth, it signifies the child's spirit entering the community. When appearing after a death it is thought to be the *shini mabui* searching for the tomb. Its appearance at other times is believed to portend the threat to the community of a malevolent female spirit intent on setting a fire. In the latter case an elaborate counteractive ritual was resorted to in the past, but I know of no recent instances of its performance, and today only the elderly seem to remember it.

AKAMATAA. A nonpoisonous snake called *akamataa* is believed to have the power to change into a handsome young man capable of seducing women. Those who fall prey to his charms will give birth to snakes. The folklore theme of a serpent bridegroom has widespread distribution throughout the Japanese and Ryukyu islands.[15]

UNI. There are folktales of demons, usually of great strength and size, who cause many tribulations for people; they are called *uni* (clearly cognate to the Japanese 'oni'). Accounts of *uni* seem limited to storytelling, at least at present.

Supernatural Punishments and Rewards

Rewards are not capriciously showered upon man; there are few gratuitous windfalls, and man must work for and deserve what he receives. The *kami*, as noted previously, are inherently neither benign nor malevolent. Even the ancestral spirits, *futuki*, though predominantly nurturant, can withhold their beneficence; moreover, they are vastly inferior to the *kami* in rank and powers. Supernatural rewards, therefore, are contingent, first and foremost, upon proper ritual action and, to a lesser degree, upon proper conduct in specific social roles and situations. Man's broadest expectations from the supernatural include good health, adequate sustenance, and sufficient offspring to ensure the continuity of his line. Okinawan religion, however, is characterized by a collectivity focus; the major ritual activities are carried out in the context of the family, kin group, community, and, formerly, the state. Within these groups, the preponderant responsibility for ritual action has been allocated to specialists; consequently, the individual layman usually plays a small and decidedly passive role in seeking supernatural rewards.

It can be stated without exaggeration, I believe, that Okinawans are in general more concerned with supernatural punishments than rewards. Perhaps this is only a truism of human nature, but possibly it is a real consequence of the system itself, which removes the ordinary person from active solicitation. At any rate, in discussions of the supernatural one hears far more about misfortunes meted out than of blessings received. I have the impression, though unsubstantiated in any systematic way, that power implies both the capacity for nurturance as well as the need to be nurturant; those who are more succorant pay for this by submissiveness, but this does not necessarily evoke gratitude.

In traditional Okinawan thinking, all forms of misfortune are viewed as products of an impaired relationship with the supernatural. This belief generally persists today, except among the well educated, but even in this group I have found high school teachers and university instructors among the clientele of the shaman. In the absence of a concept of impersonal causation, misfortune in the form of human failure, severe economic hardship, suffering, sickness, disease, insanity, disaster, etc., whether visited upon the individual or the group, can be interpreted as resulting from the action of supernatural agencies. Misfortune, especially when severe or prolonged, is considered a supernatural punishment. Such punishment is always contingent upon failure to act or upon improper action by a group or an individual, living or dead.

The primary punishing authorities in the supernatural are the *kami*. Although trouble may be definitely discerned in certain cases as arising from the action of purely malevolent spirits, the very fact of their attack is indicative of a withdrawal of support by the *kami* and ancestors. Thus, while malevolent spirits are not instruments of the *kami*, the ultimate explanation for their attack can be traced to the higher supernatural spirits. Very frequently the services of a shaman must be sought to explain these matters and to recommend proper remedial action, for the question is one of determining which spirit has been offended by the action or inaction of an individual or a group. The types of action or inaction which offend and the forms of punishment manifested by the supernatural seem to be nearly infinite (frequently I have been told, "It must be easy for you with only one *kami*"), but certain of these recur repeatedly.

Actions Precipitating Punishment or Deprivation

UGWANBUSUKU. One of the most common causes of calamity is insufficiency of prayer (*ugwanbusuku*). Cases of *ugwanbusuku* usually relate to a specific individual or household that has failed to maintain proper ritual ties with the ancestors. One family made a hasty move from a village when the household head unexpectedly secured a promising job in the city. Instead of praying to the ancestral tablets, notifying the ancestors of the proposed move, and inviting them to accompany the family, the family carelessly tossed the tablets in a bag, and a stranger (i.e., non-relative) was allowed to move into the premises. Soon thereafter the child of the family was struck down by a truck and severely injured, the job proved a disappointment necessitating a return to the country, and the house in the village suffered damage from a fire started by a neighbor's child. It was said in the village that the ancestral spirits were unhappy because they had been left stranded in the country with a stranger in their house, and that the *kami*, angered by this disrespectful treatment of the ancestors, had caused these misfortunes.

Prospective *kaminchu* (priestesses or shamans) who fail to acknowledge the call to office, or established *kaminchu* delinquent in their duties, are clear examples of persons guilty of *ugwanbusuku*. Shamans frequently ascribe their clients' difficulties to *ugwanbusuku*. Since the burden of ritual obligations is actually impossible to fulfill if they are carried to a logical extreme, it becomes a relatively simple matter to suggest some oversight which is plausible to the person concerned.

MACHIGEE. Equally as offensive to the supernatural as insufficiency of prayer is improper prayer or worship, termed *machigee* (literally, "mistakes," but, when used in a religious sense, "erroneous or improper ritual action"). Two prospective shamans claimed the same *chiji* and held prolonged and heated arguments over who was the rightful heir. Ultimately one became sick and withdrew his claim, and it was concluded that he was guilty of *machigee* and owed the *kami* an apology. In another instance, a family seeking to cure a mentally ill member prayed desperately at many famous ritual sites, including certain ones used exclusively by the former upper classes. Shortly thereafter the illness became worse, and it was said that the family had prayed "too high," beyond their own blood line. Sometimes when possessed, a shaman will see many *machigee* committed by ancestors of the client which have caused problems for the descendants.

DEFILEMENT OF A SACRED PLACE. In virtually every area innumerable stories are recounted concerning those who have suffered punishment for defiling an area sacred to the *kami*. A Japanese soldier was said to have entered a small shrine sacred to the worship of a village *kami* and attempted to remove some relics. As he emerged, a snake bit him, and he died almost instantly. A woman urinated in a tomb area and was afterwards troubled by a vaginal disorder. A student broke off a stalactite in a cave that was one of the principal sites of prayer for the chief priestess of Okinawa; on the following day he died suddenly from unknown causes, though presumably from *kami* action. A three-year-old child was crushed beneath the wheels of a cart loaded with sugar, because, it was said, her father had cut a tree from the sacred grove and used it to construct a toilet. Although at present the taboos surrounding sacred places are less stringently observed than in the recent past, elderly people continue to attach considerable importance to their observance.

VIOLATION OF SOCIAL VALUES. Supernatural punishments do not arise exclusively from infractions or neglect of prescribed ritual procedure; the *kami* also punish violations of those social norms which are accorded primacy in the value system. On the basis of actual cases handled by the shamans, I find that these fall into two broad categories. First and more commonly, punishments are meted out for action or inaction which impairs family relationships and/or continuity of the family. Second, punishment is given for actions or attitudes consistently opposed to the Okinawan conception of ideal character and behavior.

Several examples from the first category may be cited. There is virtually no strong moral condemnation of adultery per se, but repeated involvement in extramarital affairs and neglect of family responsibilities does invoke censure. Particularly reprehensible is the squandering of family resources on a paramour, for this impairs the survival and continuity of a family. Similarly, bad relationships within the nuclear family or between two linked nuclear families can cause supernatural retribution. Bad relationships between husband and wife, between husband-wife and his parents, and between parents and their first son appear to be the most disvalued by the *kami* and ancestors. Another example would be an attempt to alter the order of male succession in the family. Okinawans conceive of the first son's succession to the family property and role of household head as a natural right and duty; no matter what his disabilities or what difficulties his succession will entail, his succession ought not to be questioned. In instances where an attempt is made to alter the succession, the *kami* intercedes and shows displeasure by bringing misfortune to the family. Failure to participate in kin group rites and activities may also provoke the *kami*. In a sense, the failure to participate may be regarded as an instance of *ugwanbusuku* (insufficiency of prayer), but it also appears that sociation within the kin group has a value for its own sake. It should be emphasized that in the cases cited above, the punishment is not necessarily visited upon the wrongdoer.

A few examples from the second category might be mentioned. The cause of a wealthy man's high blood pressure was ascribed by the shaman to the fact that his greed impelled him to seek even greater riches. A housewife, jealous of her husband's close relationship with his mother, was punished by pains in her limbs. Although I have indicated that punishment in this category is less frequent than in the first, it is understood that the supernatural may punish those who are regularly greedy, envious, or jealous in nature. Such traits, strongly disvalued in daily social life, are equally disvalued by the *kami* as well.

KARII-YANJUNG. An individual's fortune results from a complex of interacting factors. It is largely determined by one's relationship to the *kami* and ancestors, which is dependent on observation of ritual obligations and respecting certain values and prescribed patterns of action. To no small degree it is also the product of inheritance, as the living may suffer from the misdeeds of ancestors. In addition, the operation of the calendar periodically alters one's fortune by making him more or less susceptible to misfortune. Lastly, there are numerous prescriptions concerning human action, violation of which will influence one's luck or fortune and render him more prone to misfortune. These are not injunctions in the manner of major taboos, violation of which brings automatic punishment by the supernatural, nor are they significant social injunctions whose transgression will bring social censure. Instead, they are conceived of as prescriptions whose observation will ensure greater freedom from misfortune. Adherence to them does not guarantee absence of misfortune, only less likelihood of its occurrence. Violation of these prescriptions is referred to as *karii-yanjung* (to break luck).

In a number of these prescriptions, belief in a negative sympathetic magic is evidenced. One does not sleep with the head to the west as the dead are laid out. The name of the poisonous *habu* snake should not be mentioned while working in tall grass or in the forest lest the creature come in answer to its name. The term for split kindling cannot be used aboard a ship carrying this as cargo, since the same term is applicable to the splitting of a hull. One old woman became infuriated when asked a question about funeral rites early in the morning, saying "You have broken the day's luck; say something bad in the morning, and it will occur in the afternoon!"

In general, *karii-yanjung* does not receive frequent recognition as a cause of misfortune; at times, however, it may be ascribed as the primary cause for a calamity. Informants tend to be vague about relating *karii-yanjung* to the reaction produced. Some feel that *karii-yanjung* simply invites attack by malevolent spirits, while others would see ultimate causality linked to the *kami*. I have the impression that many see nothing beyond a one-for-one, cause-and-effect, relationship.

NMARI-DUSHI. An individual is thought to be more susceptible to supernatural attack during his *nmari-dushi* (birth year; 'yaku doshi'). The complex of beliefs surrounding *nmari-dushi* is described in Chapter III. In essence, *nmari-dushi* occur at intervals of twelve years from the first year of life; thus, the thirteenth, twenty-fifth, thirty-seventh, forty-ninth, sixty-first, seventy-third, eighty-fifth, and ninety-seventh years of life are *nmari-dushi*. At such times one must be more cautious than usual, alert for danger, and prepared to take protective measures. In addition to *nmari-dushi*, the seventh and nineteenth years of life are also regarded as dangerous, not to mention numerous days during any given year. Informants were unable to state why *nmari-dushi* constituted a danger, but they agreed that one was not placed in a position of weakness vis-à-vis the supernatural through the action of some supernatural agent; rather, this position came about through the purely mechanical operation of the calendar. *Nmari-dushi* cannot be construed as a condition prompting supernatural punishment as when an individual is punished for a wrong act. It is a state of being which renders the person more vulnerable to supernatural attack, especially from malevolent spirits.

Manifestations of Supernatural Punishment

KAMI ARABI. A group of people, such as a community or kin group, may collectively incur the wrath of the *kami* and suffer a form of punishment called *kami arabi* (lit., "*kami* rough fire," meaning "disaster caused by the *kami*"). Common causes of *kami arabi* are said to be neglect of ritual, damage to the sacred grove (*utaki*), or any disrespectful act toward the *kami* on the part of a community, its officials, or religious functionaries. *Kami arabi* may take many forms: a high death rate (particularly among children), frequent fires, drought, epidemic, etc. A number of older Okinawans expressed the belief that Okinawa was devastated in World War II because the *kami* were displeased by the failure to maintain traditional rites; thus, the entire nation suffered *kami arabi*.

TAARI. *Kaminchu* and, indirectly, members of their immediate family may be afflicted with a specific type of punishment called *taari* or *kami-daari* (retribution, *kami* retribution). *Taari* strikes prospective *kaminchu* (community priestesses, kin group priestesses, or shamans) who reject their destined role, or established *kaminchu* who shirk their ritual obligations. Although almost any kind of misfortune afflicting a *kaminchu* may be labeled *taari*, most frequently it assumes the pattern of a genuine psychosomatic disorder. A comparison of *taari* cases from all parts of Okinawa reveals that the common syndrome includes physical weakness or sickness, inability to perform normal routine work, lack of appetite, auditory and visual hallucinations, disturbing dreams, periods of dissociation, and sometimes eye disorders in the form of partial blindness.

A seventy-year-old community priestess related that she had suffered *taari* at twenty-one after refusing to accept office. Although she was aware of the possible consequences, she had demurred, hoping to lead a normal life, but in a short time she found herself sickly and unable to perform a day's work; moreover, her sight began to fail rapidly. When all attempts at curing proved futile, she finally accepted the white robes of office, whereupon her health improved and normal eyesight returned.

All *kaminchu* were agreed that their health was conditioned by their performance in office and that any laxity could bring *taari*. Among the hereditary *kaminchu* of the community, *taari* appears to afflict only those who refuse office or who neglect their responsibilities after taking office. Its incidence is not high in this group, and less than one-third of the hereditary *kaminchu* whom I interviewed acknowledged having had *taari*. In the case of the kin group *kaminchu* and the shamans, who attain office by divine notification, the occurrence of *taari* is nearly universal. With few exceptions, virtually every shaman and kin group priestess passes through a *taari* period before accepting office; this period varies from several months to many years. Unlike the hereditary *kaminchu*, who know their *chiji*, the prospective shamans or kin group *kaminchu* must undertake the often long and anguishing search for theirs. Full recovery from *taari* must often await identification of the proper *chiji*, although the severity of *taari* usually slackens with commitment, through prayer, to undertake the search. *Taari* is regularly preceded for this group by a series of notifications (*shirashi*) from the *kami*, which should alert the individual. Consequently, when these notifications are unheeded, punishment results, in the form of *taari*. It may, of course, recur for any laxity in performance after taking office.

The high degree of anxiety engendered by the constant threat of *taari* pressures the *kaminchu* to conform to the standards of their role. Today, when many people have begun to slough off traditional rites and beliefs, the *kaminchu* attempt to observe them in the spirit of the past, regardless of personal inclinations. Although *kami-daari* is predominantly a punishment directed against *kaminchu* or prospective *kaminchu*—particularly female *kaminchu* who occupy major religious positions—any misfortune afflicting other members of a *kaminchu*'s household may be considered punishment for some failure or violation on the part of the *kaminchu*. Since a community, kin group, or household may lose *kami* and ancestral favor through delinquency on the part of its *kaminchu* member, there is some degree of group pressure to enforce conformity.

MANI-GUTU. Crucial to any understanding of Okinawan thinking is the concept of *mani-gutu*, which may be roughly equated with atavism though carrying a somewhat negative, disvalued connotation. It is firmly believed that one's conduct in this world will affect the lot of one's descendants; similarly, the activities of ancestors have conditioned the lives of the present living generations. Punishment for the offenses or misdeeds of an ancestor also may be visited upon the descendants. When an ancestor in a certain kinship status has been offensive to the *kami*, subsequent occupants of that status may be subject to punishment in the form of misfortune; thus, if a second son in a given household commits a crime, succeeding second sons in that household may be penalized. Usually, the punishment takes the form of repetition of the same type of behavior of which the ancestor was guilty. For example, the behavior of a drunkard who squanders the family wealth is certain to reappear in subsequent generations. Crimes of violence are especially abhorrent to the *kami* (as well as to society) and will inevitably cause endless suffering for descendants. In this regard, it is important to emphasize that Okinawans consider both murdered person and murderer as suffering punishment for having had ancestors addicted to violence.

Ultimately, the chain reaction of *mani-gutu* can be halted only by determining the particular set of circumstances which set off the reaction. This usually involves identification of the particular ancestor involved and then expiation through apology to the *kami* and/or other remedial action. Inevitably, this demands the services of the shaman.

ICHIJAMA. So far as I have been able to determine, the incidence of sorcery, *ichijama*, is relatively low on Okinawa. In the course of my field studies I uncovered only two recent instances of sorcery, by which I mean only two individuals *accused* of sorcery; to the best of my knowledge and that of my informants, no one has ever admitted to this. In both cases, the accused were shamans. A sorcerer, *ichijamaa* (the final vowel is lengthened, changing "sorcery" to "sorcerer"), is believed to have personal supernatural power enabling her (*ichijamaa* are usually women) to work harm against others. The characteristics of a sorcerer are moodiness, asociability, and jealousy or covetousness—traits distinctly at odds with Okinawan ideal personality. Insofar as could be determined, the sorcerer does not sell her services or indulge in black magic for the benefit of others. Sorcery is said to persist in certain family lines. If one should incur the enmity of an *ichijamaa*, who is usually motivated by intense jealousy, he will suffer sickness, property damage, fire, or other misfortune. Victims of sorcery may secure the services of a shaman, but the means of redress are quite simple. To negate the sorcerer's power, she must become so damagingly polluted that she loses supernatural support. In the case of one suspected sorcerer, two women plotted to invite her to tea and then place human feces in her drink; this, they reasoned, would cause all *kami* support to be lost. It is said that, in the past, those suspected of sorcery were socially ostracized and denied help in case of fire; they were also excluded from participation in reciprocal labor exchanges. It is my impression that the threat of being labeled an *ichijamaa* may have been a factor in social control and that the actual incidence of sorcery was rather low.

ICHIINING. The incidence of cursing, *ichiining*, is relatively greater than that of sorcery, and the circumstances of occurrence are quite different. Anyone can curse, while sorcery can be practiced only by certain persons. "Cursing" means to invoke supernatural punishment upon someone who has done a (real or imagined) injustice to the curser. The capacity to curse seems limited to a period of intense hatred directed against the guilty person; it arises, therefore, from an extreme passion or obsession, not from an ordinary dislike. Cursing is usually done by women, and in most cases it is directed against a spurning lover. For example, a married man had an affair and eventually a child with another woman; in time he grew bored, stopped seeing her, and gave no further support for the child. Her love for him changed to intense hatred and she cursed him, with the result that his son (by his legal wife) became seriously ill. The shaman recommended an apology to the woman and some money for her child.

Cursing appears to be confined to intimates, whereas sorcery, in the few stories and cases known to me, does not involve either intimates or kin. Moreover, unlike sorcery, cursing seems to have some basis of legitimacy in the eyes of society. This does not mean that cursing is valued but that the person cursing has a recognized grievance against the person being cursed. In both sorcery and cursing the person singled out for attack may not be the person who suffers the attack, although they will probably be members of the same family-household.

ATTACK BY MALEVOLENT SPIRITS. Death, disease, sickness, and other forms of misfortune may be caused by attacks of malevolent spirits, *yanamung* and *majimung*. Attack by a ghost (*majimung*) may cause death through theft of *mabui*. The spirit in an evil wind (*yanakaji*) may inflict a hideous skin disease. As stated before, Okinawans may identify a malevolent spirit as the immediate souce of the attack, but usually the attack will be interpreted as a manifestation of a more basic difficulty with the *kami* or ancestors. In this respect, the interpretations for sorcery and cursing are fundamentally the same as for attack by malevolent spirits—the individual or group has suffered some withdrawal of support by the *kami* and ancestors.

KAKAIMUNG. A common manifestation of supernatural punishment is referred to as *kakaimung* (thing attached, thing hung on, thing caught by). *Kakaimung* usually involves a bodily disorder imposed by the supernatural and most frequently indicates that an ancestor or someone recently deceased requires special prayers. A young man suffered from constant headaches and generally poor health; the interpretation was that a particular ancestor who had died of tuberculosis was now requesting special prayers. An elderly woman had severe backaches; they were said to indicate the need for prayers on behalf of a deceased sibling. A young woman had sharp pains in her arm, could not work, and suffered from disturbing dreams; these were *kakaimung* from a recently deceased classmate who wished to have a Buddhist mass ('kuyō') said in her behalf. Expectations of *kakaimung* being the explanation for bodily aches and pains are sufficiently common that clients of the shaman, after describing their symptoms, will ask, "Is this some sort of *kakaimung?*" Essentially, *kakaimung* serves as a punishing notification from the *kami* that some oversight exists in ritual obligations.

Responsibility and Accountability

The absence of a concept of impersonal causation in traditional Okinawan thinking rules out the possibility of accidental occurrences; the ultimate cause for all manifestations of misfortune can be ascribed to supernatural action. Although the *kami* and ancestors may be nurturant toward man, they also constitute the primary punishing agencies in the supernatural order. Even when attacks stem directly from the action of malevolent spirits, fundamental causality can be ascribed to a withdrawal or partial withdrawal of nurturance by the *kami* and ancestors. Supernatural displeasure may be evinced positively by infliction of punishment or negatively by withdrawal of support. Infliction of punishment or withdrawal of support by the *kami* and ancestors does not occur irrationally but arises from the omission or commission of certain action(s) by the individual or group. The types of action or inaction engendering supernatural displeasure range from purely ritual infractions to misbehavior in social relationships. Supernatural punishment, therefore, is directly contingent upon the activity of man, and, conversely, rewards are also highly contingent. Such being the case, it could be assumed that a relatively high degree of individual responsibility and accountability to the supernatural prevails in Okinawa.

Man does bear the primary responsibility for maintaining reciprocity with the *kami* and ancestors, for their nurturance is conditional upon regular performance of propitiatory ritual. As stated earlier, however, this religion is characterized by a collectivity focus; the family-household, kin group, and community (as also did the state in the past) constitute the basic ritual units of society. Within these units, major ritual responsibilities are delegated to specific individuals: community priestesses, kin group priestesses, and usually the senior female member of a household. Although these individuals may incur supernatural punishment for laxity in performance, ultimate accountability rests with the collectivity as a whole. Thus, while responsibility for performance may be delegated, accountability remains collective.

The Westerner studying Okinawan society can be handicapped by his ethnocentric focus on the individual, for the basic units of Okinawan society are families, kin groups, and communities—not individuals. The individual, as such, establishes identity only through membership in these groups. Consequently, the primary responsibilities of the individual are to the group; and, ideally, group interests take precedence, where there is a conflict, over individual self-interest. The group, in turn, is accountable for the action of individual members; this is true for both supernatural and social orders. The group, however, exists in time as well as space; current living generations are centrally placed on a continuum extending from the earliest ancestors through generations as yet unborn. Accountability, in the final analysis, encompasses the entire range of the collectivity through time; thus, a child may suffer punishment for the action of his parents or ancestors.

Individual accountability to society and the supernatural becomes enmeshed in a circularity of reasoning when viewed with respect to the transitory nature of collective accountability and the concept of atavism (*mani-gutu*). It can never be fully determined whether the individual acts as a free agent or merely in response to a predetermined sequence beyond his control. The answer to who is ultimately responsible is: no one and everyone. An intelligent Okinawan reflecting on the subject commented, "When you think about this deeply, no one is really fully responsible for anything."

Ethno-metaphysics

A consistent aspect in Okinawan thinking regarding the supernatural is the virtual absence of metaphysical speculation. So far as I am aware, there is no accounting for the origin of the universe or cosmos. As indicated above, the earliest recognized deities—the siblings *uminai* and *umikii*—are anthropomorphized spirits sent down from heaven at the order of "higher *kami*" who are not identified. This pair created the first land and produced the first people. The "creation myth" is as simple as that. The world begins with the island of Okinawa, one assumes, but "explanations" commence with the first human beings. There is, in fact, a striking paucity of any highly developed mythology. Culture hero myths, accounts of mythical epochs, or myths relating to the principal deities are notably absent or but weakly developed. Though relatively deficient in these areas, Okinawa abounds in etiological myths. One may record within a single village several different myths explaining the same custom, suggesting that myths are valued for the function of conferring sanctity upon established social practices. As a corollary, the strength of historical legends must be noted; frequently I have been surprised by the historical knowledge which an old, often illiterate, Okinawan will display. The war with Satsuma, for example, may be thought to have occurred anywhere between seventy-five and a thousand years ago, but the actual sequence and nature of events will be reasonably accurate.

The strength of historical legends and etiological myths, together with the relative absence of metaphysical speculation, reflects a primary concern with human relationships. The range of speculative interest in nature and the supernatural seems pragmatically limited to those areas directly related to man's survival and well-being.

Ethno-epistemology

There are two fundamental sources of knowledge: empirical cognition and supernatural instruction or revelation. The first is assumed to be universal and need not concern us here. Supernatural instruction, however, is limited to a few, predominantly the *kaminchu*. Such instruction may come in several ways: through hallucination, possession, hearing, or dreams. *Imi-gukuchi* (dreamlike feeling or sensation) may be equated with hallucination or waking vision; this supposedly occurs when the individual is in full command of his or her senses. It is usually an auditory and visual experience which the individual may view as a spectator or participant. Possession is of a completely different nature and may be expressed by the verbs *mutariing* (to hold, possess, carry), *nuiing* (to ride, to ride on or in), *katchimiing* (to catch), and *utchakaiing* (to lean on). In possession, an external spirit may take over full command of the body or merely be on the body in such a manner as to enable control or guidance. Hearing (*chichung*) seems to fall into a category somewhat in between *imi-gukuchi* and *mutariing* or *nuiing*. In this case, the spirit, usually the *chiji*, does not touch the body but speaks to the subject. A dream (*imi*) may also constitute a source of information and may, of course, occur to anyone, but usually its full significance can be explained only by a shaman.

Information or knowledge derived from the supernatural is received principally by those who are *saadaka nmari*; in other words, it is conferred upon those whom the *kami* have selected to become *kaminchu*. Ordinary people (*musang*, as opposed to *kaminchu*) cannot aspire to attain such knowledge by any means. In this respect, Okinawa contrasts sharply with certain of the Plains Indian tribes, in which virtually anyone could follow a prescribed procedure to obtain supernatural knowledge and power. All *kaminchu* disclaim the need for any formal training in preparation for office. Repeatedly I heard statements such as, "This is not something which you study for," or "My *chiji* tells me what to do." In actuality, of course, a new priestess in the community or kin group does learn through association with the other priestesses; however, little recognition is given to this fact, and credit for knowing what to do is ascribed to the *kami*. Similarly, the knowledge and power of the shaman are considered divinely conferred. The prospective shaman does not train with or understudy an established shaman, although many may be consulted for suggestions. A prospective shaman's search for her *chiji* tends to be a traumatic and lonely experience, but, once found, the *chiji* thereafter provides guidance.

Okinawan thinking tends to be highly pragmatic (given their definition of the situation) in the use and validation of supernaturally derived knowledge. A family confronted with serious misfortune consults not just a single shaman but seeks out several for advice or explanation and then accepts the consensus or whatever is deemed most reasonable. Similarly, the proof of becoming a shaman rests upon recovery from *taari*; the fact that the individual recovers from sickness and other misfortune characterizing *taari* constitutes proof that mastery of supernatural power and knowledge has been realized. Moreover, reputations of established shamans are constantly being substantiated or denigrated by the fulfillment or nonfulfillment of their prognostications. The supernatural as a valid source of knowledge is beyond question; it is the intermediary sources (e.g., the shamans) conveying the information, its possible interpretations, and methods of application which are questioned or tested.

Conclusion

Okinawan religious belief may be characterized as animistic, for all things, animate and inanimate, are conceived as possessed of indwelling spirits. Consequently, a rigid dichotomy of sacred and profane does not exist, such distinction being merely one of degree. The religion may be classified as "tribal," since membership is acquired by birth or residence, not by conversion or conviction. As a result, it is a nonproselytizing, nonexportable system. It is also nonexclusive to the extent that evidences of borrowing may be discerned, but this does not imply an absence of selectivity. Although the religion lacks sacred texts and a rationalized theology, the label of "primitive" seems unwarranted because of its integrative function in a literate state.

III

RELIGIOUS PRACTICES

Introduction

Religious practices serve as a means of translating belief into action and also, we may assume, provide insight into the conditions of life and the major areas of concern and anxiety. In the preceding chapter it was shown that supernatural punishments and rewards are highly contingent and that a reciprocity obtains between man and the supernatural provided ritual obligations are observed. Absence of a concept of impersonal causation gives added range to the prospect of supernatural punishment, for ultimately all manifestations of misfortune can be attributed to supernatural causation. It is not surprising, therefore, that religious practices emphasize apology, placation, and propitiation, conditioned by the event or prospect of misfortune, or that rewards are requested under the assumption that reciprocity obtains. Since the Okinawans do not appear to be excessively fear-ridden, we can assume that their system of ritual practices largely succeeds in allaying anxiety arising from the prospects of supernatural retribution or withdrawal of nurturance.

A stress on the observance of ritual obligations constitutes the keystone of this religion. Fundamentally, this is a matter of performance. Although because of its rather stylized nature the ritual action may strike the observer as purely perfunctory, the question of sincerity or feeling never arises, for in all acts, social as well as religious, there is a focus of attention on the external details of performance. Proper performance, whether in the religious or social order, is of itself held to be rewarding, and through compliance with ritual forms the individual wins the approval of associates and the supernatural.

The Calendar and Ritual Practices

Although the Gregorian calendar has been the official calendar on Okinawa since the early years of Japanese administration, the Chinese lunar-solar calendar serves as the farmer's guide in regulating the agricultural cycle, as the ceremonial calendar, and as the basis for a complex of beliefs and practices relating to the individual's personal fortune. The function of the Chinese calendar for religious life and livelihood is of considerable importance.

Most beliefs surrounding the calendar appear to be a wholesale import from China. Knowledge and use of the Chinese calendar apparently dates back several centuries in Sino-Ryukyuan relations, for the calendar and almanac were received periodically in return for tribute payments and acknowledgment of Chinese suzerainty. Its use, however, was limited to officialdom and the literate upper class. Old priestesses declare that, prior to Japanese rule and for some time thereafter, ceremonial dates were determined in the capital and that village officials were periodically notified as to when rites were to be held. As the major village rites pertained to the agricultural cycle, the farmers in turn were guided by the ritual cycle in planting, transplanting, and harvesting their major crops.

Shimabukuro[1] has suggested that, prior to adoption of the Chinese calendar, time was computed by measuring the passage of the sun over certain natural landmarks which gradually came to be regarded as sacred places of worship. Unfortunately, he cites no evidence to support this idea, and I have been unable to find any corroborating traditions. In some areas, however, the use of simple grass counters (knot records) for marking the passage of lunar time can be recalled. It is my opinion that the complex of beliefs and practices relating to the calendar is of recent introduction in the rural areas, but that in the Naha-Shuri area, especially among the upper classes, it is of considerable antiquity.

Bramsen[2] and Clement[3] have treated the operation of the Chinese calendar in detail, so only the essentials pertaining to Okinawan religion will be described here. A lunar year is ordinarily divided into twelve months alternately consisting of twenty-nine and thirty days each. The full moon thus falls on approximately the fifteenth day of each month. In order to adjust this lunar system to solar time, intercalary months are inserted in a cycle of every second, fifth, eighth, eleventh, thirteenth, sixteenth, and nineteenth year; hence in any nineteen-year period there are seven intercalary months. For example, 1960 was an intercalary year (*uruu-dushi*), and an additional "sixth" month was inserted after the regular sixth month. In Okinawa no major ceremonies are held during an intercalary month, although household rites continue as usual.

A cycle of twelve animal signs vaguely suggestive of the Western zodiac enumerates each day and year. The signs are the rat, ox, tiger, rabbit, dragon, snake, horse, goat, monkey, cock, dog, and pig. These also designate the directions (beginning with the rat as north), a bi-hourly division of the day, and the musical scale. People refer to their year of birth in terms of the animal year (e.g., *in-soo*—"dog person") and the number of cycles elapsed. A new cycle begins every twelfth year. The recurrence of one's birth year (*nmari-dushi*) in the thirteenth, twenty-fifth, thirty-seventh, forty-ninth, sixty-first, seventy-third, eighty-fifth, and ninety-seventh years of life is believed to be a time of danger and susceptibility to misfortune. It is also believed that certain combinations of the animal signs are unlucky: the dog and the monkey are regarded as incompatible, hence people born in these years ought not to marry or enter into business alliances. Certain days are considered inappropriate for specific activities: a farmer should not plant or store grain on the day of the rat; women born in the year of the horse are believed to be poor prospects for marriage, and so forth.

Running concurrently with the cycle described above is a second cycle of ten units which also applies to a sequence of days and years. These ten units are designated by the five Chinese elements—wood, fire, earth, metal, and water—each of which has a major and minor phase, thereby comprising ten in all. As the two cycles function, rat year (or day) and wood-major year (day) will recur simultaneously only every sixty-first year (day); consequently, sixty years (or days) are required for a major cycle to elapse. It is believed that the sixty-first *nmari-dushi* is the most dangerous, and great precaution must be taken at such a time to avoid misfortune. In some villages rice-planting ceremonies are held on "water" days in the belief that this will ensure an abundance of moisture to nurture the crop; but in the crucial period preceding the rice harvest, rites are held on "metal" days, since the heavily laden stalks require a metal-like strength at this time.

A third cycle of six days, unrelated to the two preceding, begins on the first day of each month and follows in sequence on each succeeding month. This cycle determines the fortune for each day. The days are divided into morning and afternoon halves which are designated good or bad. Certain days are all bad, others all good, and some a mixture of good and bad. There is some reluctance to commence any new or major undertaking on unpropitious days; consequently, it is felt that this cycle should be referred to before determining a major course of action.

A simple formula of addition and subtraction permits approximation of the tides for any given lunar day. Funerals ought to take place at the time of ebb tide, preferably low tide. For a marriage ceremony, an incoming tide approaching high tide is considered most desirable. Annual rites for ridding fields of insect pests are conducted during an ebbing tide. In the past, consideration of tide, propitious day, and the desire to bury during the daylight hours not infrequently delayed funerals for several days. The Japanese government, however, enforced interment within twenty-four hours of death, and as a result certain concessions are made now with respect to traditional requirements.

Calendrical dates and calendrical fortunes are closely watched by the senior female in the household, who is usually familiar with the details concerning each member's personal calendar history. The complexity of calendrical lore, however, is of such magnitude that the fortuneteller or shaman must be consulted for detailed analysis of personal fortunes or for selection of propitious days when major undertakings are contemplated.

There is little evidence to suggest that these practices and beliefs relating to the lunar calendar are abating; in fact, all indications suggest that they are stronger today than seventy-five years ago, when literacy and use of the calendar were not so widespread. The government, schools, and newspaper editorials have exhorted the people for years to adopt the official solar calendar; the net result has been that two New Years (lunar and solar) are now celebrated, much to the delight of the shopkeepers.

Pollution

Things or acts which pollute, defile, or render impure that which is the *kami*'s or those who seek communion with the *kami* are termed *chigarimung*. The concept of pollution includes not only that which is offensive in a physical sense but also connotes contamination of a malevolent character, implying the presence of or association with malevolent things or spirits. Because such pollution is held offensive to the *kami*, being in a state of *chigarimung* seriously impairs relationship with the *kami* and thereby renders the individual more susceptible to misfortune.

Some of the primary sources of pollution are childbirth, sex, blood, death, sickness, and disease; but other sources also exist. Tombs and the practice of bone washing, because of their association with death, are considered polluting. The former pariah caste which was restricted to the function of bell-ringing at funerals was regarded as impure and hence highly defiling. The association of death with pollution is limited to the physical fact of death and to the earthly remains of the dead; it does not extend to the ancestral spirits (*futuki*).

Certain major sites of worship, especially the sacred grove (*utaki*), may be polluted by the entrance of outsiders, particularly males. The household ancestral shrine may be contaminated by contact with a bird, a not unlikely happening with houses completely open on two sides during warm weather. The *kaminchu*, because of their close association with the *kami*, are more subject to pollution than laymen. However, a housewife may be rendered unfit for household ritual during her menses or for a period following delivery of a child. Formerly, in the town of Itoman every household hearth in the community was thrown away when a child was born; later, this practice was limited to the house of birth; today, as stoves have replaced simple three-stone hearths, it has fallen into total disuse. The interpretation was that the entire community had been polluted by a birth and that contact with the *kami* through the hearth was endangered. Fishermen are more susceptible to pollution than farmers, and if possible they will avoid a house of death, sickness, or recent birth, under the assumption that contact will pollute them and impair their relationship with the sea *kami*. A woman recently widowed may be regarded as a source of pollution. Formerly, she was secluded during the mourning period in a special mourning hut erected within the tomb yard.

Malevolent spirits in any manifestation are contaminating as well as dangerous, and certain practices may be resorted to in order to negate their effect. At present, the fear of pollution appears to be rapidly declining; thus, while a young housewife may continue to observe hearth rites as her mother (or mother-in-law) did before her, she often ignores the fact of menstruation as polluting and offensive to the *kami*. Nonetheless, for the oldest generation, most country women, and for *kaminchu*, pollution continues to be regarded as a matter deserving serious attention.

Taboo

There are a number of negative injunctions whose violation, it is believed, will bring automatic punishment by the *kami*. These are called *chiji* (taboo), which derives from the verb *chijiing* (to screen off, to fence off); the word should not be confused with its homonym, *chiji* (spirit), described in the previous chapter. Taboos involve those things and acts regarded as offensive to the *kami*. A number of taboos are directed against sources of pollution, but others relate to nonpollutive factors which also may offend the *kami* and impair man's well-being. The more stringent of these taboos apply to the *kaminchu*, who are responsible for maintaining regular ritual contact with the supernatural.

ACT TABOOS. The major act taboos surround the livelihood of the people. When the new seed beds of rice are sown, there is a general prohibition against the spilling of blood or the taking of life in the paddy. A small, edible eel which lives in paddies may not be caught until after transplanting, and some contend that a person with a fresh wound or running sore should not enter the field at this time. Later, after the rice ears have formed and prior to harvest time, many communities formerly observed an injunction against the playing of a samisen, the beating of a drum, or the making of loud noises, for fear that the ears would fall. During the most crucial period in the growth of rice—immediately before harvest, when the top-heavy stalks may easily suffer damage from wind or rain—there is a general work taboo, *un-dumi—yama-dumi* (sea closed, mountain closed). At that time, no one should enter a boat for fishing or work in the fields. Formerly, this taboo covered a span of approximately three days, but now such strictness is rare. Where still observed, it may be limited to a single day or merely to the period when the priestesses are conducting rites asking for a successful harvest. In a number of villages, especially in the north, a periodic work taboo (*yama-dumi*) survives; this falls on the eighth, eighteenth, and twenty-eighth days of the lunar month, when it is believed that *kami* descend to the mountains and fields. At such times it is forbidden to enter the mountains for wood cutting or to work in the fields. Falling at intervals of ten days, these work taboos also function as days of rest.

PLACE AND OBJECT TABOOS. A strong taboo applies to the sacred grove (*utaki*) associated with the founding *kami* of the community. Males should not enter this area, as their presence is believed to be offensive to the *kami*. The paraphernalia of the community priestess is stored out of sight and is brought out with apologies to the *kami*. Some priestesses were reluctant to be photographed or to don their white robes on other than ceremonial occasions for fear of incurring the *kami*'s wrath. Houses of sickness, death, and childbirth are taboo to the highest-ranking village priestess for a certain period of time, and, as noted before, this tends to apply to fishermen as well. A vaguer taboo surrounds tombs, placing them off limits except for funerals and ceremonial occasions; for the chief priestess of the village, tombs and funerals were taboo at all times.

STATUS AND SITUATIONAL TABOOS. In the preceding chapter it was noted that certain key statuses in the social system are considered sacrosanct and that any attempt to alter succession to these will incur *kami* retribution. The chief priestess of the village, the *nuru*, formerly spent most of her life in seclusion apart from fellow villagers and was not permitted to marry. While these practices are dead today, the belief persists that a taboo protects her position; consequently, those who marry her are reputed to be short-lived. A general taboo extends to all women in their menses, prohibiting them from entering a shrine or conducting household rites, but at present this seems to be far less scrupulously observed than in the past. During the period of the *nuru*'s menses, however, a substitute may officiate in her behalf. Fishing boats are taboo to women, as their presence would be offensive to the sea *kami*. Here, a contradiction suggests itself, for the dugouts and plank boats used in fishing are often filled with pig blood for the purpose of dyeing and waterproofing nets; yet the evidence of blood which remains on the boat is somehow not believed polluting or offensive to the *kami*. When I mentioned this to an informant, the reply was, "That is true, but the sea *kami* is a jealous female!"

SPEECH TABOOS. The divine name (*kaminaa*) of the village priestess and of the sacred grove carries an aura of taboo and should not be readily divulged. Similarly, some priestesses and shamans were reluctant to reveal the identity of their *chiji*, the particular *kami* served by them. I suspect that in some cases today, as a result of many deaths in the ranks of *kaminchu* during the war, the priestess may be ignorant of the *kaminaa*. It is difficult to assess the intent behind this taboo save that divulging the name may irritate the *kami*; however, there are suggestions that revealing these names might impair or weaken the *kami* power.

The names of deceased members of a household are often taboo to surviving members of the family. A kin term or a posthumous name obtained from the Buddhist priest may be used instead. A large number of taboos of varying degrees of intensity surround those matters referring to unpleasantries, particularly death.

TABOO DEVICES. Often the area of the sacred grove or principal shrine may be encircled by a taboo rope called *hijainna*. The taboo rope serves the dual function of indicating a tabooed area and warding off malevolent spirits. A simpler taboo device may be fashioned from miscanthus grass twisted into a loop; this is called *sang*. Pandanus leaves may also be used to indicate a tabooed place and are sometimes attached to a house gate for that purpose.

IMPOSITION AND LIFTING OF A TABOO. In theory, the power to impose major taboos is limited to the chief priestess of a community. For example, in the past the taboo on music and loud noise prior to harvest time was decreed by her, and after the grain was harvested she removed the prohibition. Moreover, when a major taboo is violated, a not infrequent event at present, it is her duty to apologize to the *kami*.

Lesser taboos may be imposed by anyone, though perhaps with lesser expectations of effect. A farmer whose paddy adjoined a road was irked by passersby who watered their horses at his field, for often the animals chewed a few stalks of grain after drinking. He therefore placed a *sang* on a stick at this spot, which served to warn others to desist from watering horses and carried an implication of supernatural retribution for violation.

Many taboos are determined by time or situation and automatically expire with a certain event. Increasingly, the strictness with which a taboo ought to be observed has become a dead letter for many, if not most. Those who have retained a strong belief observe; others may do so when it suits their convenience or pleasure. The underlying fear of misfortune undoubtedly motivates compliance in many instances.

Means of Warding Off Malevolent Spirits

A number of devices are employed in the belief that they will guard or protect persons and places from attack by malevolent spirits. The majority of these appear to be widespread throughout East Asia and in all likelihood originated in China. My informants were unable to offer adequate rationale for the operation of these techniques and devices save that they were usually efficacious. It seems that their operation is viewed as purely mechanical and probably without any inherent force or power.

SANG AND HIJAINNA. It was stated above that *sang* and *hijainna* are employed to indicate the presence of a taboo; they are also used to protect material things from malevolence. When affixed to a house, shrine, well, farm building, tomb, animal pen, etc., *sang* ensures the safety of the structure and its occupants. A small *sang* may be placed on a tray of food offerings in order to prevent ghosts from consuming the food. If a family should stay away from home or if an owner leaves his business or store, *sang* may be attached to the main entrance. Its purpose here is to warn off trespassers and simultaneously protect the building from fire and other damage which might be caused by malevolent spirits. The material used for *sang* is usually *Miscanthus sinensis*. It is fashioned in a single large loop, then knotted in such a fashion that the free ends hang down. In a field, however, *sang* may be improvised from the stalks of grain.

Hijainna (lit., "left rope"; a rope twisted to the left) is used to encircle a shrine or sacred grove. Sometimes it may be strung above a gate or across a path. It is usually fashioned from rice straw twisted to the left, contrary to ordinary straw rope, which is made with a right-hand twist. Frequently, *sang* may be attached at intervals on the *hijainna*. In appearance and function, *hijainna* bears close resemblance to the Japanese 'shimenawa' and Korean 'keumchul.'

SHIISHI. Virtually all tile-roof houses throughout Okinawa have one or more small pottery lions (*shiishi*) on the roof for the purpose of warding off malevolent spirits. They are less common in the rural areas, where, until recently, most of the houses were thatched. Many communities have *shiishi* placed at the major points of entry into the housing area; frequently these may constitute secondary sites of community ritual. The term *keeshi* (that which sends back) can be used interchangeably with *shiishi*; more recently, the Japanese term 'karashishi' (China lion) has come into currency.

ISHIGANTUU. At the intersection of paths or roads, wherever a small alley ends, and especially at all points of entrance and exit to a housing area, there is erected a small stone two or three feet in height and usually rectangular in shape. On the face are carved three Chinese characters, 'shih-kan-tang,' which Okinawans pronounce as *ishigantuu*. Sometimes a demoniac face may be crudely scratched into the stone above the characters. It is believed that the *ishigantuu* by their strategic location deny the entry of malevolent spirits, especially ghosts (*majimung*). The *ishigantuu* occurs more commonly than the *shiishi*, but the function is virtually identical, and the same term, *keeshi*, may be applied to both.

This practice definitely seems to be of Chinese origin and may be found throughout the Ryukyus, parts of Kyushu, and Taiwan; a possibly related practice has been reported from North Borneo by Yanagita.[4] He errs, however, in relating the *ishigantuu* and *bijuru* stone found on Okinawa. The *bijuru* was used as a divining stone and was also symbolic of the phallus, whereas the *ishigantuu* was employed for repelling malevolent spirits; moreover, characters were not inscribed on the *bijuru*.

CHINESE CHARACTERS. Certain Chinese characters obtained from the fortuneteller or Buddhist priest are regarded as capable of fending off malevolence. The paper on which these are written is affixed to a house or gate. In a folk-theater play, a man whose spirit is being stolen by a beautiful ghost is saved after a Buddhist priest paints these protective characters on his clothing.

SALT. A simple and highly effective technique for dispelling attack by malevolent spirits is the use of common salt. For example, a mother may sprinkle a few grains of salt on a child's head before allowing him to go swimming; it is believed that any *yanamung* or *majimung* lurking about the water in hopes of drowning a hapless swimmer will be driven off by the salt. In place of (or with) *sang*, salt may be placed on a tray of food offerings in order to ward off malevolent spirits intent on stealing the food.

HEARTH ASHES. Ashes from the hearth are also thought to be efficacious in preventing attack by malevolent spirits. Since nearly all house lots are surrounded by a wall or fence with only one point of entrance, ashes may be sprinkled at the gate to forestall entry of malicious spirits.

INSULT AND DEPRECATION. Grossly insulting language, it is believed, will discourage attack by spirits in the immediate area. When a ghost is seen, one shouts, "Eat feces!," or other obscenities; this can be even more effective if pig manure is actually hurled in the direction of the spirit. If it is determined that the ghost or malevolent spirit is female, derogatory references are made to her genitals: "big vulva!," etc.

UMAMUI. A variety of talismans and protective amulets, called *umamui* ('omamori'), are employed to ensure good fortune by warding off attack from malevolent spirits. Men drafted into the Japanese army or navy from the town of Itoman always carried with them several pinches of sand from the *utaki* for the founding *kami* of the community. After coming home, this was redeposited in the same area with prayers of thanks for a safe return. At present, seamen departing on a long voyage still follow this practice. In other areas, ashes from the hearth of the chief priestess are carried for the same purpose.

The efficacy of Chinese characters for this purpose has been noted above. In urban areas, small pieces of paper bearing characters are obtained from the Buddhist priest; these are pasted about the house at the beginning of the New Year's season.

YANAMUNG-BAREE. The general term for the exorcising of malevolent spirits is *yanamung-baree* (to exorcise an evil spirit or thing). This encompasses a wide variety of techniques and practices which may be undertaken by an individual, household, shaman, or Buddhist priest.

HAMA URII. When malevolence has afflicted a house or when it is thought to be impending, as in the case of a bird entering and alighting on the ancestral shrine or middle rafter, the household may evacuate the premises for a period of one to three days. Before departing, ashes from the hearth are sifted and placed in a smooth pile on the floor. This is covered with the wicker cover for the cooking kettle, and pandanus leaves are hung at the gate as a sign of taboo. No one enters for fear of encountering *yanamung*. In seashore communities, the family retires to the beach, hence the name, *hama urii* (beach descent); inland peoples merely remove themselves beyond sight of the housing area. For those at the seaside, bathing in salt water purifies the body and clothing; those inland sprinkle themselves with salt. After this they enjoy feasting and drinking, and neighbors are invited to participate.

When sufficient time has expired, members of the youth association remove the pandanus leaves from the gate, touching them only with sticks and yelling "*yee, yee, yee*" to frighten off any remaining *yanamung*. Then the family returns and examines the covered ashes for evidence of disturbance. If they appear undisturbed, then all is well and the malevolent spirits are considered removed; if disturbed, a shaman is engaged to contact the ancestors to determine if trouble lies in that direction. Informants stated that at the present time only one night would be spent away from the house and that often the party continues on the following day in the house. Emphasis was placed on the necessity for a party and gaiety, perhaps as evidence that tension and danger have been dispelled and the family reintegrated into the community.

NUJIFA. Whenever a person dies in the field or at any spot removed from the house, it is thought that his spirit is loose and will become a ghost if proper measures are not undertaken to transfer the spirit to the tomb. Ashes are removed from the hearth by a family member and scattered on the spot where the person died; next, more ashes are deposited at the tomb. This practice is called *nujifa* (action of pulling off) and is regarded as essential for putting the spirit to rest. It is imperative, as any spirit not safely entombed will plague the living. The hearth ashes in this context represent the family's continuity from generation to generation and in a sense represent the family spirit. At times a shaman or Buddhist priest may be hired to perform *nujifa*.

Purity, Abstinence, Asceticism, and Continence

In contrast to the Japanese, for whom spiritual purity in a large measure implies physical purity, Okinawans tend to conceive ritual purity more as freedom from malevolent spirits and things. It is true that priestesses will make an effort to wear fresh clothing and have their hair clean for a ceremony, and in the past the chief priestess of the Ryukyus spent much of her time in seclusion prior to a ceremony grooming her hair and cleaning her garments. Nonetheless, insofar as laymen are concerned, concepts of a need for physical cleanliness for ritual are relatively weak or nonexistent. Conspicuously absent from Okinawan shrine areas are basins for rinsing the mouth and hands, so commonly found within the precincts of Japanese shrines. Similarly absent is the stress on the bath and regular bathing which many observers have seen in Japan as an aspect of the synonymy of physical and spiritual cleanliness.

Acts of self-repression or self-denial as aspects of spiritual purity are predominantly limited to the *kaminchu* and more particularly to the chief priestess of the community. Formerly, these restrictions were more elaborate and rigidly adhered to than today, but there still survives some form of token compliance. Except in the case of a few old priestesses who refrain from eating meat on ceremonial days, there appear to be few restrictions regulating the intake of food or drink.

In the past, the *nuru*, the chief priestess of the community, lived much of her life in seclusion apart from fellow villagers; a special dwelling for her use was sometimes located near the sacred grove (*utaki*), which usually lies beyond the housing area. Survivals of this practice persist in scattered areas. In the town of Nago the priestess dwells near her shrine and *utaki* in a small house atop the hill behind the town. It is believed that her seclusion ensures freedom from pollution, a necessity for communion with the *kami*. On the day prior to a major ceremony the chief priestess and her female assistants may retire to the shrine or sacred grove and spend the night there in prayer. During this time the area theoretically is taboo to ordinary villagers and outsiders.

Formerly, the *nuru* as well as higher-ranking priestesses in the national hierarchy were forbidden to marry and were required to observe sexual continence during their tenure of office, which extended from the time of assuming office until death. Apparently, these restrictions did not apply to priestesses of lower rank. At present, perhaps for the last sixty years or so, the *nuru* has been permitted to marry, and I have encountered only two unmarried adult priestesses. One had a physical deformity and the other had insanity in the family, so that it was probably not for spiritual reasons that they remained unmarried. Several of the married priestesses admitted to refraining from intercourse with the husband during the period of a ceremony. In those instances where there is seclusion of the priestesses on the eve of a major ceremony, temporary continence is ensured. Linked to this practice is a vague belief that the priestesses have intercourse with the *kami* during seclusion in the shrine or sacred grove.

Ritual

The most commonly employed terms to describe ritual action are *ugwang* (prayer) and *matchii* (ceremony or rite), the latter usually rendered in the honorific form as *umatchii* ('omatsuri'). I have stressed that the

Okinawan system of belief emphasizes maintenance of proper ritual ties with the spirit world and that any laxity in performance renders those accountable susceptible to divine retribution or attack by malevolent spirits. Ritual acts, consequently, are characterized by propitiation and placation of the *kami* and ancestors, and not infrequently by manipulation as well. Although ritual procedure tends to be highly stylized, it does not appear to me that this is carried to an extreme of compulsive preciseness.

As previously indicated, the drama of Okinawan ritual is enacted chiefly within the context of three primary social institutions—community, kin group, and family-household (and formerly a fourth, the national state). The characteristic ritual activities of these institutions will be examined in greater detail in subsequent chapters. At this point, general types of ritual will be elucidated; those not to be considered later will be more fully treated in this section.

ASKING AND THANKING RITES. At an early point in my study a priestess was being questioned at length about ritual and prayer; finally she interjected, "Look, there are two main types of prayer—asking (*tatti ugwang*) and thanking (*shirigafuu nu ugwang*)—and we feel that asking is more important than thanking!" This proved to be the case in surveying the annual ritual cycle in a number of communities; in principal asking rites the white robes of office were worn, whereas in some of the thanking rites normal attire sufficed. Although thanking is involved during the harvest rite, the most important aspect is said to be the asking of the *kami* for an even better harvest in the following year.

NOTIFICATION AND INVITING RITES. Approximately one to three days before a major rite, the officiating priestess visits community ritual sites to inform the spirits that a ceremony is forthcoming and to request their attendance. In the household, similar notification may be given to the ancestors concerning any action of importance to the family. If, for example, new land is purchased, the ancestors are informed, and a copy of the deed may be shown to them. When a family moves to another community, the ancestors are notified and asked to move also; then the village *kami* are informed and subsequently those of the new community. Whenever someone dies, the ancestors and hearth *kami* are promptly advised; or if there is a new addition to the family, through birth or marriage, they are similarly told.

FERTILITY RITES. Ritual efforts to increase the food supply are conducted in many farming and fishing communities. In the town of Itoman and on Kudaka Island, where the livelihood depends on the sea, annual rites are held at the seashore for the purpose of ensuring a continued supply of fish. In farm villages, the ritual sowing (*tantui*) of the paddy of the chief priestess precedes the planting of seed beds by the farmers.

RAIN-MAKING RITES. When a drought adversely affects crops or causes wells to run dry, village priestesses conduct rain-making rites (*ama-gui*). In the time of the kingdom, whenever a drought was unusually severe, the ruler and chief priestess would participate together in rites to bring rain. On these occasions they would be assisted by the chief priestesses of all the villages of Okinawa in a concerted national effort.

INSTALLATION RITES. Whenever a new *kaminchu* assumes office, special installation rites are held. The main purpose of this ritual is to attach the *shiji* of the (deceased) predecessor to the successor.

RITES OF PASSAGE. In the past, there were a number of rites to mark the individual's transition through various social and physiological statuses from birth to death. Most of those operating at the community level have disappeared. Community participation remains for death rites in that each household sends a representative to the funeral; but, in general, rites of passage survive principally at the family level, and even here in an abbreviated form. Rites pertaining to birth, naming, marriage, birth year, etc., are performed in the house, with friends, neighbors, and kinsmen participating; but by all accounts, written and oral, these have been greatly simplified.

ANCESTRAL RITES. Households and kin groups regularly perform rites for the ancestral spirits; these will be considered in the chapters on the kin group and household. Ancestral rites appear to be wholly of Buddhist origin, and they evince a continued vigor despite an overall decline in religion.

HEARTH RITES. As noted in Chapter II, the hearth or fire *kami* constitutes a major focal point of household and family ritual deriving from the concept of this spirit as messenger between the group and higher *kami*.

TRAVEL RITES. Before any lengthy journey involving travel across water, *tabi ugwang* (travel prayer or rite) is performed. The ritual begins with prayer at the ancestral shrine followed by prayer at the hearth; from the house, a tour is made of all major sites of community ritual with prayers to the *kami* at each. When a journey extends over several months or involves great danger (as in the case of young men drafted into Japanese military service), the village or kin group priestess may be asked to pray on behalf of the individual.

MABUI-GUMI. When an individual is believed to have suffered spirit (*mabui*) loss, a ritual of restoring it to the body, called *mabui-gumi*, may be performed. Those who imagine that their *mabui* has been dropped or taken from the body may simply recite a formula encouraging its return and then go through the motions of bending over, scooping it up, and placing it on the chest. If a child should fall or suffer fright, this procedure may be resorted to as a means of calming it. A violent sneeze may also dislodge *mabui* from the body; consequently, when someone sneezes, *kusu kwee* (eat feces) is said, in the same way that we would use "God bless you" or "Gesundheit." In Okinawan usage, this expression frightens off any malevolent spirits lurking in the area who might take the opportunity to steal the *mabui*.

Formerly, a complex ritual was employed when the *mabui* was thought to have been lost or stolen. The victim was taken immediately to the pigpen (which also served as the toilet), where three small stones were picked up. These were placed inside the clothing behind the neck, and a string was drawn tightly around them on the outside, holding them securely in place. The person was then brought into the house, and a tray containing five objects—a bowl of rice, a bowl of soup, a dish of vegetables, a cup of water, and a knife—was placed before him. The stones were removed and placed in the cup of water; the knife was dipped in the water and daubed three times on the forehead or bridge of the nose. Following this, a string with seven knots was hung about the neck, and a string with three knots in it was placed around each ankle. These were worn for at least three days, preferably for seven. Upon conclusion of the ceremony, a feast was prepared and neighbors invited to attend. Here, as in the case of *hama urii*, emphasis was placed on gaiety and interaction with neighbors to comfort the individual and signify return to normality.

MEDIUMISTIC RITES. Certain of the shamans have the power to conjure up the spirits of the dead and either be possessed by them or engage in conversation with them. When possessed or in contact with the dead spirit, the shaman may use a rhythmical chant or speak in a normal voice, either her own or that of the spirit. The primary purpose of holding a mediumistic rite is to communicate with ancestors in order to determine the cause of misfortune in the family, or, if the deceased died suddenly, to learn if there were any last words.

GEOMANTIC RITES. When a tomb site is selected, a new house constructed, or a well driven, the services of a fortuneteller or shaman are sought to determine whether the *fungshi* of the site is propitious. The term derives from the Chinese 'feng shui,' a key concept in geomancy which probably was introduced into Okinawa with the establishment of a Chinese settlement several hundred years ago. Although the Chinese have ascribed several interpretations to this concept, it generally means the relationship among stars, planets, certain earth-dwelling spirits, and the physical characteristics of the landscape with respect to any given site. While the concept may be comprehended by the specialists, Okinawans usually appear to construe *fungshi* as the spirit entity occupying the site; thus, for example, annual rites are conducted by the household for *kaa nu gufungshi* (*fungshi* of the well) and *yashichi nu gufungshi* (*fungshi* of the house lot).

HOUSE CONSTRUCTION RITES. After determining that the *fungshi* is propitious, construction of the house commences. When the framing reaches completion with the placing of the ridgepole, the carpenter and other workers are treated to a party by the owner. In urban areas, at this time large bows and arrows are erected atop the frame for the purpose of fending off any *yanamung* in the area. In the rural community the priestess is invited to pray at the house and is feted at the party. This rite is called *muni agi* (ridgepole raising) and is believed crucial for protecting the house against adversity.

BOAT-LAUNCHING RITES. Before a new boat is launched, the owner, boatmaker, and village priestess pray at the shrine or sacred grove, asking for protection. Similar rites directed to the sea *kami* are then performed at the beach prior to launching.

DIVINING AND FORTUNETELLING RITES. A variety of divining rites is practiced by fortunetellers and shamans. The shamans' supernatural powers of seeing and hearing enable them to perform with a minimum of props; however, some of them do resort to crithomancy and thurifumia (respectively, divination from patterns of grains and of smoke). The former is called *ukudji*. The rice grains are first offered to the hearth, ancestral altar, or special shrine of the shaman, if she is at home. A small handful of the grain is then sorted out in three or five piles of approximately equal size. Next, the grains in each pile are arranged in pairs in the form of a circle. The various combinations of even and uneven distributions can be interpreted as the individual's fortune or as the answer to a question.

Some shamans specialize in burning incense at their shrines and then interpreting the smoke patterns as answers to questions put to them. In at least one case, a shaman used smoke patterns from her cigarette for this purpose. The underlying belief is that the *kami* or ancestors determine the emergent pattern.

A traditional fortuneteller or diviner follows Chinese divining techniques of great antiquity. Most commonly, they rely on books used in association with divining blocks or sticks and do not claim supernatural powers as in the case of a shaman. One was found to be using the abacus in place of the divining sticks or blocks, and some informants appeared to be rather impressed with this novel method.

Within the city of Naha, street stalls devoted to simple palmistry and phrenology may be found, but these practices are said to be rather recent imports from Japan. A few of the traditional fortunetellers also have knowledge of Chinese systems of phrenology and body-typing. The importance of the calendar in fortunetelling has been emphasized previously. At present, all books of fortunetelling are printed in Japan, but a few of the oldest fortunetellers still possess books in Chinese, or Okinawan versions of the Chinese texts.

Scattered throughout rural Okinawa, so-called divining stones, *bijuru* (exact meaning unknown), may be found. Such stones are believed possessed of a *kami* spirit which may furnish some indication whether a fortune or occasion is to be good or bad. These stones do not appear to have been carved but are usually waterworn limestone; the shape suggests a phallus, but such significance may be denied. In most areas they were removed or hidden at the insistence of officials who apparently regarded their usage as ill-befitting enlightened Japanese nationals. Where *bijuru* remain, they are within the confines of the sacred grove or near the communal hearth.

CURING RITES. Ritual activities relating to curing, purification, and exorcism overlap to a marked degree since they are predicated on similar belief premises. Traditional medical beliefs and concepts rest on the assumption that disease and sickness result from supernatural attack by the *kami*, ancestors, or malevolent spirits. An essential first step of diagnosis involves determination of whether the *kami* or malevolent spirits are the cause, and in serious cases this must be referred to a shaman. If the trouble lies with the *kami* and ancestors, efforts are directed toward apology and rectification; if with malevolent spirits, purgative, exorcistic rites may be conducted, and abusive, deprecatory language used. Since in the final analysis an attack by malevolent spirits suggests some withdrawal of support by the *kami*, placatory efforts may be required in their behalf as well.

PILGRIMAGE. Periodically, village priestesses (especially the chief priestess) undertake tours or visits to certain major ritual sites of the former kingdom. In the past, periodic attendance at specified national rites was mandatory for them, and present pilgrimages to those sites appear in part to be a continuation of that tradition, although there is no longer any coordination in timing. Priestesses of the kin group may also undertake pilgrimages in behalf of the group to national sites and to sites of importance to the ancestors. During their *taari* period, shamans may spend much of their time and money visiting major ritual sites in the quest to find and identify their *chiji*. At the time of assuming office, new *kaminchu* may tour certain ritual sites to introduce themselves to the *kami*.

Ordinary persons rarely go on a pilgrimage; if so, it is usually on the advice of a shaman and with the further inducement of overcoming serious personal or family misfortune. Those on pilgrimage wear no special identifying garb, and customs of begging for food or money en route do not exist; in fact, frugality and austerity would seem quite out of place at such a time, or in any major rite, for that matter.

WORSHIP FROM AFAR. As pilgrimages to distant ritual sites in behalf of a kin group or village are not made annually but usually at intervals of three, five, seven, nine, and thirteen years, priestesses pray toward those sites from certain designated points within the community. This is called *utuushi* (from *tuusung*, to pass through). A common place for performing *utuushi* is within the sacred grove.

RITUAL LANGUAGE AND BEHAVIOR. Although well educated and hence highly acculturated individuals may use Japanese in prayers to the ancestors, Okinawan enjoys almost exclusive usage as the language of ritual. In village rites, use of Okinawan by the *kaminchu* seems mandatory; occasionally this imposes a handicap, as in the case of one young priestess who had lived most of her life in Japan and spoke Okinawan with great difficulty.

Ancient religious song-poems, *umui* (frequently and incorrectly transcribed as 'omoro'), are performed in certain village rites. These have been transmitted orally for generations, and the repertoire of the oldest priestesses may include as many as a dozen of these songs. Unfortunately, in many instances their meaning has been entirely lost or has become very vague.

Priestesses and ordinary people usually pray in normal voices, but in the case of shamans the performance varies, depending on the type of shaman, her personality, and the situation. When praying or possessed, some shamans speak in a rhythmical chant; others use a normal voice or one imitating the spirit possessing them. Although the words of the shamans are rarely archaic, the substance of what they say is not always entirely meaningful, and educated Okinawans frequently accuse them of speaking nonsense. A humorous skit observed in the folk-theater had the shaman chanting a jumble of words which evoked much laughter from the audience. In witnessing and recording numerous shaman sessions I have gained the impression that this vagueness stems from a reluctance to be explicit and/or from the stylized nature of singing or chanting. As to the former, self-preservation dictates avoidance of unalterable statements or commitments for which they can be held accountable; instead the advice or message from the spirits is presented in a way that allows more than one interpretation. In the chantlike performance, the lack of clarity seems to derive in part from terseness and from the frequent insertion of proper nouns (i.e., names of historic sites of ritual and of the *kami*). In some instances it appeared that the series of names, or lines containing these, had been composed in advance, whereas other passages relating to the client were improvised on the spot. The composed portions afforded time for reflection on the improvised sections, and since the names recited were impressive in their import to this religion, it was likely that they were also employed to evoke a favorable response from the listener. No evidences of ventriloquism, of speaking in tongues, or of resorting to nonspeech utterances were encountered.

The language employed in addressing the *kami* is rich in the utilization of honorific, exalted, and deferential forms of speech. Like Japanese, Okinawan verbs can be used in humble, neutral, and exalted forms. In the use of honorific prefixes and suffixes, Okinawan is undoubtedly even richer than contemporary Japanese. There is also a large number of words for ordinary things and actions which are employed exclusively for religious matters. For example, water offered to the *kami* or sacred water is referred to as *ubii*, not by the common term for water, *miji*; for other offerings to the *kami* there are *uchatoo* (tea), *ubuku* (cooked rice), *ukoo* (incense), *umiki* (rice wine), etc., terms which are not commonly used for these things.

In general I would say that ritual behavior is characterized by restraint and decorum, and that highly charged emotionalism is absent. Fear, awe, thrill, love, inspiration, humility, frenzy, and hysteria, as manifestations of religious behavior, are rarely overt. A qualified exception must be made for the shamans in that some of them exhibit manic or hysteric behavior at times; but those shamans whose behavior tends toward the extravagant are viewed as poor ones, and it is assumed that a proper relationship with the *chiji* has not been achieved. Outlandish behavior may be expected during the *taari* period; thereafter, control of the body and emotions should be secured. In contrast to what has been written of shamans in certain cultures of Siberia, Africa, and India, the performance of the Okinawan shaman seems rather mild. The relative absence of overt emotionalism does not, however, signify light treatment or disregard, for the threat of supernatural attack or deprivation remains as a spur to ritual activity.

RITUAL OFFERINGS. Few limitations apply to the nature of ritual offerings, but incense constitutes the single indispensable item for all ritual occasions, and large quantities are stocked in even the smallest rural stores. Wine or stronger beverages distilled from rice, millet, or potatoes rank second to incense in frequency of use as offerings. In many villages ritual wine is made by the priestesses several days in advance of a ceremony. Formerly, fermentation was induced by chewing the grain and allowing saliva to act as a catalyst. This practice encountered strong discouragement from school teachers and government officials and was discontinued on Okinawa during the decade or so preceding World War II, but in the more remote areas of the southern Ryukyus it reportedly continues among a few of the old priestesses.[5] For household rites, tea is commonly substituted for wine in the interests of economy.

Some informants contended that uncooked foods and grains should be offered to the *kami* and cooked foods to the ancestors. I found little evidence of this as a consistent practice or even as a commonly stated ideal. The shallowness of Buddhist beliefs is well attested by meat offerings tendered the ancestors at the altar or tomb. Okinawans rarely express any prejudice against meat as some Japanese, at least verbally, are inclined to do; traditionally, they have been pig raisers, and, where finances permit, pork dishes constitute a portion of the offerings in major rites of the household and kin group. Meat dishes are far less common in community rites, perhaps due to expense. Some community priestesses stated that, while meat was suitable for ancestral offerings, it should not be offered to the *kami*; a few indicated that they did not eat meat on ceremonial days.

As a general rule, it can be said that there are no blood sacrifices and that the idea is rather abhorrent to Okinawans. A partial exception may be made for the following particular rite held during time of pestilence or high mortality in a community. A pig or cow is slaughtered and its bones and meat hung on ropes surrounding the shrine and across principal paths leading into the community. Portions of meat are distributed among the villagers, especially the children. The offerings of flesh and bones are intended not for the *kami*, however, but for the malevolent spirits assumed to be carrying the pestilence. The rationale is that these spirits will stop to eat the flesh and will not invade the village or its shrine.[6]

The usual food offerings to the ancestral spirits and *kami* tend to be the same as those consumed by man, though they are more elaborate and varied. Food offerings are never wasted, and feasting usually follows the rite; unconsumed food is carried home by the participants for their families to share. In a few villages, I have seen certain wild food products—sago palm starch and pandanus keys—used as offerings; the sago palm in particular figured importantly as a famine food until the recent past. Very frequently, an inedible food dish (*minnuku*) is set in among offerings to the ancestors in the belief that malevolent spirits will consume this and leave the good food untouched.

At present there are numerous indications, well attested by the old people, that ritual offerings have become less elaborate and perhaps less a matter for concern than in the past. To a large extent the complete impoverishment of the island and its people during the war necessitated economizing, but even with the prosperity of recent years the new precedent survives; moreover, government officials, school teachers, and newspaper editorials regularly admonish the populace to curb any extravagance in religious activities.

RITUAL FEASTING AND DRINKING. As noted above, food offerings to the *kami* and ancestors are not wasted; feasting and drinking usually follow all of the principal rites. In the household, regular offerings to the ancestors and the hearth *kami* on the first and fifteenth of the month coincide with the morning meal and are in fact the ordinary fare consumed by the family. For the major annual rites, a variety of elaborate feast foods is prepared, and the men and older women consume considerable quantities of alcoholic beverages. At such times, an atmosphere of conviviality prevails, and there is an obvious pleasure in oral satisfactions.

Although mass participation in community rites has declined markedly in recent decades, the priestesses and their entourage still spend the afternoon or day following a principal rite in feasting, drinking, and dancing. This is called *kami ashibii* (*kami* play), and it is a time for pleasure in eating, drinking, dancing, singing, and joking.

In some urban homes, especially among the better educated, such eating and drinking appear to be the principal remnant of what was once an important religious rite; this pertains particularly to rites relating to the *kami*. Ancestral rites have evinced a greater tendency for survival among all groups.

RITUAL PARAPHERNALIA AND DRESS. No special paraphernalia or attire is demanded for household rites, but the ritual activities of the *kaminchu*, shaman, and fortuneteller may require a number of accessories. For all major ceremonial occasions, female *kaminchu* of the community and kin group don white robes of linen or cotton atop their regular clothing. Simple cloth headbands are frequently worn nowadays by the priestesses, but in many areas the garland (*chinumaki*) of leaves is still to be seen. This style of ceremonial headdress appears to have been widely distributed throughout all parts of the Ryukyus and certain areas of aboriginal Taiwan. The chief priestess of the village wears a necklace of round beads with a large claw-shaped stone, called *mitama*, suspended in the middle. The latter are identical in size, shape, and color with the Japanese 'magatama' associated with the prehistoric Yayoi and Tomb Culture periods. Traditionally, these stones have been symbolic of the authority of the chief priestess, and in one community where a priestess carelessly misplaced hers, the office was given to the finder by the king's officials. A drum, offering trays, and a large fan constitute the remainder of paraphernalia used in communal rites today. The kin group priestesses bring a small wooden box, called *binshii*, to communal rites; this serves as a container for rice grains, wine cups, and incense used in the offerings, but it also is regarded as representative of the entire kin group.

The use in community rites of masks and disguises made of leaves is sporadic but widespread in the Ryukyus. Since this practice tends to be associated with remote and isolated villages, it might be assumed that it represents the survival of a once extensive usage. So far as I can judge from written sources and informants, these disguises were not worn by the *kaminchu*. In the Okinawan area, masks are still employed by women in at least one annual rite on Henza Island off the east coast, and the use of leaf disguises is reported from scattered communities along the isolated northeast coast, always in association with the *shinugu* rite. This practice is not to be confused with the lion-mask dance (*shiishi mooyee*), which can be found in many villages and which the priestesses do not regard as having any religious significance.

The dress of the shaman and fortuneteller in no way differs from that of ordinary people. Some of the shamans operate with ritual props—rice grains, smoke, abacus, drink, etc.—used in divination or in communication with the spirits, but others operate wholly without props, except for incense. The fortuneteller, on the other hand, needs books and divining sticks or blocks.

In the past, there was a practice of ceremonial transvestism, called *winagu nati* (lit., "becoming female"), which permitted certain males to enter the sacrosanct sacred groves, normally taboo to them. When participating with the state priestesses at Seefa Utaki, the most sacred site of the nation, even the chief ministers of state were required to affect female guises. Insofar as can be determined, this was a temporary ritual requirement and was not associated with any pathology or behavioral deviance.

RITUAL PARTICIPANTS. The principal roles in religious action are reserved for women, with the men performing as ritual servants or occupying purely passive roles as spectators. Community and kin group *kaminchu* conduct major rites in the name of the collectivity, with the membership participating as passive spectators, if at all. Within the household, major ritual activities are carried out by the senior female member, usually the wife or mother of the male household head; this pertains to ancestral rites as well as to hearth rites. The virtually complete female domination of ritual activity in all spheres reflects an implicit tenet of belief that females are spiritually superior to males.

RITUAL SITES. Any place of regular ritual performance may be called *ugwanju* (prayer place). While *ugwanju* are of many types, the essential, minimal item identifying such a place is a censer; thus, the heart of the sacred grove, usually without any structure, contains a censer beside a large rock or under a great tree. Four types of *ugwanju* might be designated on the basis of affiliation: national sites formerly of importance to the state religion, ritual sites of the community, places of kin group ritual, and household ritual sites. These may overlap to a degree. For example, certain community sites are used by specific kin groups also; yet each group preserves certain sites for its own principal use.

Religious Art and Symbolization of the Supernatural

One of the most impressive aspects of Okinawan religion to the outsider is the marked underdevelopment of religious art and design, and by all indications this is an old and persistent characteristic. The pure white robes of the priestesses, the simplicity of their other adornment, and the lack of any colorful accessory paraphernalia epitomize a consistent plainness. The traditional styling and mode of construction for shrines (with thatched roof and plain walls) do not serve to distinguish them obviously from other structures in the community. These edifices are without any external or internal color or decorative design. The *utaki* (sacred grove), consisting of a clump of trees with a censer at its center, is simplicity itself. Shrines for the community hearth contain little more than the three stones depicting the hearth and perhaps a shelf where offerings can be placed. The *kami ashagi*, a focal point for the public aspects of community rites, consists of a thatched roof and no walls, with only posts or stone pillars for support of the roof; its floor is the earth, as in the case of most old shrines, and a rude log serves as a seat for the priestesses. In recent decades there has been a tendency to rebuild decaying shrines in the tradition of Shinto architecture, complete with 'torii.' According to some informants, this was dictated by practical necessity during the period of extreme Japanese nationalism prior to World War II; more recently, it can be attributed to admiration for things Japanese.

There are no carvings, statuary, or images of the ancestors, and virtually none of the *kami* aside from a few masks. A mask representing the hearth *kami* (*fii nu kang*) was formerly kept in some kitchens, with oil applied annually to its lips in the belief that only good would be said of the family when this deity reported to the higher *kami* at the end of the year.[7] This practice has been widely reported from North and South China and may be considered a Taoist import. The lion-mask dance, referred to previously, appears to be widespread throughout parts of Ryukyu, Japan, and Korea; this too is of Chinese origin.

The obvious void in the area of religious art and symbolization of the supernatural does not indicate a lack of creative imagination on the part of Okinawans, for in other fields of artistic expression they have acquitted themselves well. Okinawan dyeing and weaving techniques have been highly acclaimed in Japanese art circles, and their lacquer ware is reputed to be among the world's finest. This situation apparently derives from the nature of the belief system, which has failed to arouse any emotional response that finds an outlet in creative expression. It is indicative of an essentially pragmatic approach to the supernatural, placing greatest emphasis on the avoidance of malevolence that may derive therefrom.

IV

RELIGIOUS ORGANIZATION
AND SPECIALISTS

Religious Organization

Traditionally, Okinawan religious organization has been subsumed within the contexts of four social institutions: the state, community, kin group, and family-household. It has not existed as a separate entity indirectly affiliated with these groups but rather as a component part thereof. This is to say, the major institutions of Okinawan society have each maintained specific religious functions as a part of their inherent processes and in that capacity have constituted ritual groups. Consequently, the basic determinants for an individual's membership in a given ritual group have been those of birth and/or residence. Such membership has been automatically conferred and is incumbent upon all members of the collectivity; it is not rationally arrived at on the basis of personal preference, though at the present time recalcitrant members may fail to participate. In the final analysis, these divisions have been all-inclusive, for not only has the system been without sectarian schisms but foreign systems have largely failed to achieve any substantial organized following.[1]

THE STATE. Prior to the Japanese annexation in 1879, the whole of the kingdom was organized for religious as well as political ends. An official hierarchy of hereditary priestesses ranged from the village through the districts and regions, culminating in the office of the chief priestess, a close relative of the ruler and virtually his equal in rank. This was not a pluralistic state but rather a single system composed of two mutually complementary facets: a religious hierarchy of females paralleling a political hierarchy of males. The upper echelons of the religious hierarchy persisted for some time after the dismemberment of the political state, but, lacking any support or encouragement from the new government, these too gradually withered, disappearing completely in 1944. At the village and town level, however, vestiges of the lower echelons still remain and continue to function.

COMMUNITY. The Okinawan community constitutes a ritual group for the performance of ceremonies relating to the welfare and livelihood of its membership. The large urban complex of Naha and Shuri (representing the amalgamation of many formerly independent communities) no longer preserves any ritual organizations;[2] however, certain of the towns—Nago, Motobu, Itoman, etc.—though semi-urban in character, continue to do so. Those rural communities of upper-class origin, the so-called *yaadui*, have been founded in the last two hundred years, long after the establishment of the national hierarchy, in a period when Confucian thinking held sway in the upper classes, and they have not developed a community religion. All commoner villages, however, theoretically continue to function as ritual communities despite wartime destruction of shrines and depletion in the ranks of the hereditary *kaminchu*. My survey, covering more than 120 communities, indicates that approximately 60 per cent of the population resides in communities preserving some degree of organized community ritual.

Ritual activities at the community level are closely correlated with the agricultural cycle, the major concern of the people's livelihood. Rites are conducted by the *kaminchu*, who attain office on the basis of birth in certain households which customarily have held exclusive right to occupy these positions. Although the *kaminchu* alone conduct village rituals, in the past the entire community participated as ritual observers and joined with the *kaminchu* in the festivities which usually followed. In many villages today, though there are exceptions, only the *kaminchu* and a few older people show much interest in ritual affairs.

KIN GROUP. All Okinawans are organized into patrilineal kin groups by virtue of birth for the males and of marriage for the females, and at present the sole *raison d'être* for the kin group seems to be its ritual function. Thus, while but 60 per cent of the population remains organized into community ritual groups, theoretically the entire population is organized for ritual purposes on the basis of kin affiliation.

Kin group ritual activities are performed by female *kaminchu* called *kudii*, but, unlike the *kaminchu* of the village, they do not hold their positions on the basis of inheritance or membership in a specific house. The essential qualifications for becoming a *kudii* are *saadaka nmari* (high-*saa* birth) and birth in the kin group. Ritual action in the kin group focuses primarily on the male ancestors and their wives.

FAMILY-HOUSEHOLD. There are two major focal points of worship in the household: the hearth and the ancestral tablets. As noted before, the principal ritual duties are borne by the senior female member of the household. Thus, despite an emphasis on patrilineal descent and patrilocal residence, female domination of household ritual remains consistent with the pattern for the state, community, and kin group.

Religious Specialists

The Okinawan religious scene is dominated by two principal roles, those of priestess and shaman. Several other specialists occupy secondary roles: the fortuneteller, Buddhist priest, pariah, sorcerer, and healer. Despite some overlapping in functions, these roles may be clearly defined.

The priestesses are concerned primarily with propitiating the *kami* through ritual efforts conducted on behalf of the specific ritual group which they represent. The shamans, on the basis of preternatural powers of possession, seeing, and hearing, are largely involved in determining the causes of misfortune and directing remedial action. The fortunetellers, through extensive knowledge of ancient Chinese occult lore, determine personal fortunes, though, unlike the shamans, they are unable to do this through supernatural powers. They also select propitious sites and dates for important activities. The Buddhist priests may conduct funeral rites, and the pariahs formerly played a vital role in escorting the deceased's spirit to the tomb. Sorcerers perform no socially approved function but indulge in black arts to the detriment of their associates. Lastly, the healer cures sickness and disease by reciting formulas and prayers. It should be noted that the fortuneteller, Buddhist priest, and pariah spirit-leader are males, while the others are female; the former group is positively associated with beliefs and practices of foreign origin, whereas the latter, at least from this vantage point in history, appear to be more indigenous. The priestesses (*kaminchu*) outnumber all of the others combined and serve the interests of organized groups, while the remainder are principally concerned with the individual.

KAMINCHU. Formerly, there were many ranks and grades of *kaminchu*. Today their numbers are greatly depleted, and only those of the community and kin group remain. As previously noted, the word *kaminchu* means *kami* person, and individuals who bear this title are believed to have been born with *kami* rank (*saadaka nmari*) and to possess *kami* spirit (*shiji*). It is the function of the *kaminchu* to propitiate and control the *kami* in the interests of the group which they represent. The higher-ranking female *kaminchu* are believed to have the power to invoke *shiji*, necessary for promoting fertility of the soils and growth of the crops. The term *kaminchu* is without any connotation of gender, but it usually implies the females, who are higher in rank than the males. The distinction between male and female *kaminchu* may be made by the terms *winagu-gami* (sister *kami*) and *wikii-gami* (brother *kami*), or more politely, *uminai-gami* and *umikii-gami*, although the more common practice is to designate the individual by his or her official title. These priestesses will be considered in greater detail in subsequent chapters relating to the community and kin group.

The dominant roles in ritual activities are held by female *kaminchu*, with the male *kaminchu* supporting them as ceremonial aides or servants. The office of *kaminchu* is held for life, and retirement in favor of a successor is not practiced. Community *kaminchu* inherit office by occupying a certain kinship status—usually that of first son or first daughter—within a household which has traditionally filled this position. Kin group *kaminchu*, overwhelmingly females, attain office by virtue of high-*saa* birth, the quality being first detected by the older women of the kin group and subsequently confirmed by a shaman. Moreover, a woman must be born into the kin group in which she holds office; consequently, she serves in her brother's or father's kin group rather than her husband's.

Age is not a factor in the selection of *kaminchu* for office; the sole prerequisites are *saadaka nmari* and, in the case of the village *kaminchu*, heredity as well. One account[3] maintained that in the Ryukyus a woman is eligible to become a priestess at sixty-one, implying that a complete calendrical cycle must first elapse before taking on this "dangerous" role. This definitely is not the case in the Okinawan area, nor did I find it to be so in areas of the southern Ryukyus where I studied. Moreover, it is commonly believed that a *kaminchu*'s ritual effectiveness is enhanced through many years of service to the *kami* and that through her the community's or kin group's position is similarly enhanced vis-à-vis the *kami*. The most respected priestesses, consequently, are those who have been in office for a few decades. An old informant in one village in northern Okinawa stated, "We have a young *nuru*, too young now, but after she takes care of the shrines and the *kami* which she possesses for many years, she will become better."

The source of a *kaminchu's* knowledge and power derives from the level of her birth with respect to spirit rank and possession of *kami* spirit; therefore, she professes to attach little importance to training for her role. Nonetheless, when a high-ranking *kaminchu* reaches old age, her successor may begin to accompany her in all ritual activities and endeavor to master the sacred songs (*umui*) and ritual procedure. Thus, while the importance of training is verbally disclaimed ("The *kami* tells me what to do when the time comes"), such training is resorted to of necessity. Moreover, the death of many *kaminchu* in World War II so rapidly depleted their ranks that many successors were wholly unprepared to fulfill the duties of office.

When not in use, the traditional dress for the *kaminchu* (the simple white robe of linen or cotton) is stored in the home of the *kaminchu* or, sometimes, in the case of the *nuru*, kept in the main village shrine. Some *kaminchu* related that these robes were burnt every twelve years on completion of a calendrical cycle, but this does not seem to be a widespread practice and may in fact be a recent innovation. Female *kaminchu* wear white headbands—purple in the case of *nuru*—to which a garland of leaves and twigs is sometimes affixed. Customarily, on ceremonial occasions the *nuru* wears a necklace containing one or three large, claw-shaped beads, usually colored. At least two *nuru* were found who possessed bronze mirrors among their paraphernalia; these were without any ceremonial function, but it should be noted that the same claw-shaped beads and bronze mirror constitute two of three sacred treasures of the Japanese Imperial Family. Except for that worn on ceremonial occasions, the *kaminchu's* dress is indistinguishable from that of lay persons.

As a group, the community *kaminchu* are not characterized by behavior patterns which might be regarded as deviant; however, the method of their selection renders them somewhat atypical of the general population today. The fact that the position is retained for life brings the average *kaminchu* into office in the middle years of life, so that most present *kaminchu* have had less schooling than the younger half of the population. More often than not they are Okinawan speakers, either by preference or through inability to speak good standard Japanese; consequently, their outlook is predominantly Okinawan, and they tend to be rather conservative. The higher-ranking female *kaminchu*, especially the older ones, evince an all-consuming interest in and dedication to their calling, but the younger priestesses are more concerned with the affairs of their households and livelihood and tend to regard their duties as onerous. It is tempting to ascribe these differences between the generations solely to culture change, particularly to the influence of education, but considerable evidence seems to indicate that the traditional pattern has always been for the young not to show much concern for religious matters, increased interest coming only with the middle and late years of life.

By virtue of their close association with the *kami*, it is deemed imperative that *kaminchu* avoid all manner of pollution which might render them unfit for ritual action. Traditionally, this has applied more stringently to the higher-ranking female *kaminchu* than to the others. Formerly, the *nuru* and all those above her in the national hierarchy were forced to remain celibate during their tenure of office; while this practice has fallen into disuse, a number of lesser restrictions designed to ensure her purity still prevail. To no small degree these restrictions limit her full participation in village life, cutting her off from a number of common social events, such as births and funerals, which mark village life. In some villages her social isolation is made more real by the fact that her residence is apart from the main cluster of dwellings. The effect of this partial physical and social isolation tends to reinforce the common conception of her as an associate of the *kami* and hence as unlike ordinary people. The older priestesses particularly, accustomed to many years of this manner of living, seem to have their thoughts and attention on decidedly other-worldly matters. It is not difficult to imagine that fifty to seventy years ago they were venerated as holy people, and quite possibly felt themselves to be such.

Relationships among the *kaminchu* are generally cordial; such differences as do exist remain well concealed, for it is believed that discord will impair their relationship—and hence that of the group—with the *kami*. There is, moreover, a conscious feeling of providing an example for the group, and *kaminchu* are wont to describe themselves as persons of good character.

The compensations, real and psychic, which accrue to the *kaminchu* for the performance of their duties have altered considerably in the past fifty years. Formerly, they were accorded the highest status in the group; the *nuru*, for example, officially ranked above the village headman and was equal in rank to Shuri-appointed gentry officials. The *nuru* and her chief assistant, the *niigami* (root *kami*), enjoyed economic security through large landholdings held in perpetuity, not subject to reallotment under the communal landholding system. Today their status is largely determined by age factors; the older people accord them their traditionally high status, whereas the young view them with indifference or embarrassment. The land reforms of 1899–1903 substantially altered their economic position by placing their lands in the hands of male relatives. Nonetheless, despite a decline in social and economic status, many *kaminchu* still appear motivated by a strong sense of duty in the belief that responsibility for the welfare of the group rests largely with them. The increasing indifference of the group toward their activities often gives rise to the feeling that they are sacrificing themselves for the sake of the group.

Even the severest critics of the *kaminchu* do not accuse them of pursuing a profit motive in the execution of their duties. They are not customarily remunerated for their services, for it is believed that a reward for *kami* service would be highly demeaning to the office, if not actually insulting to the *kami*. Small gifts of grain, food delicacies, or wine may be given to the *kaminchu*, but a set fee in terms of money or goods is neither demanded nor expected. In the past, ritual expenses for offerings, travel, etc., were borne by the community through a levy on each household, but today in many villages the male political leaders are increasingly loath to allot funds for ritual purposes. Where this lack of support has occurred, the *kaminchu* themselves now meet these expenses, though sympathetic individuals may voluntarily contribute assistance.

Undoubtedly, the fear of *kami-daari* (*kami* curse) constitutes the major factor in compelling reluctant *kaminchu* to conform to the demands of their role; the strength of this belief has been made all the more obvious by modernization, which has provided new opportunities and temptations encouraging defection. Male *kaminchu*, especially, appear increasingly reluctant to endure their inferior ceremonial status. This changed attitude undoubtedly derives from the influence of Japanese culture, which accords the male a higher status in all spheres of action, religious as well as secular.

An educated male *kaminchu* in a certain town stated that he felt ashamed to appear in public rites as a mere servant to the women and had therefore ceased to participate, but the fear of *kami-daari* impelled him to visit regularly all places of worship and apologize to the *kami*. The *nuru* scorned him for his refusal to participate and stated that he would die from *kami-daari* as soon as the "true" successor to his office appeared. The threat of supernatural punishment seems ever present; in fact, virtually every *kaminchu* interviewed expressed the belief that *kami-daari* would strike those derelict in duty.

At present, the status and privileges of the *kaminchu* may be said to be greatly reduced from what they were fifty years ago; despite this, the burdens of their office have increased rather than diminished. For many of the younger *kaminchu*, especially the males, the threat of divine retribution seems to be all that binds them to their duties; yet, notwithstanding the pressures of change and the defection of the young, the older *kaminchu* continue to perform their traditional rites, confident in the belief that they are maintaining the welfare of their group.

The *kaminchu* or *kudii* of the kin group do not differ markedly from the community *kaminchu* in their role function; both may be described as priestesses. With respect to role recruitment, however, they are quite distinct. The kin group *kaminchu* goes through a self-recruitment procedure similar to that of the shaman, which will be described in the following section.

YUTA.[4] The principal functions of the shaman (*yuta*) relate essentially to the absence of a concept of impersonal causation in traditional Okinawan thinking, so that all manifestations of misfortune ultimately can be ascribed to supernatural action. The *yuta*, with preternatural powers of seeing, hearing, and possession, are regarded as uniquely equipped to discern the causes of misfortune and to suggest or direct remedial action. They are commonly called upon when misfortune strikes or when any unusual, and hence seemingly ominous, events transpire.

My study of a dozen shamans and their clientele in 1960 and 1961 revealed that approximately 80 per cent of the problems brought to their attention involved matters of health, ranging from purely somatic disorders to those of an obviously psychic nature. Examples of other problems considered by them included dream analysis, lost items or money, suitability of a selected mate with regard to spirit compatability, adoption, ancestral matters (tomb, ritual, property), selection of a house site, severe economic hardship, contact with a recently deceased person, and even politics. The range of their activities encompassed spirit possession or mediumship, curing, exorcism, divination, retrocognition, and prayer. Very few, if any, would claim proficiency or attempt specialization in all of these areas; usually their reputations rest on accomplishment in one or two.

According to the estimates of central police headquarters in the capital, there are approximately two thousand shamans. My estimate, based on a shaman census taken in several areas, would place that figure several hundred lower, somewhere in the range of one shaman per six hundred persons. In any event, they overwhelmingly outnumber the 350 medical doctors (private and government physicians) as of 1961. Shamanism has been and remains predominantly associated with females, although a few male shamans can be found. The latter, however, do not comprise more than 5 per cent of the total by my estimate. Male shamans tend to be regarded as more deviant than their female counterparts. One informant commented, "There are not many male *yuta*, and some of them seem like *wikiga-winagu* [male-females, i.e., homosexuals]. We always think of them as a little crazy." Despite this fairly common conception of them, no cases of transvestism or homosexuality were found. Their assumption of a role identified with females alone may suffice to categorize them as effeminate. Moreover, the strikingly common characteristic of male shamans whom I encountered was a major physical disability—one was totally blind, two were crippled, and another was debilitated by an advanced case of tuberculosis. These handicaps obviously precluded many normal male roles.

Shamans may be found in all areas of Okinawa, but they are more heavily concentrated in the towns and cities. This may corroborate Harada's observation[5] that in Japan shamanism tends to prevail in those areas permitting a greater individualism, i.e., the towns and cities. However, in Okinawa governmental efforts to outlaw this practice in the past may have driven the shamans to seek anonymity in larger population centers. In recent years a heavy influx of rural people into the urban areas also may have contributed to the concentration of shamans there. In the country, it is said that a *yuta* does not derive many clients from her own village and that people prefer to consult those outside the community.

Like the priestesses, *yuta* are believed to be selected by the *kami*. A basic requirement, therefore, is that the prospective shaman or *kaminchu* be born with *saadaka*. For the hereditary priestesses of the community there is seldom a question as to who is *saadaka nmari* (of high-*saa* birth), but for the shamans and kin group priestesses, who are essentially self-selected, the presence of high *saa* must be confirmed by an established shaman or fortuneteller, preferably the former. It is believed, however, that most prospective *yuta* and *kudii* are unaware of their destined roles and obligation to serve and that, consequently, the *kami* must resort to notifications (*shirashi*). These *shirashi* may take the form of general misfortune, illness, disease, disturbing dreams, or strange or unusual occurrences; an accompanying hallucinatory experience is a certain indication of *shirashi*. At this point some individuals will suspect that their difficulties relate to *kami* matters and will consult a shaman. A very few, on visiting the shaman and learning that they are *saadaka*, will accept their role and wholeheartedly commit themselves to finding their *chiji*. This early recognition and ready acceptance of the role is termed *duu-wachi* (self-recognition). The overwhelming majority, however, attempt to continue normal lives by trying to ignore these *shirashi* (notifications) and the shaman's interpretation. As a consequence, they become victims of *taari*, the psychosomatic disorder described in Chapter II. *Taari* may cover a period ranging from several months to many years, and supposedly relief is not obtained until the prospective shaman or kin group priestess succeeds in identifying her *chiji*. This is accomplished by visiting many sites of prayer and by consulting with many shamans for clues. Final identification of the *chiji* usually occurs in a hallucinatory experience, sometimes during a dream. Thereafter, the individual bears a lifelong obligation to serve the particular *kami* so identified.

After an abatement or marked reduction of *taari* symptoms, the individual is regarded as having mastered this affliction with supernatural assistance. At this point, others may informally request assistance with their problems, and gradually a clientele develops in this fashion. My informants repeatedly insisted that they had not intended at the outset to establish a business but that they had been pressured into doing so by others who were impressed by their experiences and recovery. They were equally insistent that they had not learned their new role from any established shaman and that their instruction was derived from the *kami*. This point of view is subscribed to by the general population, though, of course, the new practitioners have the opportunity during the *chiji* quest to observe many shamans in action and to become familiar with many ritual sites. I have found that occasionally a person in *taari* may be placed in the care of an established shaman and may even reside in the latter's house for a period of time; but this is not regarded as a novitiate, since the purpose is to help or cure, not to train. In general, though not without exceptions, *yuta* relationships tend to be characterized by intense rivalry or jealousy, *yuta wanai* being a common expression to describe this.

The life histories of most shamans reveal long records of marital discord and intrafamily conflict: frequent divorces; sexual incompatibility; fighting with spouses, siblings, in-laws, and parents. Their lives are often characterized by frequent and vaguely defined illnesses—stomach disorders, constant headaches, asthma, neuralgia, skin disorders, etc.—which fail to yield to medical treatment, modern or traditional. All of them contend that their childhood, adolescence, and adult lives were decidedly different from those of ordinary people, and the frequency of hallucinatory experiences stands out as a persistent trait. Although a matter of serious concern, hallucinatory experience (*imi-gukuchi*) is not positively disvalued in this culture, and informants spoke with little hesitancy about their experiences.

In general, shamans tend to have had less formal education than most people, but they give the impression of being well above average in intelligence. Some are capable of rather extraordinary feats of memory, being able to retain household names, birth years, birth orders, and brief personal histories for the entire membership of a household on a single hearing and to repeat these in a prayer or chant. They are highly articulate and usually succeed in dominating any conversation. They frequently express anxiety over any slackening of ritual efforts which will bring a recurrence of *taari*. As a group, while intelligent and articulate, they are obviously disturbed; the important fact is that they have successfully implemented or adjusted their personality disorders to a socially approved role.

As stated before, the *kudii* of the kin groups go through an identical process—notifications, *taari*, and *chiji* quest—in attaining office. It must be further noted that some *yuta* also function as *kudii* in their kin groups, although the two roles, those of shaman and priestess, have quite distinct functions. I do not mean to imply by this that all *yuta* serve as *kudii* or that all *kudii* become *yuta*; on the contrary, this is not true for even a majority in either group; but some duality does occur. A crucial factor here is the type of *chiji* identified. For a prospective *kudii* it must be a remote ancestral spirit of the kin group, most frequently the *chiji* of a predecessor in office. For a shaman, so far as I am aware, the *chiji* is not that of a predecessor, as there are no established shaman lines. Moreover, the *chiji* of a shaman need not be a remote ancestor in their line, even though shamans may attempt to claim more than a spiritual kinship with their *chiji*. Consequently, acceptance by the kin group of the *chiji* appears to be one selective factor. It is also significant, I believe, that the type of shaman who serves as a *kudii* is usually an *ugamisaa* (prayer person), who relies primarily on prayer to contact the supernatural, rather than an *uranaisaa* or *chiitatiyaa* (diviners), who rely principally on spirit possession. Viewing both groups (*yuta* and *kudii*) collectively, I have the impression that the latter are less aggressive verbally, less disturbed, more subdued, and more dependent personality types than the shamans.

The clients of the shamans are mainly females, in keeping with the fact that the senior female of a household acts as ritualist on behalf of the family. Given the collectivity focus which characterizes Okinawan culture, it may be said that nearly all households number themselves among the clientele of the shaman. Recordings of shaman-client sessions revealed that households of high-ranking government officials, university staff members, school teachers, and businessmen—not to mention laborers, farmers, and fishermen—were included. As a rule, each household sends a representative to visit the shaman shortly after New Year's, or at least during the first six months of the new year, in order to obtain the fortune for each member. Otherwise, any crisis situation may prompt a visit. When a family member is ill, it is usually the senior female who visits the shaman and who then cajoles or adjures the afflicted individual into following the shaman's advice. When an illness is severe or prolonged, there is a tendency to consult a number of shamans and to employ a variety of medical techniques concurrently. Widespread reliance on shamanism stands out as a persistent feature of contemporary Okinawan life.

Those shaman sessions which I have witnessed were relatively mild. Although it is widely believed that a *kami* or ancestral spirit may take possession of the *yuta*'s body while in communication, I seriously doubt that a trance or state of dissociation from reality is regularly attained, at least not in any routinized or controlled manner. On one occasion I photographed a blind *yuta* during possession; later he expressed irritation over this disturbance, although the only disruption had been the click of the shutter, indicating that he had been in complete control of his faculties. Parenthetically, it must be noted that no evidence of epileptics performing as shamans was found, nor was there any evidence of attempts to induce a trance through starvation or other means. The word *yuta* is said to derive from the verb *yuyung*, meaning "to tremble," "to shake," or "to rock to and fro." Although widely used, this term is regarded as derogatory by the shamans, who prefer to be called *kaminchu* or *hanji* (judge).[6] Moreover, my informants insisted that only a poor *yuta* who had not yet completed *taari* would tremble or shake. Nonetheless, I have seen a few perform in this manner, and in the southern Ryukyus (Miyako and Yaeyama) this is common to the performance of shamans and priestesses alike. Currently, at least, the performance of the Okinawan shamans provides only a thinly stylized simulation of trance.

The standard fee for a visit to the *yuta*'s house is fifty cents (U.S.); if she is called to a house, a charge of several dollars, plus transportation and meals, may be exacted. A shaman may earn more in a single hour than a laborer in a day. Besides the fixed fees for their services, they often receive gifts, especially food (fruit, cakes, or rice). Many *yuta* are able to support themselves from their professional earnings; others, who are less popular, may have part-time occupations. The most successful inject a goodly element of showmanship into their performance which impresses clients and adds to their reputation. Most commonly, clients are told that their difficulties stem from a lack of ritual or improper ritual and that the ancestors are displeased. Advice for remedial action is shrewdly offered in such a way that responsibility for effective action rests with the client. There are no penalties for failure in advice or treatment aside from a loss of clients and income.

It is difficult to determine whether the *yuta* are increasing at present; certainly they are maintaining their numbers far more successfully than other religious functionaries. Some informants expressed the opinion that the number of *yuta* has actually increased in the postwar period; more likely, relaxation of the old law prohibiting shamanism has enabled them to practice more openly, thereby creating an impression of increased numbers. In either case, the persistence of shamanism stands out in marked contrast to the over-all trend of decline and disintegration for Okinawan religion.

SANJINSOO. Practitioners engaging in fortunetelling, divining, and geomancy and deriving their knowledge from books rather than the supernatural are called *sanjinsoo* (the characters indicate the meaning of this term to be "explanation of yin and yang principle"). The older term *hanji* (judge) may still be applied to them, but, as noted before, it has come to mean *yuta* as well. The Japanese term 'ekisha' (fortuneteller, diviner) has found increasing currency. Unlike the *kaminchu* and *yuta*, who profess high spirit rank and *kami* guidance, the *sanjinsoo* claim no supernatural powers, eliciting their prognostications instead from the lunar almanac (*kuyumi*), the *I Ching*, and numerous other books on occult lore. Traditionally, this profession has been exclusively for males, and formerly it was dominated by the upper classes, for in the old kingdom those of the gentry class who failed the state examinations for entrance into the bureaucracy were said to have entered the professions of teaching or fortunetelling. The commoners, of course, were illiterate, since all education was denied them save what might be garnered by living as servants in upper-class houses.

The major functions of the *sanjinsoo* include determining fortunes (*unchi*), selecting propitious times for specific actions (such as buying, selling, moving, traveling) or events (engagement, marriage, and funerals). In addition, they perform geomantic rites to locate places of good *fungshi* (*fungshi nu yutasang*) for wells, tombs, and buildings Occasionally, they are called upon to suggest personal names, as their knowledge of Chinese characters is respected, and during the early postwar period they were frequently asked to select new family names for impoverished families who reasoned that the change might improve their fortunes. During *nmari-dushi* (birth year) a person (or representative) may visit the *sanjinsoo* to chart a course of action for the year. Soon after the lunar New Year one member of each household, usually the senior female member, will visit the *sanjinsoo* to discuss the family's fortune for the forthcoming year; this is called *hachi unchi* (first fortune) and is identical to visiting a *yuta* for the same purpose.

Formerly, the *sanjinsoo* acquired his knowledge through many years of study with an established *sanjinsoo*. Prior to the dissolution of the Okinawan kingdom in 1879 a few were said to have gone to China for study.

Since that time some *sanjinsoo* have studied in Japan, particularly in the Osaka area, where a number of Okinawans have settled. Others have learned from reading books on the subject. The books and methods of the *sanjinsoo* were originally developed in China and were probably introduced into Okinawa after the fourteenth century, when a Chinese community was established in Kume, now a part of Naha. During the past fifty years, however, Japanese books on 'eki' have replaced the older Chinese and Okinawan texts, as only a very few of the oldest *sanjinsoo* are now able to read Chinese texts or Okinawanized versions thereof. A number of *sanjinsoo* also specialize in the study of Okinawan history, and as a group they tend to be well informed on this subject. Their knowledge of local history has its practical use in the reconstruction of genealogies for families and kin groups, an important function in a culture which prizes ancestry and continuity. Like the *kaminchu* and *yuta*, they tend to be more Okinawan in outlook and manner than the general population.

Fortunetelling and divination are performed by using six wooden blocks or forty-nine bamboo sticks; these are rotated between the palms and then cast or arbitrarily divided. The pattern in which they turn up or divide is then looked up in books in which possible combinations have been worked out. It is believed that a *kami*, usually *uting nu kami* (the heaven *kami*), determines the result; consequently, most *sanjinsoo* maintain a small shrine for this *kami* within the living room, and the divining sticks or blocks may be offered to this shrine before a fortune is read. *Sanjinsoo*, at least in conversation with a Westerner, tend to de-emphasize the importance of the *kami* and to stress instead the books which they believe to contain the wisdom of the ages. It seems not unlikely that the shrine and suggested influence of the *kami* are concessions to popular concepts concerning the role of the supernatural in determining personal fortune.

The dress of the *sanjinsoo* does not differ from that of the general population, although one *sanjinsoo* in his late eighties affected the dress and hair styling of the former gentry class. During the time of the old Okinawan kingdom, when this profession was limited exclusively to the upper classes, they naturally dressed as befitted their rank. At present, most *sanjinsoo* are men in the middle and late years of life; not a few educated men (by Okinawan standards) turn to this profession for a means of livelihood after their retirement. One informant, for example, was a retired primary school principal. As the texts which they employ demand an extensive knowledge of characters, the *sanjinsoo* may be looked upon as men of learning and erudition; in conversation they will readily describe themselves as scholars (one insisted that he was a scientist). Their behavior is marked by decorum and aloofness, in keeping with the image of a learned man in this culture. Formerly, their status was high, in part because of their class affiliation but also because Okinawan culture has traditionally accorded high status to learning. Today their status has suffered a sharp decline, although they are still accorded some degree of respect by older people. Significantly, today's new elite does not scorn them, perhaps because the 'ekisha' continues to flourish in Japan. A high-ranking police official stated, "Before the war there was a strict law against the practice of shamanism, but there were many *yuta* nonetheless. However, there was no such law against the *sanjinsoo*." Why? "Because they have a 'konkyo' [foundation or basis] for advice. We could only punish them if they gave advice which was not in their books." This same individual went on to relate how a *sanjinsoo* had once accurately predicted his brother's death at sea.

The standard fee charged by a *sanjinsoo* is fifty cents; this provides an income, if steadily employed, considerably above the earnings of a laborer. Although they might command a higher status than the *yuta* in erudition, it is felt that their powers are decidedly limited. As one informant put it, "A *sanjinsoo* can only tell you if your luck is good or bad; he cannot explain why." The fact that their advice is without supernatural basis lessens their effectiveness in the eyes of ordinary people; consequently, for serious matters of misfortune the services of a *yuta* are preferred or considered mandatory.

The *sanjinsoo*, like the *yuta*, do not form an organized group, and relationships among them are generally lacking in cordiality, as competition is keen. For the *yuta*, whom they regard as arch foes, they have only contempt and scorn; the most derogatory charge which they can level against a rival *sanjinsoo* is to accuse him of "*yuta* methods." This charge has some basis in fact, for some *yuta* have invaded the *sanjinsoo* ranks and placed fortuneteller signs outside their homes in order to attract clients.

General opinion seems to be that the number of *sanjinsoo* has increased but that their erudition is not as great as in the past. An eighty-year-old *sanjinsoo* noted, "When I was a boy in Kume Mura [originally the Chinese district in Naha], all the great *sanjinsoo* could read Chinese with ease. Several of the great *sanjinsoo* who lived there had even gone to China for study. Today, most of them are in comparison untrained, virtually illiterate, and of lower-class origin; they read a few simple books and claim to be *sanjinsoo*. The numbers have increased, but the quality has decreased."

BOOJI. Although sectarian Buddhism constitutes a negligible factor in Okinawan life, there are scattered throughout the island, chiefly in the cities and towns, a few Buddhist priests—*booji* ('bozu')—who tend small temples and officiate at funerals. Their presence at funerals, however, is by no means universal; poor families readily dispense with their services. The presence of a *booji* at a funeral might be regarded as an indication of the family's affluence rather than an attestation to its Buddhist piety. In addition to this function, *booji* sell protective amulets and sometimes are called upon to perform certain exorcistic rites.

During a funeral the *booji* prays at the house just before the palanquin is carried from the yard; he walks near the head of the procession to the tomb and there prays once again before the casket is entombed. He usually departs before the funeral rites are completed. His prayers are rendered in a Japanese version of Sanskrit, pronounced with a decidedly Okinawan accent; consequently, what he says is unintelligible to all, often to himself as well. His utterances are punctuated by the ringing of a small bell held in his hand. Several informants separately stated that the *booji*'s performance during the strain of funeral proceedings struck them as ridiculous and evoked an irresistible desire to laugh.

The talismans or protective amulets which the *booji* sells may be carried by the owner. More usually they are hung about the house in the belief that they will drive away all manner of *yanamung*. They are generally mere slips of paper bearing printed characters recognized for their efficacy in combating malevolence or promoting good fortune.

The *booji*'s exorcistic practices are usually limited to *nujifa*, the removal of dead spirits believed to have become ghosts. When a child drowned in a small river near a certain village, someone remembered that a man had drowned at that spot nine years earlier. It was believed, therefore, that his ghost had caused the child's death and that subsequently the child's ghost would endeavor to find another victim, and so on in an endless cycle. The belief exists that the ghost of one who has died a violent or unnatural death must hover near the spot of death and that it will find no rest (i.e., will be unable to enter the tomb) until it causes a death. Consquently, a *booji* was called to pray at the scene of death and to escort the spirit to the family tomb in the hope that a cycle of deaths would thereby be averted.

An infrequent yet important function of the *booji* relates to the disposal of corpses unclaimed by relatives. If an individual brings public disgrace upon the members of a kin group, he or she may be refused interment in the common tomb. Those guilty of gross criminal acts or of suicide are most likely to be rejected. (In the latter case, Okinawan culture bears greater similarity to Chinese than to Japanese culture.) In such cases, the *booji* is called to cremate the body (Okinawans do not ordinarily practice cremation) and inter the ashes with simple rites in the temple or temple yard. No members of the family pray for the person's spirit and no ancestral tablet is made. This is considered an extremely drastic action, for it is believed that those who die without descendants to pray for them are condemned to wander endlessly without rest and will cause endless tribulations for the living.

The popular attitude toward the *booji* seems largely conditioned by his association with death; he does not occupy a very high status or command much respect in the eyes of ordinary people. Men seem especially contemptuous of him and joke about his long-windedness and easy life. Grudgingly, perhaps, it is recognized that his services contribute in some measure to a successful interment of the deceased, an important accomplishment if the living are to avoid being plagued by ghosts.

NIMBUCHAA. Prior to the battle for Okinawa in 1945 there existed a pariah caste whose members were called *nimbuchaa* (*nimbuchi*-person: one who recites 'nembutsu,' a Buddhist prayer or invocation). Primarily, the *nimbuchaa* were identified with the occupation of bell ringing at funerals. Most of the *nimbuchaa* were located in the Anna Mura district of Shuri and the Kakinohana district of Naha; those in the latter area were said to have been used exclusively by the royal family and nobility, while those in the former area were used by the gentry and commoners. In the rural areas, one or two *nimbuchaa* families were said to be found in each *majiri* ('son'). During the period of the kingdom, gentry families summoned one *booji* and two *nimbuchaa* for their funerals; the commoners were permitted to employ but one *nimbuchaa* and usually could not afford a priest. According to some informants, the royal family and nobility summoned as many as their wealth would allow or the individual's status demanded. As soon as a death occurred, a *nimbuchaa* was called to the house; generally, he was not permitted to enter the yard but was stationed at the gate, where he would sit striking his bell until the body was taken to the tomb. It is said that the *nimbuchaa* led the procession to the tomb, continuing his din until interment.

Formerly, the *nimbuchaa* were segregated into special districts and were forbidden to marry outside their caste. Moreover, their very presence was considered polluting to others; a well-known legend concerns Okinawa's famous *juri* ('geisha'-prostitute) poetess, Yushiya Chiru, who was inadvertently polluted by an affair with a *nimbuchaa*. Although the Japanese abolished class distinctions during the early years of their administration, public opinion forced the *nimbuchaa* to continue their hereditary occupation, but by the 1930's and early 1940's their employment at funerals had become irregular. Wartime dislocation of the entire Okinawan population presented the opportunity for them to desert their profession and segregated districts, enabling them to spread into all parts of the island, and the area of their settlement in Shuri reverted to fields after the war. Today most people acknowledge that this discrimination was grossly unfair and that such practices are not in keeping with the new way of life.

It is not known who the *nimbuchaa* were originally or how they came into such a low status.[7] They bear some resemblance to the Japanese pariah group, 'eta,' who were (and in some areas still are) segregated into special districts and forbidden by public opinion to marry outside their caste. Their traditional occupations, however, are decidedly different; butchering, hide-working and sandal-making tend to be the occupational specialties of the Japanese 'eta.' The 'eta' do not now have a religious function, although it is commonly acknowledged that their origin has some connection with Buddhism. On Okinawa this would certainly seem to be the case; their name alone would suggest this (although as a polite euphemism they were addressed by the term *kaniuchi*, bell striker).[8] Unfortunately, for our purposes, historical accounts and even present-day Okinawan and Japanese studies have made little mention of the ritual activities of *nimbuchaa* aside from a few fleeting references. At the tomb, however, it was their function to recite the *nimbuchi* ('nembutsu') or Buddhist invocation, in addition to striking their bell, and it is definitely known that the 'nembutsu' ritual was introduced into Okinawa in the years 1603–1605 by the Japanese monk Taichū Shōnin of the Jōdō Sect.

All *nimbuchaa* were said to be members of the Jōdō Sect, and their Shuri settlement contained a small temple for the worship of Amida. One aged informant stated that this sect had incurred public disfavor by its belligerent missionary zeal and that all its followers may have been gradually relegated to this lowly status as a consequence. Certainly Jōdō is not held in high esteem today, and one of the great villains of Okinawan history and folklore was the nefarious Jōdō priest Kurukani Jashi, whose evil talents so terrified the populace that he was at last ordered assassinated by the king. Undoubtedly, the *nimbuchaa* developed their function after the introduction of Jōdō and the 'nembutsu'; it is a moot question, however, whether they existed as a pariah group or possessed any religious function before then. The practice of bell ringing at funerals is widespread throughout East Asia, but on Okinawa alone this practice was ascribed to a specific hereditary group with a pariah status. Significantly, in the southern islands of the Ryukyus they seem to have been regarded as ordinary commoners, not outcastes.

YABUU. Those who employ traditional methods of healing and curing are called *yabuu*. This term applies to two distinct types of medical practitioner. The first is a male who has received formal instruction in traditional Chinese medical practices of bone setting, acupuncture, moxacautery, blood letting, and the use of certain potions and salves. These men have been trained by established practitioners or have attended schools in Japan; the leading *yabuu* in the kingdom are said to have received their training in China. Although their numbers are declining as the numbers of modern physicians increase, their practice is still regarded as a legitimate one, and they are licensed by the government after passing an examination.

The second type of *yabuu* is usually a female who relies primarily on the curative powers of prayers and formulas, although she may also possess an extensive knowledge of plants and their medicinal uses. It is said that in the past the male *yabuu* were to be found in the urban areas, while the female *yabuu* predominated in rural villages. The former were engaged by the upper classes and the latter by the peasantry; in effect, the educated upper classes preferred the more empirical Chinese techniques of healing, whereas the illiterate relied to a greater degree on magical methods. Both systems, however, appear to be in consonance with Okinawan concepts of sickness and disease.

The absence of a concept of impersonal causation has been repeatedly stressed; sickness and disease are considered products of a supernatural agent—*kami*, ancestral spirits, and malevolent spirits. Effective treatment thus demands diagnosis to determine the specific causal spirit. Even though a male *yabuu* may adequately set a broken bone, it is necessary to determine why the break occurred and which supernatural agent was responsible. Consultation with a *yuta* would not only help recovery but would prevent recurrence of misfortune. Sickness and disease caused by the *kami* or ancestors require prayers and action to correct the situation which has displeased them. Illnesses believed to result from sorcery, ghosts, or other malevolent spirits demand purgative and exorcistic techniques, curses, formulas, and also prayers to solicit *kami* assistance. Chinese curative techniques of acupuncture, blood letting, and moxacautery are well suited to the concept that malevolence must be purged or effaced. Tattooing as a remedial technique is also practiced. Even today, Okinawan preference for medical treatment that cuts, punctures, burns, etc., is remarkable; antibiotic shots, for example, have found widespread and almost instantaneous acceptance, whereas modern concepts of sanitation and disease prevention have made a relatively slight impression on the masses.

Sakima[9] has defined *yabuu* as "medicine man," which would imply a curer who employs magical techniques with the aid of a spirit helper or other personal supernatural power. This definition could only apply to the female *yabuu*, not to her male counterpart, who utilizes Chinese healing techniques. Moreover, although some describe the female *yabuu* as a type of *yuta*, so far as I am aware there is no consistent process by which the *yabuu* acquire their role, nor do all of them claim personal supernatural powers as do the *yuta*. The consistent trait is use of prayers and formulas in curing. Country *yabuu* are usually older women, and there are indications that this has been a traditional pattern. Their knowledge is generally acquired from close female relatives, usually a mother or mother-in-law. Consequently, there is some tendency to recognize *yabuu* households or *yabuu* lines, although no strict rule of inheritance obtains. It is equally obvious that some *yuta* specialize in curing and become *yabuu*.

The *yabuu* are in decline, although they still outnumber the modern physicians. Older people in the rural areas, especially women, continue to utilize their services. The more common practice, however, is to engage a physician for treatment and a *yuta* for explanation.

ICHIJAMAA. The Okinawan sorcerer (*ichijamaa*), described in Chapter II, was for me the most elusive of the ritual specialists, in that I did not have the opportunity to interview any *ichijamaa* and was forced to rely on informants for what are essentially hearsay accounts. Sorcery is a common folklore and folk-theater theme, and it is one of the recognized causes of sickness or other misfortune. According to Okinawan belief, anyone may curse, but only *yuta* and *ichijamaa* have the power to work sorcery. In two recent cases, the accused were *yuta*, but it is clearly recognized that not all *ichijamaa* are shamans. *Ichijamaa* utilize their power exclusively for asocial ends, whereas the *yuta* work for socially approved ends. A *yuta* who resorted to sorcery would be regarded as one with a false *chiji*.

An *ichijamaa* is believed to be possessed by a malevolent spirit which has been inherited from one of the parents. Among male *ichijamaa* this passes from father to son and among females from mother to daughter. It is customary, therefore, to recognize *ichijamaa* lines, and people are said to refrain from marrying into a family which is believed to have this trait. Most *ichijamaa* are females; only a very few are males.

As noted before, *ichijamaa* are said to have asocial natures and to be jealous and covetous of others and their possessions. Behavior of this sort is highly disvalued by Okinawans, and it is easy to believe that extreme manifestations render an individual susceptible to the accusation of being a sorcerer. An *ichijamaa* who dislikes someone or covets his possessions may cause him to become sick by projecting foreign objects into his body or may cause his tools to break or his animals to sicken. This is said to be done by secret rites known only to the *ichijamaa*, but apparently possession of some part of the victim's body, such as a lock of hair, renders the action more effective. It is also believed that a sorcerer has the power to possess another person and to cause the loss of *mabui*. If the *ichijamaa* is known, the victim may curse or throw pig dung in her direction, but more commonly the victim is unaware of the sorcerer's identity or that the misfortune has been caused by sorcery, and it is a *yuta* who first discerns this. The *yuta* also may perform exorcistic rites designed to remove any foreign object or spirit from the victim's body, possessions, or house area. Apparently, the *yuta* does not directly enter into combat with the sorcerer; no accounts of battles between shaman and sorcerer were reported.

It is difficult to make any meaningful assessment of the incidence of sorcery in contemporary Okinawa. Educated people readily scoff at these accounts and label them with the Japanese term 'meishin' (superstition). Yet among the oldest generation, women, and the uneducated, belief in sorcery seems quite genuine. The case of a Naha *yuta* who in 1956 extracted large sums from neighbors in return for not doing sorcery against them indicates that some fear of sorcery exists. In this instance the police were asked to intervene. It is said that in the past suspected *ichijamaa* were socially ostracized, denied the assistance of fellow villagers, and enjoined from participation in reciprocal labor exchanges (this might still be the case). There appear to be effective means for handling recognized cases of sorcery; moreover, sorcery is not commonly cited by the *yuta* as a cause of sickness or misfortune. Difficulties with the *kami*, ancestral spirits, or ghosts take precedence, at least today, over sorcery. I therefore do not regard the Okinawans, of today or the recent past, as sorcery-ridden.

V

STATE RELIGION

The Ancient Cult

Archaeological remains have thus far provided few clues as to the nature of ancient Okinawan religion, but several sites have yielded a number of the large claw-shaped beads of the sort still worn by the village priestesses as part of their ceremonial attire, suggesting that the prehistoric people might also have used these for religious purposes. Moreover, extensive deposits of artifacts in and around the major sites of national worship indicate that these places have been frequented since early times. It is to be hoped that more systematic research will eventually shed further light on this matter.

While the earliest documentation of Okinawan history begins in the late twelfth century (largely derived from Chinese accounts), the first written versions of the creation myth date from the seventeenth century, following several centuries of contact with China and Japan. Three sources contain the earliest written versions of this myth and have been intensively studied by Okinawan and Japanese scholars. They are *Ryūkyū Shindō-ki*, written by the previously mentioned Japanese monk, Taichū Shōnin, and published in 1648; *Chūzan Seikan*, compiled by the Okinawan statesman Haneji Tomohide (Shō Shōgen) in 1650; and *Omoro Sōshi*, a collection of 1,553 religious songs (*umui*) compiled from 1531 to 1623. Unfortunately, the language of the last work is archaic and has been cumbersomely recorded in the Japanese syllabary, so that even Okinawan scholars are not in agreement as to the meaning and significance of these songs.

Spencer[1] has shown that Taichū's version of the creation myth is somewhat simpler than Haneji's and has suggested that political considerations may have dictated a greater elaboration. The evidence of Japanese, and to a lesser extent Chinese, influence in Haneji's version is considerable, and it is to be stressed that he wrote after the Satsuma conquest of 1609, whereas Taichū gathered his material in 1603–1605, several years before that event. For example, Haneji relates that the mythical founder of the first Okinawan dynasty was Tenson; the identical name and characters are used in Japanese history for Ninigi, grandson of the sun goddess (Amaterasu ō mi kami) and grandfather to the Emperor Jimmu, who founded the Japanese state. Tenson's dynasty lasted for twenty-five generations and supposedly extended over a period of nearly eighteen thousand years! Shunten, legendary founder of the first historic dynasty (*ca.* A.D. 1187), was claimed by Haneji to have been sired by Minamoto Tametomo, a famous Japanese warrior who had been exiled after the temporary defeat of his clan in 1156. History records, however, that Tametomo never left his place of exile in the Izu Islands, which extend off the coast of Honshu in a southeasterly direction from the mouth of Tokyo Bay. But Haneji's fanciful creation ultimately became a popular legend in both Japan and the Ryukyus and the subject for a novel in Tokugawa Japan. Shunten's name appears to have been copied from that of the legendary Chinese ruler Shun, renowned for his great sagacity. In substance, much of Haneji's writing about early Okinawa appears to be fabrication, evidencing liberal borrowings from Japanese and Chinese historical traditions.

The versions of the creation myth given in *Ryūkyū Shindō-ki* and in the *Omoro* relate that the creator deities were Amamikyu (Amamikyo) and Shinerikyu (Shinerikyo). Haneji's version mentions only Amamikyo, but the *Kyūyō*, said to be a later Chinese version of Haneji's work, names both deities.[2] Okinawan and Japanese scholars have speculated at considerable length on the significance of the female deity's name; curiously, little attention has been directed toward the male, Shinerikyo. The most popular interpretation has been that Amamikyo represents a tribal name. Higaonna[3] declares that scholarly opinion believes the Amamikyo were the Amabe of southern Kyushu. Frequently,[4] the name Amami, which applies to the largest island group lying between Japan and Okinawa, is cited as evidence that the Amabe passed through that area on their migration to Okinawa. Unfortunately, these "scholarly opinions" are actually baseless speculation; very little is truly known about the Amabe in early Japan, save that they were one of the hereditary 'be' or guilds and that they were fisherfolk. Ascribing the first settlement of the Ryukyus to them on the basis of only a partial similarity of names seems hardly justifiable, nor does the identification of deity, tribe, and guild say much for logic.

The extant oral version of the creation myth, which was recorded in Chapter II, merely related that two sibling deities—*uminai* or *winagu-gami* (sister *kami*) and *umikii* or *wikii-gami* (brother *kami*)—created the island and the first people. Although I was unable to elicit any mention of Amamikyo or Shinerikyo save among those who had read history or had been influenced by others who had, it is possible to account for the name of the former as the product of the difficulty encountered in transcribing Okinawan speech in another language (viz., Japanese or Chinese). In certain of the *umui* which I recorded, mention was made of *amami*, *amami kang ganashii*, and *amami kami nu ganashii mee*, which, old informants stated, refers to the heaven *kami*, more commonly called *ting nu kami* at present and rather vaguely conceptualized as the supreme *kami*. The first people are frequently said to be the *amanchu* (heaven person or people, i.e., descended from heaven). Similarly, their period—the beginning of time—is called *ama nu yuu* (age of heaven) or *kami nu yuu* (age of the *kami*). I am inclined, therefore, to reject all theories that Amamikyo was a tribal name or that it represents a proper name at all and to believe that it merely designates heaven *kami* or heaven person. The name Shinerikyo affords no easy decipherment, for there appear to be no cognates in extant oral traditions, although Arakaki Magoichi (in personal conversation) expressed the opinion that this may once have had the simple meaning of "male *kami*" or "person" (in the Chinen-Kudaka dialect, *shii* means "male"). It is to be stressed that these names were originally transcribed in Japanese and were subject to the limitations of the Japanese syllabary, hence the original Okinawan pronunciation and the meaning have been largely lost thereby. It is to be hoped that future studies of these materials will incorporate a more rigorous linguistic approach than has been utilized heretofore. Because of the many inaccuracies in recording and evidences of fabrication in the early written accounts, I am inclined to regard the surviving oral myths as more truly representative of ancient traditions.

Old Okinawans believe that the island of Kudaka, approximately two miles off the southeast coast, was the area of first settlement and the place of origin of the Okinawan people. They will often refer to it as a *kami* island, and traditionally it has been treated as one of the focal points of national worship.[5] Kudaka is a rather barren, low, wind-swept island whose people eke out a meager existence by fishing and planting millet and wheat in the sandy soils. From Kudaka, it is said, the first people moved to the Chinen district on the mainland, opposite Kudaka, settling in the area of Seefa Utaki, which during historic times has been regarded as the most sacred place on Okinawa. Because of water shortages (the *utaki* is located on a steep ridge about one hundred meters above the sea) the people moved about one mile south along the coast to the site of the present village of Hyakuna in Tamagusuku district. Here the first rice is believed to have been planted in a field called Miifudaa; this field and two nearby springs, Ukinju-Hainju, became important sites of pilgrimage and continue as such to this day. From this area, it is said, the people eventually spread over the entire island of Okinawa.

Seefa Utaki symbolized, then, the place where the first ancestors lived on Okinawa, and until dissolution of the kingdom it was the most sacred site for national worship conducted by the chief priestess of the land. So, too, in every Okinawan village, aside from those established in recent times, there is an *utaki*, which constitutes the most sacred site for communal worship. Such places, as previously noted, are said to be *shijidakasang*. Trees and shrubbery are never cut there, and in the past males were forbidden to enter. It is commonly believed that the *utaki* represents the site where the village founder lived or prayed, and that the *kami* worshiped there is in fact the village founder or the *kami* to which the founder prayed. It is thought that on ceremonial occasions this *kami* descends to the *utaki*, and only the highest-ranking village priestess possesses the power to invoke this spirit. Some measure of the importance attached to these places may be seen in the fact that the annalists of the Okinawan kingdom carefully listed all *utaki* of the land; Miyagi[6] relates that for the northern area (Kunigami) alone 133 *utaki* were recorded.

Taichū's version of the creation myth declares that the first fire was brought from Ryūgu, which in Chinese and Japanese folk-belief is conceived of as a dragon palace resting on the bottom of the sea; but this does not constitute a part of the contemporary belief, which regards *ruugu* or *duugu* (Ryūgu) as the residence of the sea *kami* (*unjami*). Yanagita[7] has attempted to relate the names (name?) *nirai kanai* (according to Okinawan scholars, *niiree kanee* or *giree kanee* is the correct pronunciation), mentioned in the *Omoro* and *Ryūkyū Shindō-ki*, to Japanese beliefs concerning Ryūgu and to elicit their significance in Ryukyuan mythology. He believes that *niiree kanee* referred to a sort of paradise in the sea to the east from whence fire was obtained and where the dead sojourned. These terms do not constitute an active part of contemporary belief, and even many old Okinawans appear to be wholly unfamiliar with them. Moreover, Yanagita[8] himself acknowledges that the terms have not been recorded (in recent times) on Okinawa. However, I was able to record *giree kanee* in an *umui* sung by the *nuru* of Itoman, who explained that *giree* was an old term for bone washing and that *kanee* had the meaning of "beach." Formerly, bone washing, usually one to three years after death, was done on the beach, so that the bones might be washed and purified in salt water. While the priestess was reluctant to relate these terms to any belief in a paradise, as Yanagita has attempted, it was conceded feasible to speak of a dead person as going to *giree kanee* in the sense of having posthumous existence. The word *niiree*, which seems to have been used interchangeably with *giree* in the ancient songs, has the meaning of "roots" or "origin." The old system of burial prior to the adoption of Chinese-style tombs (it may still be found on the island of Kudaka) was to place the body in a small wooden casket on the beach; then, after bone washing, the bones were placed in a small urn and secreted in a cave or niche along the shore. It is a matter for conjecture whether, as Yanagita contends, *niree kanee* (or *giree kanee*) once constituted the Okinawan paradise, for today the Buddhist paradise, *gukuraku* ('gokuraku'), occupies this position, although, as will be shown, popular Buddhism can boast less than three hundred years on Okinawa.

Many scholars have assumed that a fire cult constituted the focal point of ancient and modern Okinawan religion, but I was informed at the Shuri Museum, which periodically conducts archaeological research throughout the islands, that thus far the three-stone hearth which symbolizes the *fii nu kang* has not been found in any prehistoric site. Certain of the ritual practices surrounding the hearth, as I have noted, are obviously of Taoist origin. For example, the practice of smearing oil or sugar on the mouth of the mask or picture depicting the hearth *kami* (before its departure for heaven to report on the family's activities throughout the past year) has been widely practiced in China.[9] More significantly, hearth rites show their greatest development in those areas—the Naha-Shuri district and adjacent areas of southern and central Okinawa—where Chinese influence was strongest, whereas elsewhere in the Ryukyus these practices are notably weaker or even nonexistent. My research in the Yaeyama Islands of the southern Ryukyus revealed that the hearth rites there are associated with the Okinawan administrators sent down by Shuri after the conquest of 1501. Yanagita Kunio (in personal conversation) has suggested that while the main practices relating to the hearth appear to be Chinese, there may have existed an earlier, simpler form of hearth worship onto which these were grafted. A similar view is expressed by Miyagi,[10] who believes that practices relating to the *fii nu kang* were distorted at an early date in the Naha-Shuri district by Taoist influences and that the older practices are better preserved in northern Okinawa, but my investigations in that area failed to provide any corroborative evidence for this claim. In my view, hearth rites appear to be of less importance there, and the only practice exhibited in the north and not found in central and southern Okinawa is that of hanging in back of the hearth the jaw bones of pigs that have been raised and consumed by the family.

Spencer,[11] basing his study largely on Iha's work[12] and brief interviews with three *nuru*, emphasizes fire worship as the central facet of ancient and modern Okinawan religion. Apparently, he failed to discern that the main function of the *fii nu kang*, at least in recent times, has been to provide a link between the household or community and the higher *kami*, not to serve as a primary object of worship itself. He further declares that the duties of hearth worship were carried out by virgin priestesses and that in every household the eldest daughter was consecrated to this task, going so far as to liken them and their associates to the Vestal Virgins (Iha[13] made the same analogy). This is an attractive speculation, for it shows a parallel to early Chinese practices[14] and bears some measure of authenticity; until recent years the village priestesses and all higher-ranking priestesses were required to remain celibate during their lifetime in office. However, no present evidences, historical records, or traditional myth familiar to me substantiate the contention that in every household the eldest daughter was custodian of the hearth and in charge of household rites, let alone the suggestion that she was consecrated to a lifetime of celibacy in attendance on the hearth. On the contrary, all informants agreed that household rites were the responsibility of the senior female member of the family—the wife of the household head or his mother. Furthermore, Miyagi's chart[15] based on his study of the old records lists the person in charge of household rites as the 'kemuri no amu' (properly, in Okinawan, *kibui nu amu*) or mother of the house (literally, the word *kibui* means "smoke," but it may be used as a classifier in counting houses). Spencer[16] also incorrectly states that she is called 'okode' (properly, *ukudii*), a term which applies to the priestesses of the kin group and not to a household ritual specialist. Lastly, Spencer creates the impression that the hearth cult formed the core of the state religion, but my investigations found no evidence of the existence of the hearth in shrines above the village level. The *fii nu kang* was neither enshrined nor worshiped in the shrines of the four highest-ranking state priestesses, and old gentry and noble families still residing in Shuri regard the *fii nu kang* as solely a household deity. Unfortunately, Spencer's ideas have been uncritically accepted and repeated in recent studies of Okinawan history and culture.[17]

Both the oral and written versions of the creation myth relate that the first men were rulers and the first women priestesses, which agrees with traditional practice in ascribing to the latter control of ceremonial life. Miyagi's analysis[18] of political and religious structure in the Okinawan kingdom shows that prior to the reign of Shō Shin (1477–1526), when the state was centralized and feudalism abolished, males occupying a leadership position—king, minister, feudal lord, warrior, village head, kin group head, and household head—were paired with female religious specialists, and that they were likened in written accounts and legends to the sibling creator deities, *uminai-gami* and *umikii-gami*. It appears, at least in the case of the ruler and chief priestess, that the pairing was more than symbolic and that they were actually siblings; thus, the ruler, according to early accounts, administered the land as the brother *kami*, and his sister conducted ritual in his behalf as the sister *kami*.

Although the exact nature of their relationship in early times is not certain, Nakahara[19] conjectures on the basis of his study of the *Omoro* and surviving practices of recent times that the main function of these women was concerned with control of the mana-like *shiji* (Nakahara, it will be recalled from Chapter II, takes the position that *shiji* was an impersonal supernatural power). The physical and charismatic power of the male leader supposedly was directly dependent on possession of strong *shiji*; and his *shiji*, which could be expended or diminished, required constant renewal and replenishment. As only females had the power to invoke and attach *shiji*, these men were dependent upon a close female relative who could be trusted to confer and sustain their *shiji*; most commonly this task was charged to a sister or perhaps a wife. Nakahara believes that originally the women who controlled *shiji* were shamans, who exerted their powers through a spirit mediumship attained after lengthy periods of seclusion, but that with the establishment of a national religion and the fixing of their office on a hereditary basis it came to be believed that their powers were inherited from the predecessor in office; thus, possessional shamanism gave way to a hierarchy of priestesses. The establishment of a national religion and a political bureaucracy also served to effectively divorce the real kinship bond which theretofore linked the female religious specialist with the male leader, except for the king and his sister.

The political significance of the female religious specialist in Okinawan culture shows an interesting parallel to that in early Japan.[20] Until Haneji's tenure as prime minister (1666–1696), when he reduced the chief priestesses to a rank below that of the queen, the ruler and chief priestess were at least coequal in rank. There are indications, however, from early history, religious songs, and accounts of Chinese and Japanese visitors that the female religious specialist may once have ranked above her male counterpart. Sakima,[21] who investigated a number of these early sources, expresses the belief that the ultimate authority regarding control of the state rested with the chief priestess and that the male ruler merely exercised control in her behalf. He notes[22] that a Chinese visitor to Okinawa in 1606 stated that in ancient Okinawa the chief priestess stood above the king in rank. Apparently, troops were sent to battle in the name of the chief priestess, not that of the king. There is evidence also that matters of justice were often entrusted to these women. A Buddhist monk from Satsuma who stayed on Okinawa for six years sometime during the period 1573–1592 observed[23] that the power to decide and punish crimes was held by priestesses and related that on one occasion they employed a poisonous snake to dispatch a robber whom they had convicted. It was apparently this state of affairs that led a Chinese traveler in 1683 to assume that there were no courts of law, since he observed no male judges. Sakima recalls[24] that, until recent years, in the more isolated areas of Okinawa the *nuru* was asked to determine a man's guilt by lifting the *bijuru* stone; if it felt heavy, he was declared guilty, if light, not guilty. Taichū also stated that the priestesses were the guardians against crime and that they meted out justice

with a vengeance. Some feeling that the *nuru* held a sacro-temporal power
still persists; several aged informants likened her role to that of a policeman and stated that it was the practice of gentry officials to confer with
her whenever there was crime or disorder in the village. Sakima sees the
priestesses of early Okinawa as possessed of an unlimited spirit power
('reiriki,' the same characters which Nakahara employs for *shiji*) and as
greatly feared and venerated by all the people.

The history of Okinawa, particularly from the sixteenth or seventeenth
century, reveals a steady reduction of the powers once held by these women.
Undoubtedly, contact with China, which became regular from the late
fourteenth or early fifteenth century, brought the influence of Confucianism and its stress on the superiority of males, and the penetration of
Japanese Buddhism (dating from the late sixteenth and early seventeenth
centuries), emphasizing the ancestral cult through the male line, contributed
significantly toward establishing a political climate favorable to curbing
the power of the priestesses. Thus, in 1650 Haneji wrote in the *Chuzan
Seikan*[25] that a government based on a religious belief which left its direction to females would be in disorder; when he subsequently became prime
minister, a number of measures were instituted toward curtailing their
powers and disassociating them from active participation in political
affairs.

While our knowledge of the ancient religion is fragmentary, it is
possible to reconstruct some of the broad essentials of the system, parts
of which persisted through historic times and in some instances still
persist. The people regarded themselves as the offspring of two sibling
creator deities and hence of divine descent. Their major sites of worship
appear to have been the sacred groves or *utaki*, believed to be the first
sites of settlement or the earliest sites of worship. Judging from the early
religious songs, all natural phenomena were apparently believed possessed
of supernatural spirit. From early times, ritual life was dominated by
women, whose ability to control the spirits and/or an impersonal supernatural power was regarded as of such magnitude that political power as
well may have resided with them. Thus, male political leaders exercised
control in their behalf and were dependent upon their bidding. There was
a close kinship relation between the female religious specialist and the
male political leader, repeatedly likened to the relationship between the
sibling creator deities.

Establishment of a State Religion

Historic accounts reveal that in the early phase of Okinawan history the country was divided into a number of petty principalities, each headed by a hereditary chief or lord (*aji* or *anji*) whose territory was called *majiri*. Each *aji* was assisted in his administration by a priestess, called *chimi* (the Japanese reading for her title is 'kimi').[26] Again, according to early accounts, their relationship was that of siblings; the *aji* ruled as the *umikii-gami* while the *chimi* sustained him as the *uminai-gami*. Okinawans refer to this early period as *aji nu yuu* (age of the *aji* or manor lord), which they believe followed the *kami nu yuu* (age of the *kami*) or *ama nu yuu* (age of heaven).

A centrally administered state controlling the entire island did not emerge until after 1429. Prior to this time, the *aji* warred among themselves, and their territories changed hands many times. The common misconception of a unified state previous to this time arose largely from the deliberate attempts of annalists to confer respectable antecedents—a lengthy history of royal succession showing hegemony from mythical times—upon the ruling family. Actually, the "royal line" of the old kingdom reveals at least six dynastic changes within the first three hundred years of history, and adding the dynasties of the southern and northern kingdoms makes a total of eight in that period. Much of the purported history of early Okinawa relates solely to the series of *aji* who secured control of the central area of Okinawa around Urasoe and Shuri, which subsequently became the capital of the kingdom. An old Okinawan scholar stated, "Before Shō Hashi (1422–1439), any *aji* who was strong enough to conquer a large territory would claim to be ruler, but actually they did not rule all of Okinawa."

Around the beginning of the fourteenth century, three petty feudal states had emerged as the unions of the various *majiri*; they were called Hokuzan, Chuzan, and Nanzan; these were the names given them by Chinese annalists.[27] The kingdom of Nanzan originated on the southeast coast near the present village of Tamagusuku, but when trade contacts were established with China, the seat of government was moved to the west side behind the present town of Itoman. The Chuzan kingdom arose in the Urasoe district directly north of Shuri but early removed to the latter site, which afforded excellent defensive positions and close proximity to the ports of Naha, Machinato, and Tomari. Far to the north, on the western tip of Motobu Peninsula, the Hokuzan kingdom created its capital. During the fourteenth century these states competed for Chinese recognition and trade, but the issue was ultimately resolved in 1429, when Shō Hashi, an *aji* of Sashiki Majiri (which had belonged to the ruler of Nanzan), completed his conquest of the entire island. After unification, the main castle sites for the three kingdoms—Tamagusuku, Shurigusuku, and Nakijingusuku—were treated as places of national worship, but, significantly, the Chinen-Kudaka area was accorded precedence over them as the most sacred.[28]

At the time of unification, the strict hierarchy of religious offices such as existed in later times does not appear to have been operative; rather, as I have noted, each official, and perhaps every male occupying an important status in society, was paired with a female aide, a religious specialist who manipulated the spirit world in his behalf. According to tradition and early accounts, their relationship was based on a close kin tie, usually that of brother and sister. The king was paired at the head of state with his sister, the *chifijing ganashii mee* (*chifijing* may be cognate to 'kifujin,' noble woman or peeress, while *ganashii mee* are extremely polite honorifics used for *kami* and persons of exalted rank). The regional governors and chief ministers of state—peers of the realm and usually close relatives of the ruler—were paired with their sisters, who were called *chikasa* (one who is in charge; hence, one in charge of ritual matters). In each *majiri*, the *chimi*, who, according to tradition, were sisters of the *aji*, aided them in administration of the fiefs. At the village level it seems that the *niigami* (root *kami*), who was a daughter of the founding house (and hence founding kin group) of the village,[29] presided as the chief priestess, while her brother served as titular head of the kin group and village. Lastly, in every household the male head functioned as its political representative in village affairs, while his wife or mother controlled domestic ritual matters. At all levels, therefore, the relationship was based on a close kin tie, and it would appear that religion in this form at least was not operating in the public interest but for the personal welfare of the individual or kin group.

Unification of the island did not bring genuine security to the Shuri government, for each *aji* continued to maintain a retinue of armed followers and posed a constant threat to internal stability. During the reign of Shō Shin (1477–1526), however, the feudalistic structure of the state

TABLE 1

RELIGIOUS HIERARCHY, OKINAWAN KINGDOM

POLITICAL OR SOCIAL UNIT	TITLE OR POSITION
Nation	*Chifijing ganashii mee* Shrine: Chifijing Udung Family: Shō *Chikasa kumui* Family: Shō
Region	*Ufu su nu mee* Shrine: Shun-dunchi Family: Bing Region: Central Okinawa *Ufu su nu mee* Shrine: Makang-dunchi Family: Hintunaa Region: Southern Okinawa *Ufu su nu mee* Shrine: Jibu-dunchi Family: Taaba Region: Northern Okinawa *Ufu amu** Tomari Mura Sobe Mura Kume Jima Iheya Jima Miyako Jima Ishigaki Jima
Village	*Naru kumui* Name of household: *nundunchi*
Founding kin group of village	*Niigami, niitchu* Name of household: *niiyaa*
Household	*Kibui nu amu*

* One *ufu amu* for each place listed.

was destroyed, and private possession of arms was forbidden as was the practice of self-immolation after the death of one's lord. The *aji*, their families, and retainers were requested to establish permanent residence in the capital; only a handful of them in the northern area powerful enough to resist managed to remain in their fiefs (until 1723). This movement of the *aji* and their retainers to Shuri was not without plan, for they were carefully settled in predetermined locations within the three wards (Mihira) of Shuri. The northerners from Hokuzan kingdom were moved into Nishi-hira; those from the central kingdom, Chuzan, were located in Fee-hira, while the southerners from Nanzan were settled in Maaji-hira. Miyagi has shown[30] that these wards were not arbitrarily created but probably represented ancient divisions of Shuri, most likely the coalescence of three separate villages into a single settlement.

While the new state was gradually modeled on that of China, in substance its character was uniquely Okinawan. The Chinese system of nine ranks and eighteen grades was adopted for the purpose of fixing the hereditary social rank of nobility and gentry. While the structure of an egalitarian civil bureaucracy was established and public office was theoretically determined by achievement in an examination system, in practice only the upper classes were permitted to compete, and the very highest administrative posts were reserved exclusively for the upper nobility who were close relatives of the ruling family.[31] Rigid standards of class distinction were created for dress, housing, occupation, justice, mobility, etc., thereby conferring a castelike form upon society, and with the passage of time these standards became increasingly restrictive.

At this time a complete reorientation of the religious system was begun by the government, and a national hierarchy of priestesses was established with the *chifijing* at its head (Table 1). Although the *chifijing* continued for a time to be recognized as the king's equal, she was removed from the castle and relocated in a new shrine on the opposite side of Shuri. Thereafter, the king alone ruled from Shuri Castle—not the pair as before. The younger brothers of the ruler were permitted to retain a personal priestess, *chikasa*, who prayed in their behalf; but if later practices are any indication, this prerogative was not passed on to their sons, being restricted solely to the brothers of the ruler.

Religious control over the three regions coinciding with the former kingdoms was bestowed on three priestesses, probably of commoner origin, who heretofore may have been priestesses for the three communities which came to make up the three wards of Shuri. The priestess who received the office controlling northern Okinawa served at Jibu-dunchi[32] in the Jibu area of Nishi-hira, where the northerners had been settled; the priestess controlling the central region officiated at Shun-dunchi (Shuri Tunchi) in the Akata section of Fee-hira, where the people from the former Chuzan kingdom were now located; and the priestess in charge of southern Okinawa (Nanzan) lived at Makang-dunchi in Yamagawa of Maaji-hira. Apparently, these women were deemed suitable for elevation to this high position by virtue of the fact that they were not aligned with any powerful family and would therefore owe their allegiance solely to Shuri Castle. They were not, as Spencer[33] suggests, priestesses of important families in the realm; Miyagi[34] points out that their class status could not have been high, as their *tunchi* rank was equivalent to that of a village priestess. These women were called *ufu su nu mee* (*ufu* = great; *su* = head or ruler; *nu* = of; *mee* = before or in front); many written accounts give their title as 'o amu shirare,' which was unfamiliar to my informants and which appears to be a mixture of Japanese and Okinawan. The *ufu su nu mee* officiated as the chief priestesses for the regions under their control and maintained contact with the priestesses of the villages; in the national hierarchy, they stood midway between the chief priestess of the nation and those of the villages.

The *chimi*, who, it will be recalled, conducted ritual for the *aji* or feudal lord of the *majiri*, were assigned no role in the new religious system, and efforts were made to abolish their office. The feudal lords were consequently deprived not only of fiefs and retainers but of any religious backing as well. It is thought[35] that there were approximately thirty-three *chimi*, equal to the number of *majiri*, at the time of centralization, and when the *Chūzan Seifu* was compiled late in the seventeenth century only five or six were said to remain. Most likely, that figure represents the number of *aji* in the north who had withstood the government's efforts to resettle them in Shuri.

In 1532, the office of *nuru kumui* was established as a part of the national religious hierarchy; the *nuru* conducted ritual at the village level and ranked directly below the *ufu su nu mee* of the region.[36] It is not clear when the *nuru* originated, but Okinawan scholars generally acknowledge that the office represents a relatively recent development in Okinawan culture.

While Iha[37] regards the office as a political creation of the early sixteenth century, he cites evidence to show that *nuru* appointments were being made nearly a century before centralization and creation of the state religion. Apparently, these women were usually appointed from families politically favorable to the ruler. Instances are also cited of women receiving this appointment as a reward for their virtue; on the other hand, on at least one occasion the office was bestowed on an ex-mistress of the ruler. Origuchi[38] declares that the *nuru* are not basic to Okinawan religion and that their office was created for political purposes. I found that the *nuru* does not come from the founding kin group of the village, which indicates that the *nuru* and her kin group were at one time intrusive elements; moreover, the fact that the *nuru*'s house is usually the founding house for her kin group suggests that its existence in the village may have resulted from her appointment. Traditionally, and so far as I know without exception, it is the *niigami* who represents the oldest and founding kin group of the village. It seems not unlikely that the purpose of the *nuru*'s appointment was to curb the religious power of the dominant kin group in the village. The political power of this kin group was similarly curbed by Shuri's assignment of a gentry official to administer the village; this office, unlike that of the *nuru*, was not hereditary. Thus, the dominant political and religious figures in the villages henceforth owed their appointment and allegiance to Shuri and, at least in the beginning, were without any blood tie in the community. On attaining office, each successive *nuru* received a letter of investiture from the government and journeyed to Shuri to pray with the *ufu su nu mee* of her region; thereby her tie with Shuri was maintained.

I have sought to stress that prior to centralization and the dissolution of feudalism there existed a close kinship relation between male leader and priestess, but after this time the two were completely dissociated save at the very top level, in the royal family, and at the other extreme, in the ordinary household. The highly individual-oriented, domestic cult of early times was now replaced by a state cult focusing on the broader interests of the whole society. The hereditary religious and political powers of feudal lord and kin group head were effectively negated or abolished. This system, created in the late fifteenth and early sixteenth centuries, continued to function with few changes until the breakup of the kingdom in 1879.

The State Priestesses

CHIFIJING GANASHII MEE. The chief priestess for Okinawa and all island dependencies of the small kingdom was called the *chifijing ganashii mee* and was selected from among the daughters of the reigning Shō family; customarily, she was an elder sister or the eldest daughter of the ruler. According to legend and historical accounts, in early times she was not permitted to marry, but from the seventeenth century widows or divorced women were allowed to accept the office, although they were required to observe continence in office. As in the case of all *kaminchu*, the office was held for life and retirement was unheard of.

Until the reign of Shō Shin (1477–1526) the *chifijing*'s shrine, Sunuhiyan Utaki, was located within the gates of Shuri Castle, and there are evidences that she played an active role in the affairs of state. It is said that on one occasion she forced the abdication of a ruler after receiving a divine oracle.[39] Shō Shin or his ministers, however, had the *chifijing* removed to a new shrine, Chifijing Udung, on the opposite side of Shuri (near the present site of the Shuri Junior High School), where it remained until the early twentieth century. Within this shrine, three *kami* were worshiped: Kunkung Ganashii Mee, Ufu Jimi Nu Mee, and Bideeting. Kunkung was believed to be the *kami* spirit of the first *chifijing* and therefore the same *kami* as the *chifijing*. Ufu Jimi Nu Mee was said to be the *kami* spirit who controlled all weather phenomena relating to the growth of plant life; informants expressed the belief that this *kami* had once been a living person, perhaps the first ruler or one of the early *chifijing*. Bideeting was worshiped as the *kami* who produced future generations; this represents a borrowing from the Buddhist and Hindu pantheons (Sarasvati in Sanskrit). In Japan this *kami*, Benten or Benzaiten, is one of the seven *kami* of good fortune, but these do not form a part of Okinawan belief. Formerly, there was a Buddhist temple to Bideeting in Shuri, but there seems to have been no direct connection between this temple and Chifijing Udung; significantly, Bideeting is not worshiped in the rural areas.

Although ritual offerings and prayers were made on the first and fifteenth of each month to the *fii nu kang* in the kitchen of Chifijing Udung, this *fii nu kang* was regarded as a household *kami* not in the same category as the above three. I was reliably informed that there were no public shrines for the *fii nu kang* in Shuri.

It was the *chifijing*'s function to officiate at national rites and to pray regularly for the health of the ruler and the prosperity of the country. Apparently, her ritual powers were conserved exclusively for the major ceremonies of state and were not expended on day-to-day ritual; this task was delegated to her chief assistant, *ufu-gui* (great solicitor), whose duties entailed saying daily prayers to the three *kami* and assisting the *chifijing* on major ritual occasions. This woman, who was of commoner origin, came from the island of Kudaka, which in Okinawan mythology is recognized as a *kami* island and the site of first settlement. Another assistant of the *chifijing* was the *wachi jichi*, who was charged with the care of ceremonial paraphernalia. Unlike the *chifijing* and *ufu gui*, who dressed in the sacred white ceremonial robes, this woman wore ordinary clothing, but she was selected for her virtue from among the older unmarried or widowed gentry women of Shuri. A third assistant was the *utchi nu hanshi*; it was her duty to direct the management of the household and particularly the cleaning of the shrine. Like the *wachi jichi* and all other women who worked there, she was selected for her character and was usually of gentry rank. The last assistant to the *chifijing* was called *hanshi nu taari* and was concerned with the preparation of ceremonial offerings of food and drink. Like the *ufu gui*, she was of commoner origin and came from Kudaka Island. In addition to these women, there were a number of female servants who served at the shrine. All appointments to this shrine were for life, but usually older women beyond their menses were preferred for these positions. It is said that each woman was carefully selected for her character and virtue and that appointment to this shrine was considered a high honor. No males were permitted to reside in the shrine area or to serve the *chifijing*; the great room, *ufu yaa*, where the *kami* were enshrined, was said to be taboo to all males.

Many stories are still related of the restrictive life which these women led. All were required to observe continence, and, because of the need to avoid contamination, they were largely cut off from regular outside contacts. It is said that they arose at dawn each morning to perform *amichujiing* (purification by cold-water bath) and that much of their time was devoted to grooming themselves and their garments to maintain their purity. They were not permitted to eat meat of any kind (Okinawans are a pork-eating people), which was regarded as highly polluting. During menstruation or sickness they would not enter the *ufu yaa* for fear of offending the *kami*. Except for the funeral of a ruler or *chifijing*, they did not attend funerals or visit houses of birth or sickness or any place which might expose them to contamination. It is even said that they were not permitted to die in this shrine but were removed to another place whenever death was considered imminent. The severest restrictions applied to the *chifijing*, who spent much of her life in seclusion, conserving her powers and avoiding pollution.

Although Chifijing Udung was maintained by the government as state property, the *chifijing* received an annual rice tribute from the Chinen area, where Seefa Utaki is located; this stipend amounted to 200 'koku,' or slightly less than 1,000 bushels.

CHIKASA KUMUI. Second in rank to the *chifijing* but without shrines or financial support from the state were the *chikasa kumui*. These women served as priestesses to the younger brothers of the ruler. They were usually the eldest daughters or sisters of the men they served. They prayed regularly within the male's household for his welfare and that of the ruler. Apparently, the *chikasa* were confined solely to those houses headed by a younger brother of the ruler, hence the ascension of each new king saw the creation of a new set of *chikasa*. As a limited form of concubinage was practiced, each monarch usually had several brothers. Only on the occasion of the most important of national rites, such as the pilgrimage to Seefa Utaki, did they participate in public rites; at these times they served as chief assistants to the *chifijing* and occupied positions above the *ufu su nu mee*. Ordinarily, however, they functioned as household priestesses. Unlike the *ufu su nu mee*, they exercised no control over other *kaminchu*; in fact, it is said that they did not wear the white robes symbolic of the true *kaminchu*'s office. While their exact purpose defies certain comprehension, one old informant reasoned that if a ruler had died childless a younger brother would in all likelihood have succeeded him; hence, there was a need to have someone in the household to pray for the potential successor's health and good fortune.

UFU SU NU MEE. We have seen that in the three wards (*mihira*) of Shuri there were the three *tunchi* (*mitunchi*) presided over by the *ufu su nu mee*, who ruled, for religious affairs, the three regions of Okinawa. In the national hierarchy they ranked directly below the *chifijing*, although in state ceremonies they yielded second place to the *chikasa*. Their office was a hereditary one, held by virtue of birth as first daughter of a specific household; thus, the priestess for Shun-dunchi came from the Bing family, the Makang-dunchi priestess from the Hintunaa household, and the Jibu-dunchi priestess from the Taaba family. For their support, the government assigned them certain large land tracts on the outskirts of Shuri; these bore their title (e.g., Jibu-dunchi-ji), were held in perpetuity, and were worked by commoners. They also were said to receive large quantities of grain and produce, brought to them for first-fruits rites by the village *nuru* of their region.

Until the annexation of 1879, it was their first duty to pray for the health of the ruler and the prosperity of their region. On the occasion of national rites they joined with the *chifijing* and *chikasa*, but otherwise they enjoyed little regular contact with them. Like the *chifijing*, much of their life was spent secluded within the confines of their shrine, attended by only a few servant women; it was equally incumbent upon them to avoid all sources of pollution and constantly maintain their ritual purity. Unlike the *chifijing*, however, they were considered unsuitable for office if widowed or divorced, and they were required to observe a lifetime of chastity. One of their major functions was to install each new *nuru* of their region. The *nuru* was first required to journey to Shuri and pray with the *ufu su nu mee*; she then received a letter of appointment from the government, confirming her status. For national rites, the *ufu su nu mee* sent announcements to the *nuru* of their region through regular government channels.

TUCHI NU UFU YAKUU. Until sometime in the eighteenth century there existed an official state diviner; Iha[40] describes him as a magician who selected propitious dates for state ceremonies. Little information concerning this office may be found, but it appears that at one time this man exerted great power. Iha relates that there is a record of one's having been executed, but his power was so greatly feared that the king ordered the body interred in the royal tomb in hopes of placating the spirit. Among Confucian-oriented government officials there appears to have been considerable resentment against his powers, for Haneji is said to have declared that the office represented a superstition and deserved to be abolished. But Iha notes that an account dating from 1707—a decade after Haneji's demise—indicated the position was still extant.

JUUNINSUU. Until the termination of the monarchy, a National Council of Ten (Juuninsuu) directed and determined policy in religious matters; this body was headed by the *chifijing* and high-ranking government officials. According to an old male informant of upper-class origin, the council was equivalent to the Umuti Juugunin, or Supreme Council of Fifteen, which guided the political affairs of state and was headed by the king and his prime minister.

UFU AMU AND NURU KUMUI. Ranking below the *ufu su nu mee* were the *nuru* of the villages. The role functions of these women will be considered in the next chapter. In a number of areas, however, there were priestesses who were somewhat above the *nuru* in rank and who exercised control over an area of considerably greater importance than a single village or cluster of villages. These women were often titled *ufu amu* (lit., "great mother"), and all available evidence indicates that these offices originated as political appointments.

On the main island of Okinawa there were two *ufu amu*: Tomari *ufu amu* and Sobe *ufu amu*. Tomari, now a part of Naha, was the principal port for Shuri and hence of considerable importance for a trading nation. Sobe was a small settlement east of Naha (and is now a part of that city), and the Sobe *ufu amu* presided over the annual tug-of-war in Naha. So far as I could determine, both offices have been vacant for many years. On the offshore islands of the Okinawa area, there were two principal *ufu amu* offices, the *chimbee* of Kume Island and the *anganashii* of Iheya Island.[41] The present *chimbee* of Kume Jima (*Kumi nu chimbee*) believes that she represents the twentieth generation in this office, which commenced with the eldest daughter of the Chinaha *anji* who was sent to govern Kume. The office of *anganashii* on Iheya Jima is now vacant, but it is said that the first *anganashii* was the elder sister of Shō En (1470–1476), who founded the last dynasty.

On the islands south of Okinawa, the *nuru* office was never established at the village level; however, after the conquests of Miyako and Yaeyama, the Shuri government established *ufu amu* in each area. In the city of Ishigaki, capital for the Yaeyama area, there is still an *ufu amu* who presides as chief priestess over the nine islands. This office was conferred on her family in the early years of the sixteenth century for support rendered to Shuri in the conquest of 1501. Similarly, in Hirara, the principal city of Miyako, there was formerly an *ufu amu* (*upamp*) who had also been appointed from a local family favorable to Shuri.

1. Looking south along main highway through Naha.
   (Photo courtesy USCAR.)

2. Main street in Itoman.

3. Coastline of Kunigami-son, northwest Okinawa.

4. Paddies in Kanegusuku, southern Okinawa.

5. Washing clothes at communal well in Itoman.

6. Transplanting rice. (Photo courtesy F. R. Pitts.)

7. Old-style farmhouse.

8. Townspeople ascending hill to *nundunchi* at Nago on ceremony day.

9. Approach to Seefa Utaki.

10. Seefa Utaki, principal shrine of the Okinawan nation.

11. *Kami ashagi* in Sakiyama.

12. Censer in *utaki* (sacred grove) at Katsuu.

13. *Nundunchi* (shrine-residence of the *nuru*, chief village priestess) at Hedo.

14. Three-stone hearth representing the hearth deity (*fii nu kang*).

15. *Kami ashibii* (period of *kami* play or festivities) at *nundunchi* in Itoman.

16. The Itoman *nuru* (chief priestess).

17. *Niigami* (root *kami*, second-ranking village priestess) and *nuru* (chief priestess) of Itoman, with *munchu kaminchu* in foreground.

18. *Niigami* and *nuru* of Itoman.

19. Ozato *nuru* at *kami ashibii.*

20. Boat racers at *nun-dunchi* after *harii* (Itoman).

21. Village officials participating in well-purification rite.

22. Shaman conducting rite to purify well.

23. Taboo rope (*hijainna*).

24. *Ishigantuu* (stone with Chinese
    characters to ward off malevolent spirits).

25. *Sang* (grass taboo marker).

26. After *muni agi* (ridgepole-raising
   rite); arrows are to fend off
   malevolent spirits.

27. Burial urns (*jiishigaami*) of former upper class, on exhibit at Shuri Museum.

28. Commoner-class burial urns.

29. Commoner-class patri-sib (*munchu*) tomb.

30. Funerary paraphernalia at tomb door.

31. *Bijuru* (divining stone) at Shuri Museum.

32. Mask for lion dance.

The *nuru* office was established in the Amami group of islands north of Okinawa during the period of Shuri control, and in scattered villages *nuru* may still be found there. I do not know whether an *ufu amu* office was created there or not; if so, I would presume that it might have been in the present city of Nase, Amami Oshima. Since the Shimadzu are reported to have attempted to suppress the *nuru*, forcing them to function *sub rosa*, it seems likely that an *ufu amu* would not have existed long under their administration.

National Rites

For a small island nation without any great natural wealth or resources, agriculture constituted the basis of national livelihood, and, not surprisingly, the major ritual events related directly to the agricultural cycle. The majority of state rites were identical in substance with those to be described for the village in the following chapter and will not be treated here. However, ritual offerings of the first fruits to the *ufu su nu mee* constituted an important phase of the ceremonial cycle. Each *nuru* was charged with the responsibility of bringing the first fruits (*mujukui nu hachi*) of the rice, wheat, millet, and potato harvests to her regional *ufu su nu mee*; some of these products were in turn offered to the *chifijing* and the ruler. In addition to the basic food crops, certain special crops of the various districts were brought in as well; thus, from Kanegusuku, famous for rush mats and linen cloth, the first harvested sedge and hemp were taken to Shuri. From the village of Kudaken in Chinen-son, the *nuru* annually brought in the first vegetables of the year harvested from a field near Seefa Utaki, and these, it is said, were served to the ruler. Rice harvested from the paddy in Tamagusuku, which was believed to be the first on Okinawa, was also taken to the ruler. Symbolically, the ruler and high priestesses were the first to partake of the new crops, and I was told that by this practice the government was able to judge the condition of every harvest.

In early times, *agari mai* or *agai maai* (touring the east) were the major national rites observed by the kingdom; these ceremonies occurred in the second and eighth lunar months. The first *agari mai* was timed to coincide with the offering of the first wheat on Kudaka Island. At this time, the grain was not yet ripe for harvest, which takes place in the following (third) lunar month; but supplicatory ceremonies, as I have stressed, take precedence over thanking rites, and on this occasion a few unripe sheafs of wheat were cut and offered to the *kami* with prayers for a good harvest. During this *agari mai*, the king, court, *chifijing*, *chikasa*, *ufu su nu mee*, and all the *nuru* of the land journeyed from Shuri to the Chinen and Tamagusuku areas on the southeast coast. There they performed rites at the sacred sites relating in mythical tradition to the creation and first people. Then the entire party crossed to Kudaka to participate in the offering of the wheat. In the eighth lunar month, *agari mai* was held again, with Seefa Utaki as the focal point; this time, rites were performed for the first ancestors who had settled on that site. Traditions still exist in Okinawa and scattered areas of the Ryukyus that the eighth lunar month constituted the New Year in early times.[42] Arakaki tells (in personal conversation) of traditions that the *chifijing* did *agari mai* in the fifth lunar month, traveling to Tamagusuku, where the first rice paddy was located, to participate in offering the first rice ears to the *kami* and asking for a good rice harvest. Haneji is said to have opposed *agari mai* as a drain on the national treasury, and from 1673 the king and court ceased to participate; instead, a representative of the ruler was sent with the priestesses. The *chifijing* and other priestesses in the national hierarchy seem to have carried on as before, except that the visit to Kudaka was curtailed and *utuushi* (worship from afar) was performed from Seefa Utaki while facing toward Kudaka. While reasons of economy were said to have dictated the abandonment of this ceremony by male officials, it is to be noted that Haneji was prime minister at this time and that he viewed the indigenous system as based on superstition. Moreover, the fact that Seefa Utaki was taboo to all males required that the king, prime minister, and all officials wear female attire while on pilgrimage there; undoubtedly, this practice became an increasingly sore point as Confucian ideology gained ascendency among the leaders of government.

When a ruler died, all the *nuru* of the land were summoned to Shuri. There, according to one old *nuru* whose predecessor had attended the state funeral of Shō Iku in 1847, the *nuru*, *ufu su nu mee*, and *chifijing* gathered in a great circle around the bier and sang *umui*. Thereafter, all of them went into seclusion (*yugumui*) for one week. Later, the *chifijing* and widowed queen journeyed to Seefa Utaki to inform the ancestral *kami* of the king's death, and they remained there overnight in the sacred grove.

Installation rites for a new *chifijing* were conducted at Seefa Utaki with the *ufu su nu mee* and all *nuru* in attendance. The Kudaka *nuru* officiated at these rites, and it was she who placed the sacred jewels, *mitama* ('maga-tama'), about the *chifijing*'s neck. This ceremony was referred to as *unaraurii* (*un* = *utaki*, *ara* = new, *urii* = descent; hence, the descent of the *kami*), and it was believed that the new *chifijing* received her predecessor's *kami* spirit at this time.

It was stated in Chapter I that although normally there is an abundance of rainfall, the porous nature of the soil renders farmland susceptible to drought if several rainless weeks should pass. Legend relates that during the reign of Gihon, one of the early "kings" (*ca.* thirteenth century), a drought of great magnitude persisted until the entire island was reduced to the point of starvation. Feeling his relationship with the *kami* to be at fault, the ruler ordered a pyre built for himself and climbed atop it; as the fire was ignited, so the legend goes, a heavy rain began to fall and extinguished the blaze. The hill where his pyre was built, Amatchiji in Tama-gusuku, remained the site for national rain-making rites (*ama-gui*) until the end of the nineteenth century. Whenever a drought became a matter of national concern, the *chifijing*, *ufu su nu mee*, and *nuru* met at Amatchiji to perform this rite. In the rural areas, it still remains a part of the *nuru*'s function to conduct *ama-gui* when a lengthy period of drought threatens the livelihood of her village.

In addition to the rites described above and those reserved for the next chapter relating to the agricultural cycle, prayers were conducted by the *chifijing* and *ufu su nu mee* at the time of the vernal and autumnal equinoxes and again at the summer and winter solstices. In the rural areas, these rites are not observed by the *nuru* as a part of communal ritual, but in recent times, perhaps concurrent with the spread of the calendar into the rural areas, they have been incorporated into domestic ritual.

Chinese and Japanese Influences

It was noted above that, from the sixteenth and seventeenth centuries, history reveals a persistent effort by the government to reduce the powers of the priestesses. As the tiny island state emerged on the East Asian scene, regular contact with the great neighboring states brought an influx of new concepts and beliefs which radically altered the attitude of officialdom toward the indigenous religious system. For five hundred years Okinawa served as a tributary to the Chinese state and maintained regular trade contacts through an Okinawan settlement and factory in Fukien Province. The great intellectual stimulus which Okinawa received from China came from Confucianism, which first influenced the transformation from feudalism into civil bureaucracy, creating a state structure that persisted until 1879. Satsuma's covert political domination from 1609 served to facilitate Japanese missionary activities and the adoption of the Buddhist ancestral cult in the island.

Some perspective as to the timing and character of the changes that took place can be gained from briefly examining the major recorded events of the seventeenth and eighteenth centuries pertaining to religious life. Although Buddhist missionaries from China, Korea, and Japan visited Okinawa prior to the seventeenth century and succeeded in establishing a few temples in the Naha-Shuri area, it was not until that century that Buddhism was able to secure any real foothold. Taichū, as previously noted, introduced the 'nembutsu' ritual of Jōdō Shinshu, whose followers, the *nimbuchaa*, came to play an important role in funeral rites. According to Buddhist priests, it was in the same century that ancestral tablets were adopted, and during the latter part of that century the upper classes began to construct genealogies, causing the government in 1689 to establish an office for examining these and attesting to their accuracy. All upper-class genealogies count their first generation from that time, as all preceding generations were designated *kami* (*futuki*). In 1768 the king set a precedent which the entire nation was eventually to follow by performing *shiimii* (Japanese, 'sei mei'; Chinese, 'ching ming') rites at the ancestral tomb. It appears that by the end of the eighteenth century Buddhism had attained its present form on Okinawa.

We have seen that during Haneji's tenure as prime minister (1666-1696) a number of alterations were made in the state hierarchy, and active participation by male officialdom in national rites was brought to an end. In 1667 the *chifijing*, who hitherto had been ranked equal to the king, was demoted to third place after the queen. Then in 1677, history records, the office of *chifijing* was actually conferred on the queen.[48] Participation by the king and court in *agari mai* was curtailed in 1673 for reasons of governmental economy. In his writings, Haneji was critical of the priestesses and their powers and attacked the state diviner; undoubtedly, Haneji, the outstanding scholar-statesman of Okinawan history, had been deeply influenced by Confucian thought.

During the eighteenth century the government attempted to counteract the influence of the *yuta*. In 1728 they were forbidden to operate in the urban areas. Then in 1736 the practice of shamanism was outlawed. Although shamanism was repeatedly condemned by the government and similar measures were later enacted by the Japanese, it continues to flourish to this day. Sometime during the eighteenth century the office of the *tuchi nu ufu yakuu*, or state diviner, was abolished as a superstition.

In 1724 the government granted permission for unemployed gentry to migrate from the Shuri area and take up farming in the country, for a marked population growth among the upper classes had occurred, creating a shortage of jobs and opportunities for them in the capital. Thereafter, many of the so-called *yaadui*, or scattered villages composed of upper-class settlers, were founded in the rural areas; it is said that a new village appeared at the rate of one every four years during the remainder of that century.[44] Significantly, no *nuru* were appointed to these villages, indicating that the matter was no longer of concern to the government or of necessity to the upper classes. Consequently, to this day *yaadui* villages are devoid of any organized community religion or priestesses.

Although the main attack on the indigenous religion was delivered by the government, certainly its actions can be attributed to influences originating abroad, particularly, I believe, to Confucianism and Japanese Buddhism, both of which stress male superiority and consider a woman only in relation to her husband, father, or son. Such a concept was decidedly alien to Okinawan tradition and values. I have noted in examining upper-class genealogies, for example, that daughters and wives were formerly listed as well as sons, but in recent generations this practice has become less common. In spite of these changes, the indigenous religion has shown amazing resiliency. Although Buddhism has established itself on Okinawa during the last three hundred years, its principal function remains confined to an area which was but slightly claimed by the native system. As Origuchi[45] states, ancestral worship is not a basic concept in Okinawan religion, and Buddhism as it exists on Okinawa is basically a cult of the dead. Aside from this, Okinawan Buddhism has little to show—only a handful of sectarian followers and a few temples. Apparently, Buddhism did provide a more satisfactory system for handling the troublesome spirits of the dead than had existed previously; the indigenous religion, as we have seen, is largely concerned with propitiating the productive forces of nature and with avoiding punishment or withdrawal of support. The fear of ghosts and the misfortune they are capable of inflicting appears to be a deeply embedded trait, and surely a religion which offered ancestral tablets and ancestral rites and taught that the spirits of the dead, if properly worshiped, would become agents for good, afforded some measure of relief from that fear. The result has been that these aspects of Buddhism have been so woven into the skein of Okinawan belief that their alien origin is barely recognized.

Japanese Prefecture (1879-1945)

Japanese annexation effected the immediate dissolution of the government and the gradual disintegration of the state religion. The first result of the new order was the forcible removal of the king, Shō Tai, and a sizable retinue of court officials to permanent exile in Japan. The *chifijing*—daughter of the previous king, Shō Iku—remained in Shuri to care for her shrine and to maintain ritual obligations as before, but she died in 1909 at eighty-four years of age, and the office was left vacant for some years. Then a widowed daughter of Shō Tai accepted the office, for, as one old informant said, "this was regarded as too important an office to be left vacant." The office, however, faced new problems. When all upper-class stipends were abolished by the new government, the *chifijing* lost her main source of income. Then it is said that economic necessity (political pressure?) forced the Shō family to sell her shrine, Chifijing Udung, to the Japanese government for use as a student's dormitory; consequently, the last *chifijing* was without income or shrine.

The offices of *ufu su nu mee* similarly suffered from the changes introduced by Japanese control; most devastating was the loss of all income with which to sustain themselves and their shrines. Two of their families were forced to leave Shuri along with the general exodus of impoverished gentry and to seek their livelihood elsewhere. In the final decade of the nineteenth century, the last *ufu su nu mee* died, and no hereditary successors were available for the office. For a time the three *tunchi* remained vacant; then they were consolidated into a single shrine, and a widow from a gentry family assumed the duty of praying there. Regular contact between the *nuru* of the villages and the *ufu su nu mee* had ceased, and the loss of the *ufu su nu mee* removed the only link between the *nuru* and *chifijing*, leaving both in isolation.

For a time, the community *nuru* continued to carry on much as before, but gradually their high status deteriorated. The first blow came with the land reforms of 1899–1903, which transformed the system of communal land tenure into a system of private ownership. The large landholdings of the *nuru* heretofore held in perpetuity by her were now transferred to the male household head. In many cases these holdings were dissipated by grants of land to younger sons on the occasion of their establishing separate households; or frequently the *nuru* married into another house and was unable to take her land. Somewhat later, universal grammar school education became available in the rural areas, serving to further undermine the *nuru*'s position by depreciating Okinawan culture, glorifying things Japanese, and insisting on acceptance of state Shinto. The male *kaminchu* became increasingly restive and reluctant to maintain their role as ceremonial servants.

The lack of any central coordination for nationally observed rites served to produce numerous local variations in both their timing and nature. The *nuru* were no longer brought together for national rites. Their sense of unity was soon lost, and they were left to the rather limited contacts and insular thinking of their native villages. By the time of World War II, the *ufu su nu mee* were long dead and their offices vacant. In 1944, one year before the American invasion, the last *chifijing* died, leaving the *nuru* as the last vestige of the state religion.

VI

COMMUNITY RELIGION

Introduction

One of the basic institutions of Okinawan social life is the village-community. Although almost a third of the population now resides within the urban cities and semi-urban towns, the bulk of the population may be found in the 570 rural villages. In the typical village, "the number of houses is rarely fewer than fifty or sixty, usually from seventy or eighty to two hundred,"[1] and there are approximately five members per household. The average village, therefore, is a primary community wherein all members share a face-to-face relationship. A typical village displays a tightly nucleated settlement pattern, and this close physical unity goes hand in hand with a deep consciousness of social unity. The old Okinawan refers to his village as *shima*, which literally means "island," and in a figurative sense the typical village does constitute an island, with its closely grouped houses perched on high ground, often buried in deep foliage, and surrounded by open fields. In the recent past, this physical isolation was buttressed by a strict rule of endogamy and by governmental prohibitions on changing one's place of residence or occupation. The spirit of internal unity was enhanced by a system of communal land tenure and by an emphasis on reciprocal labor exchange, and apparently from ancient times the village was "basically a cooperative body."[2]

It was noted in Chapter I that two or three variant settlement patterns exist, particularly the *yaadui*, the small scattered settlement created in most cases by upper-class settlers since 1724. As the *yaadui* never developed an organized community religion, our attention will focus on the old nucleated farm villages and the seaside farming-fishing villages. It should be emphasized, however, that despite rapid commercial and population growth in recent decades, the towns still preserve some features of an organized religious life. For that matter, some of the cities have but recently lost this. Shuri, as indicated in the last chapter, formerly possessed a threefold division for religious purposes. Similarly, Naha now represents the union of many villages into a single city; some of these villages formerly had priestesses and communal rites. We may safely conclude, therefore, that until recent years virtually every community of reasonable antiquity was organized for ritual purposes and possessed a hierarchy of hereditary *kaminchu*.[3]

Traditionally, the village has derived its sustenance from subsistence agriculture; a number of coastal villages and small island communities have combined fishing with farming, but for the overwheming majority farming has been the basis of their livelihood. As noted above, sweet potatoes, rice, wheat, millet, pineapple, sugar cane, and vegetables are the major agricultural products, with potatoes, rice, and vegetables forming the bulk of the diet. Prior to World War II, virtually every household owned a horse or cow for heavy farm work. Pig raising appears to have been practiced since prehistoric times, and in the kingdom each farm household was required to keep several pigs. The consumption of pork, however, has been largely limited to ceremonial occasions and celebrations. Until 1899–1903, when the Japanese introduced their form of private property, a system of communal land tenure facilitated by periodic redistributions obtained for most of Okinawa and its island dependencies; extreme fragmentation and scattered holdings remain today as the heritage of that system. Formerly, cloth was woven in every home for tax payment and home consumption, but during the past fifty years there has occurred a marked decline in home-produced products, which have been displaced by those of modern industry.

Today the village is linked to the outside world to a greater extent than ever before; moreover, its integration into the greater national society is proceeding at an accelerating rate. The folk-community of the past is undergoing a transformation which in the not distant future will have the people of the villages differing from the urbanites only on the basis of residence and occupation. In this chapter we shall be concerned with Okinawan religion as it functions at the community level. Some of the institutions and practices which will be described are no longer operative, but these were formerly an integral part of community life and hence must be examined for their relevance to the subject.

Social Organization

HOUSEHOLD. The basic social unit within the village is the family-household (*yaa*), for the community is conceived of as an association of households bound together in a relationship of equality. The concept of political participation by households is basic to the thinking of the villagers; thus, while universal manhood suffrage now obtains for all municipal and national elections, within the community active political participation is limited to male household heads functioning as the representatives of their households. In effect, each family has but one vote and one voice in village politics. Similarly, in ceremonial life when it is said that "everyone" participates, it is usually meant that one woman from each household attends as the representative of her family.

The household contains as its core the nuclear family of husband, wife, and their offspring. For the firstborn son, patrilocal residence obtains, but younger sons establish neolocal residence after marriage. The position of household head always passes to the first son, and at the present time he inherits the bulk of the family property, although most fathers try to provide younger sons with a small amount of land. Formerly, when the system of communal land tenure was in effect, the first son's inheritance was limited to the family house and lot. A first son bears the responsibility of caring for the ancestral tablets and supporting his parents in their declining years.

A household constitutes an economic unit, with each member working for the livelihood of the group. The average farm family owns less than an acre of arable land, which is usually subdivided into nearly a dozen widely scattered plots. Division of labor on the basis of sex is rather flexible; thus, while in general the duties of the wife center on household chores and child rearing and those of the husband are concerned with farming and/or fishing, these divisions are not held fast. A wife may do nearly as much farm work as a man, although the heavier tasks are usually assumed by the male. Similarly, weaving cloth or mats is considered a woman's task, but men, particularly the old men, may engage in these activities, much depending on the size of the family and the urgency of the situation. At harvest or transplanting time, every member of the family is occupied from dawn to dusk in these activities; but at other times when the weather is bad or agricultural duties less urgent, men as well as women may engage in weaving, ropemaking, child tending, etc. In fishing villages, virtually all farm work is done by the women, and in some villages where the men are away at sea much of the time, most political offices below the rank of headman are held by women. Household ceremonial life, however, is regularly dominated by the eldest female member of the family.

Family names are relatively new for commoners and were first adopted after the Japanese annexation of the Okinawan kingdom, but all households in the village, today as in the past, possess a household name, *yaa nu naa* or *yaa n naa* ('yago'). It will be shown in the following chapter that the *yaa n naa* tends to define a household's descent status within its lineage, but a few *yaa n naa* indicate a hereditary status of a given household within the community. Foremost among the latter is *nundunchi*, denoting the shrine-residence of the *nuru*, chief priestess of the village. Another prominent household name in virtually every village save the *yaadui* settlements is *niiyaa* (root house) or *niigang-yaa* (*niigami* house); this name always indicates the founding house of the village. *Niiyaa* is the birthplace of the *niigami* (root *kami* or priestess) and *niitchu* (root man), who are also referred to as *uminai-gami* and *umikii-gami*. In ceremonial affairs, the *niigami* ranks second to the *nuru* among the village priestesses, while her brother, the *niitchu*, holds the position of the highest-ranking male *kaminchu*. Occasionally, the term *kuni muutu* (country origin) may be applied to a *niiyaa*. In many villages, an *ufu yaa* (great house) may be found; this often indicates a household which in the past occupied a politically paramount position in the community. This may have been the former residence of a Shuri-appointed gentry official or the residence of a commoner family whose members were regularly appointed to positions of leadership by the Shuri government.

The *yaa n naa* does not merely designate a particular family in the village but implies as well a specific house lot within the village where that family has traditionally resided. Great importance is attached to retaining possession of the family house lot, for here, it is believed, lies the family's main link with the ancestors. House lots and household names seldom change. Even today the individual is usually referred to in terms of his household name and kin status within that household, not by his family or personal name; thus a man may be described as the second son of a certain *yaa n naa*, or a woman as the grandmother of a certain *yaa n naa*. In the final analysis, the individual maintains his social identity through the family, and the concept of an individual independent of this association has been wholly foreign to the thinking of villagers.

LINEAGES. Each village is divided into several lineages, the number and size depending upon the village population. In Kanegusuku, which had a population of 507 in 1954, I found eight lineages; the smallest consisted of but four houses, while the largest possessed more than sixty houses. The lineages are segments of larger patri-sibs made up of a number of lineages commonly located in the various communities of a given area.[4] The major function of a lineage concerns ancestral rites and the care of the dead. Usually, a lineage possesses a common tomb for all members or may share a tomb with related lineages in neighboring villages. Today the lineages are without any other function, although prior to the dissolution of the kingdom a lineage was said to be accountable for the actions of its member houses. Several terms are used for the lineage, *hara* (side or line), *firugi* (splinter), *ichimung* (lit., "one thing," but written in Japanese as "one gate"), and *fichi* (connection) being the most common. Villagers usually refer to a given lineage by a name to which the word *hara* is suffixed.[5]

NEIGHBORHOOD. The smallest political subdivision of the village is called *kumi*.[6] Another old term, *haru* (field),[7] also finds common usage. In the past, there tended to be an identity of neighborhood and lineage, hence the concept of *haru* as kin group as well as area. Today, as the result of population movement in the past fifty years and particularly as the consequence of wartime dislocation, the *kumi* may best be regarded as a neighborhood. The member houses of the *kumi* work together on labor details, particularly the government-sponsored road-maintenance corvée; they also cooperate in reciprocal labor exchanges for harvests, house construction and repair, and other tasks demanding a sizable expenditure of labor beyond a single family's capacity. Considerable importance is attached to maintaining good neighborly relations, and in actual fact the average farm family could not function without the cooperation of its neighbors. Most families have shared a close physical proximity to neighboring households as far back as they can trace their residence in the village, and the fact that they are often closely related further strengthens their unity.

MOIETY. There are possible indications of the existence of moieties in the Okinawan villages of the past. Today the existence of pseudo-moities may be found in certain communal rites, particularly the annual tug-of-war and boat races.[8] The division is commonly conceived of in terms of *agari* and *iri* (east and west), less frequently *shimu* and *wii* (lower and upper). It is sometimes said that one side is male and the other female, likening the two to the sibling creator deities. In Yaeyama, southernmost of the Ryukyu Islands, a moiety-like division has an even greater function in community rites; moreover, although no traceable kin relationship can be established for all the "moiety" members, a strong feeling persists that they are related by blood.

AGE GROUPS. Certain social groups organized on the basis of age have traditionally played an important function in village life. Prior to this century there existed three organized age groups within the village. The *wakamung-gumi* (youth group), consisting of all unmarried males age thirteen and above (although these age groups included both sexes, in practice only the males played an active role), formed the village guard and performed certain necessary labor tasks for community benefit. In each village there were one or more houses termed *yagamayaa* (noisy house), which functioned as working area for young women or as sleeping quarters for the young men as well as meeting places for both sexes. Almost complete sexual freedom was allowed to the unmarried youth of the village. Above the *wakamung-gumi* was the *suu-gumi* (father group), made up of all married males (i.e., household heads) to the age of fifty or fifty-five; this group was most active in village affairs and furnished the leadership for the community. The last group was the *ufu suu-gumi* (grandfather group), the elders of the village, who, while not playing an active role in the village life, wielded the ultimate authority in matters of public concern. They ordinarily functioned as advisors to the *suu-gumi*. Each of the groups was headed by a chief or *kashira*.

With the assumption of Japanese control, these groups were gradually displaced by organizations sponsored by the national government as devices for greater political control and for stimulation of modernization. The *wakamung-gumi* was replaced by the national 'seinenkai' (youth association), which, despite impressive aims for cultural and economic improvement, amounts to little more than a social club at the village level. As a parallel to the young men's association, the young women are now organized into a 'joshi seinenkai' (young women's association). Those who formerly constituted the *suu-gumi* are now members of the 'nōgyō kumiai' (agricultural cooperative association), while their wives participate in the 'fujinkai' (women's association) and, recently, the parent-teacher associations. Each of these organizations is tied to larger district, regional, and national groups largely managed or supervised by the national government. The various age groups were formerly self-contained units within the village, but the new organizations have been potent factors in bringing the villager into contact with the outside world. Significantly, membership in these groups is automatically conferred and is not achieved as a matter of choice; hence, the groups tend to be all-inclusive in village membership.

CLASS. In the Okinawan kingdom, society was divided into two principal classes: *hakusoo* (cognate to 'hyakushō,' farmer, but with the broader meaning of "commoner") and *yukatchu* (good people—hence, upper class). The *hakusoo* were of two types: the urban merchant, artisan, or laborer, and the rural farmer. The *yukatchu* were divided into gentry and nobility. From the time of Shō Shin, as previously noted, most members of the upper classes had their permanent residence in Shuri, but after 1724 a number of them periodically migrated to the country areas and established new farming villages. The farmers of commoner ancestry designated themselves *jiinchu* (natives) and referred to their upper-class neighbors as *chiruunin* (immigrants or temporary residents). There was very little social contact between the *jiinchu* and the *chiruunin*; the land of the latter was often very poor, and they were much despised for their haughty manners amid poverty. Within each district (*majiri*) there were Shuri-appointed gentry officials, but these men were subject to rotation, and their appointments were not usually made hereditary.[9] They were not integrated into the village, since, aside from their administrative function, they did not participate in community life. Intermarriage between *yukatchu* and *hakusoo* was very rare.

One of the highest-ranking commoners within the village was called *shiminchu* (ink person, i.e., one who could write); this individual had usually acquired a rudimentary knowledge of characters while serving in a *yukatchu* house. Afterwards, his ability enabled him to obtain a position as a clerk in the lower echelons of the state bureaucracy, but the *shiminchu* were highly respected in the village and were regarded as virtually of gentry status. It was also possible for commoners to purchase titles, but this was said to require 160,000 'kwang,'[10] and the purchasers were despised by other gentry. In prestige and high social status, the *nuru* (with her family) was the highest-ranking individual in the village. She had the largest landholdings in the community, and they were not subject to periodic redistribution. Her *yaa n naa* was suffixed with *tunchi*, indicating her rank to be equivalent to gentry status. In the eyes of the villagers she was paired with the gentry official, and, significantly, she prayed for his health as the *chifijing* did for the ruler.

Class distinctions are said to have been significant, particularly with regard to marriage, until the decade before World War II; today these distinctions are regarded as meaningless by all except the very oldest people and a few of the old gentry and nobility still residing in Shuri. Landlordism has not developed in rural Okinawa, so there are no great disparities in wealth among village families; moreover, the destruction caused by combat during World War II tended to level all social and economic distinctions. At the present time, new classes are emerging, but as yet the villages lag behind the urban areas in this development.

Social Control

The chief mechanisms of social control within a village that has traditionally functioned as a corporate body and wherein aggressive assertion of individuality is equated with selfishness are seldom expressed in overt form. As is so often the case where the membership of the community enjoys a face-to-face relationship, fear of ridicule, criticism, noncooperation, silent treatment, and possible ostracism suffice to compel the individual to comply with the general will of the community. One is impressed at the outset by the homogeneous character of the village, a natural outcome of the common experience and cultural heritage which all members have shared. While past restrictions on movement and exogamous marriage have been lifted, the average villager nonetheless has enjoyed but a limited range of contacts in his or her lifetime. The small size of the village and close physical proximity of households combine with the all-consuming demands of subsistence agriculture and serve to confine the individual to a narrow environment; consequently, the range for independent action tends to be rather narrow and inflexible. The individual must consider every act in terms of the consequences not only for himself but for his family as well. Although the family and kin group are no longer legally responsible for the actions of their members, the individual is still primarily regarded by the state as a member of a family group and is so duly recorded in the official household registry ('koseki'). The feeling persists that one's mistakes as well as one's achievements are shared with the family. As a consequence, all of these factors serve to curb individualism and insure the homogeneity of the community. Conformity and honoring one's obligations are major cultural values. The surrogate for this marked lack of emphasis on the importance of the individual is provided by a close ego identity with the group—family, kin group, and community (and, in recent times, the state).

Factions within the community are rarely tolerated or allowed to develop, and so great is the fear of rift through discord that few official acts are initiated without first securing unanimity and agreement, considerable emphasis being placed on presenting a facade of unity and tranquillity to the outside. Problems of discord and internal strife within the village are, as much as possible, kept from the attention of outside authorities. By briefly examining a few of the self-policing practices formerly employed, we may gain some insight into the nature of social control as exercised in an overt form.

NMA-DIMA. In the past, as I have noted, considerable sexual freedom was permitted the young people of the village; but when a girl was discovered carrying on a love affair with a man from another village, she was subjected to verbal chastisement and often physical punishment by the village. If the couple were caught together, the male was usually given a beating. Frequently the girl and sometimes the male were placed astride a board or log and paraded about the village by the members of the *wakamung-gumi*. Usually, the girl and her parents were afterwards subjected to a public scolding before a village meeting. Marriage with an outsider was permitted only on payment of a large fine (*tima*) in liquor or money to all unmarried men and youth of the village. This was called *nma-dima* (horse fine) or *nma-zaki* (horse 'sake'), with reference to the simulated ride on horseback given by the *wakamung-gumi*. Obviously, exogamous marriage was not easily condoned, and old informants attest that it was rather infrequent in the past.

KURUU. Those who consistently ignored the community will or made themselves a general nuisance to their neighbors were likely to become *kuruu* (the black one). Fouling a village well, refusing to participate in communal labor corvées, or indulging in sorcery made one liable to this charge. Those who were designated *kuruu* received the silent treatment from the entire village; all forms of social interaction with them were forbidden. They were, in effect, completely ostracized from village life. If the house of one who was *kuruu* caught fire, no assistance was rendered; in fact, anyone who consorted with or in any way interacted with a *kuruu* was also liable to be designated *kuruu*. It is said that a *kuruu* had either to make amends to the community—by public apology and providing enough liquor for a party for all men of the village—or leave the community. The consensus of opinion, however, seems to be that certain families tended to be *kuruu* because of "bad blood" and that such undesirable households were best expelled from the village.

TIIFICHEE. When a crime or theft occurred within the village and the miscreant was not immediately apprehended, the technique of *tiifichee* (hand holders) was employed. All villagers were summoned to the village meeting place, the nature of the offense was described, and the culprit was asked to confess. If there was no response, all youths and adults were herded together in a small area; then a rope was held across a path of exit by two officials. Every individual was required to find a partner (not a close relative) and march down the path hand in hand toward the rope. It was believed that a person of bad character or a known suspect would have difficulty in finding a partner and hence would be left to walk the path alone and thus be publicly exposed as the guilty party. If this failed, then the officials decided who was guilty and pulled the rope taut as the guilty one approached. In some villages, it is reported, *tiifichee* was held near the end of the year whether there had been a crime or not; the difficulty or ease with which one found a partner served to indicate to one and all each individual's status with regard to the rest of the village. In this way, it was believed, each person would strive to merit the respect of his neighbors and fellow villagers.

FUDA. In virtually every Okinawan community until the termination of World War II, one or more tag ('fuda') systems were employed. In many villages where sugar was the cash crop, a 'fuda' was used to prevent illegal consumption of sugar (the government subsidized and encouraged sugar production as a contribution to the war machine) during a greater part of the year. The 'fuda' was usually a wooden board to which a cord was attached so that it might be worn about the neck. If anyone was caught eating sugar, he was forced to wear the 'fuda.' The wearer was then required to pay a small fine in money to the village office each day until such time as he or she might apprehend another violator. It therefore behooved the possessor to lurk about the cane fields waiting for someone to steal sugar. Many stories are related of families which were impoverished by a member who was unable to pass on his 'fuda.' The 'fuda' method was also used to keep the wells clean. Before the war, most schools employed a 'fuda' to keep the students from speaking Okinawan and to ensure that they spoke only proper Japanese ('hyōjungo'). An errant student was required to wear the 'fuda' much like a dunce cap until such time as another student used Okinawan in the classroom. Although the practice is now generally regarded as undemocratic, I heard reports of current resort to it in some of the rural schools.

The above practices were cited as examples of the manner in which self-policing was exercised by the village; their effect was to make every individual his neighbor's keeper. While most of these practices are virtually moribund now, the spirit of purpose implementing them is decidedly alive and vigorous. The village continues to function as a corporate body whose individual members must strive to cooperate, compromise, and comply in the larger interest of that body. Cooperation takes precedence over personal achievement, and all social actions interplay against that background. The concept of community is founded on the belief that the communal body constitutes a major social institution of society and that its interests are paramount over those of any individual, household, or group of households. One of the major functions of the community in the past (and to a lesser extent today) related to the religious life of its members. For ritual purposes, the village constitutes a religious community in the fullest sense of the word. The physical village, its inhabitants, and the religious group are one and the same. There are no religious factions or, in theory at least, dissenters; one holds membership by virtue of birth and residence. The dominant orientations of ritual action are directed toward the basic economic activity—agriculture—and toward the health and safety of the membership. In the minds of its adherents, the community religion maintains the welfare of the village. The burden of ritual life is carried by hereditary specialists, but these persons always function for the benefit of the collectivity, not in their own interest or for that of their staunch supporters. Thus, today, while not a few may disclaim any interest in community religion and may often withhold their support from ritual events, they are never excluded from the prayers and rites, which are still conducted in their behalf as well. The very thought of excluding them from the benefit of religious action would not occur.

Religious Organization

Traditionally, ritual activities for the community have been conducted by hereditary specialists who inherit their office on the basis of membership within certain family-households. With few exceptions, religious offices descend through the first-son line of these houses; thus, the female *kaminchu* tends to be the first daughter of a first son, while the male *kaminchu* is always the first son of the house possessing such an office. With the notable exception of the *niigami* and *niitchu*, there is rarely more than one community *kaminchu* within a given house. Frequently, the *yaa n naa* identify houses possessing a religious office, the most common example being that of *nundunchi*, where the *nuru* resides.

Belief holds that all *kaminchu* are born with high *saa* (*saadaka nmari*), and commonly this must be determined or attested to by a shaman or fortuneteller. In the particular case of the community *kaminchu*, this screening amounts to a mere formality, as it is felt that the *kami* have already indicated the proper individual by house and birth order. Religious offices are held for life; consequently, the *kaminchu* never retires, resigns, or fully delegates this responsibility. The female *kaminchu* completely dominate all ritual matters, while the male *kaminchu* are relegated to the role of ceremonial servants.

Wartime casualties, which extinguished many families, and the inroads of modern education have combined to produce many depredations in the ranks of the community *kaminchu*; only in a few outlying areas was I able to find a complete complement of religious offices, and in most villages a number of positions are vacant. There is, moreover, some regional variation, but I have attempted to present an exhaustive coverage and will indicate local differences.

NURU. Foremost among the village *kaminchu* ranks the chief priestess, *nuru kumui*,[11] who plays the dominant role in the ceremonial affairs of the community. In the preceding chapter I stressed that the *nuru* apparently originated as political appointees of the Shuri government; whatever the circumstances might once have been, the *nuru* are now fully integrated into village life. However, some *niigami* expressed the opinion that their office was more basic, pointing out that a *nuru* might control two or more villages, whereas a *niigami* was to be found in every old village.

Without exception, the *nuru* bears a close relationship to the *yaa n naa* of *nundunchi*; in the past she was always the first daughter of this house and resided there throughout her lifetime. Formerly, she was not permitted to marry, but during the past fifty years this injunction has become a dead letter, and of twenty-four *nuru* interviewed I found only two who were unmarried. Contingent upon her marriage, several changes have occurred with respect to her residence and successor. In not a few villages a strong feeling persists that the *nuru* must never leave *nundunchi*, even for marriage; as a result, her husband is required to reside at *nundunchi* and to assume her family name. This practice, however, has not been without difficulties, for it has placed two nuclear families of the same generation under a single roof—that of the *nuru* and that of her brother, the first son of *nundunchi*. The Japanese land reforms of 1899–1903, as I have noted, conferred ownership on the male household head in the first-son line; this resulted in placing the *nuru* and her husband in a position of dependency on the largess of her brother (her husband would be a younger son, usually without property). The situation has also engendered dispute as to whether her daughter or her brother's daughter should be the successor. To avoid these problems, a few communities have resorted to the expediency of permitting the wife of the first son of *nundunchi* to become *nuru*, but most villages reject this practice and continue to demand that the *nuru* be a daughter of *nundunchi*. Consequently, in many villages a simple compromise has been effected whereby the *nuru* resides in her husband's house but returns to *nundunchi* for all ceremonial events. In this case, her successor continues to be her brother's first daughter.

In addition to officiating at all major rites within her village of birth, a *nuru* usually controls religious matters in one or more (usually two) neighboring villages. Common belief holds that these villages were founded by emigrants from the *nuru*'s village, and usually an actual blood relationship can be traced through the male line from one or more lineages in the satellite village to those of the parent community.[12] On ceremonial occasions, the *nuru* first officiates within her native village and afterwards travels to each of the satellite communities for nearly identical performances. At this time she is accompanied by one or more of the male *kaminchu* from her village, not by any of the female *kaminchu*. She formerly toured her satellite villages while riding on a white horse, but this practice has been dispensed with in recent decades.

The office of *nuru* confers on its occupant a semi-divine status. Formerly, her household was the most prosperous in the village by virtue of her extensive landholdings, *nuru-ji* (*nuru* fields). She additionally enjoyed an exemption from all labor, her field work and firewood being provided by the village. Although these privileges no longer accrue to her, many villages continue to defer to her by granting a blanket exemption from all communal labor corvées. It is still believed, therefore, that her duties demand that she be kept as free as possible in order to attend to them. Similarly, belief demands that she avoid pollution and maintain her purity for maximum ritual effectiveness. Although she now marries, she may refrain from sleeping with her husband during ceremonial periods. She does not attend funerals or visit houses of sickness or houses where a death has recently occurred (time limitations on this taboo vary from village to village). If a ceremony falls during her menses, a substitute may preside in her place. Older Okinawans express the belief that her constant attention to *kami* matters (*kami-gutu*) has the effect of improving her character and even enhancing her physical beauty. Many still believe that the fortune of the community rests largely upon the effectiveness of her actions as intermediary between the community and the *kami*.

NIIGAMI. Occupying a rank second only to that of the *nuru* is the *niigami* or *niigang* (root *kami*), who represents the founding house, *niiyaa*, of the founding lineage for the village. Except for new villages (and the upper-class *yaadui* settlements), every old commoner village possesses a *niigami*; thus, while there is on the average one *nuru* for every three villages, there is virtually a one-for-one identity of *niigami* and villages. In satellite villages, the *niigami* functions as the highest-ranking priestess in residence. On the occasion of major ceremonial events, when the *nuru* visits her village, she functions as chief assistant.

In the previous chapter it was suggested that the *niigami* may once have been the chief priestess of the village, being later supplanted by the state-appointed *nuru*. The *niigami* is the first daughter of *niiyaa*, but as marriage restrictions have never applied to her, within the memory or knowledge of my informants, she has been free to marry and usually resides in her husband's house, returning to *niiyaa* only for ceremonial occasions. Although the *nuru*'s functions frequently carry her outside the village, the *niigami* has been restricted to her village of birth. One *niigami* likened her position in this respect to that of the Japanese 'ujigami,' or tutelary deity.

In a number of communities, particularly the larger ones (e.g., the town of Nago) two or more *niigami* may be found. In such cases it appears that two or more settlements have coalesced into a single community, but one of these *niigami* is always regarded as senior and her house considered the first in the area. Where two or more *niigami* exist within a single community, the title *ufu niigami* (great *niigami*) or *waka nuru* (assistant *nuru*) is conferred on the senior *niigami*.

UTCHI-GAMI. A lesser female *kaminchu*, found in only some communities, and then only in those containing a *nuru*, is the *utchi-gami* (meaning undetermined), who functions as an assistant to the *nuru*, often substituting for her when she is polluted or otherwise indisposed. Unlike the *niigami*, who rarely comes from the same lineage as the *nuru*, the *utchi-gami* is usually born in the same lineage as the *nuru*. Shimabukuro[13] ascribes to her a vague function in the past of praying for the welfare of the Shuri-appointed official; I was unable to uncover any recollection of this. It is said that this was usually the function of the *nuru*; perhaps Shimabukuro based his contention on the fact that one of the village officials was titled *utchi sabakui*. The term *utchi-gami* tends to be more common in Kunigami (the northern area of Okinawa) than elsewhere. In the southern and central areas, this role is called *ii-gang* (squatting or sitting *kami*, suggesting perhaps a subservient position with reference to the *nuru*) or *umeeii* (*u* = honorific, *mee* = before, *ii* = squatter).

NIITCHU. The *niigami* will always be found paired with a *niitchu* (root person) who is the first son of *niiyaa* and hence usually her brother. This pair is referred to as *uminai-gami* and *umikii-gami* (sister and brother *kami*), likening them to the sibling creator deities in their roles as representatives of the founding house of the village. The status of the *niitchu* in ceremonial action is decidedly inferior to that of the *niigami* and other female *kaminchu*, but he stands at the head of the male *kaminchu*, directing them in their duties as ceremonial servants. In this capacity he bears the title *ufu shiidu*.[14] When the *nuru* travels to her satellite villages, the *niitchu* of the parent community usually accompanies her. Unlike the *niigami*, who leaves *niiyaa* after marriage, the *niitchu* remains there as household head; he is also recognized as the titular head of his lineage. Below the *niitchu*, there are a host of male *kaminchu* who play but a very minor role in ceremonial life; the most common of these will be briefly described.

NIIBU-TUI. During certain of the major rituals it is the function of one male *kaminchu* to serve the ceremonial wine to the priestesses and other participants; he is called *niibu* (ladle) or *niibu-tui* (ladler).

NMA-TUI. Formerly, when the *nuru* made her ceremonial rounds of the satellite villages, the *nma-tui* (lit., "horse holder") walked ahead, holding the bridle of her horse. Today he precedes the *nuru*'s procession in village rites, clearing a path through the spectators. He is sometimes called *nma n jaa* or *nnjaa* (lit., "horse caretaker"), as in the past it was his duty to feed and groom the *nuru*'s horse.

UCHIWA SHIIDU. The *uchiwa shiidu* (fan *shiidu*) carries a large fan fashioned from pandanus leaves, with which he fans the *nuru* during the long hours of ceremony. In the event of rainy weather or very hot sun he holds an umbrella to shield her from the elements.

TEEKU-GAMI. The only musical instrument used in accompaniment to the singing of the sacred songs (*umui*) is the drum. This is kept by the *teeku-gami* or *teeku shiidu* (drum *kami* or *shiidu*). I was unable to determine whether the playing of drums was exclusively a male function in the past; at present time the female *kaminchu* may do so, but this usually occurs in the play period (*kaminchu ashibii*) which follows the formal rites.

SHIMANPEE. In a number of the villages of Kunigami one or more males have the duty of cleaning and preparing the ritual sites. They are called *shimanpee* (lit., "village parent"), but in most villages this task is assigned to the youth association or to individual households on a basis of rotation. One of the clearest indications of the strength of community religion was the extent to which these groups cooperated with the *kaminchu* in performing this task. In the town of Itoman, for example, it is now necessary for the *kaminchu* to hire laborers to perform this service.

SAJI. In the past, each house within the village was required to make contributions to all rites conducted by the *kaminchu* on behalf of the community. For the rice and wheat harvest, contributions were made in grain; on other occasions, a tithe called *usakati* ('sake' fee) was levied. Several male *kaminchu*, *saji* or *sajakai-gami* (receiver *kami*), collected these for the *nuru*. In some villages of Kunigami these men bear the title *sagung-gami* (searcher *kami*). Except for the more remote areas where less change has occurred, this office has fallen into general disuse.

SUUDEE. In most villages the task of collecting *usakati* is now carried out by representatives, *suudee* ('sodai'), of the various neighborhoods (*haru*). These men are elected yearly by their neighbors or are appointed in rotation by the village officials. The amount of tax is determined by the officials, collected by the *suudee*, and turned over to the *kaminchu* for their ceremonial expenses. The *suudee* are generally older men and household heads.

SANNANMUNG. Formerly, when the fermentation of ceremonial wine was initiated by the chewing of grain, a young woman or girl was selected for the task. She was required to have sound health and an attractive appearance. Before chewing, her mouth was rinsed with salt in order to ensure her freedom from pollution. Each year the *kaminchu* appointed a different woman to perform this function throughout the ceremonial year. In some areas these women were called *sannanmung* (meaning undetermined); they were not regarded as *kaminchu*. During the last two decades this practice has been abandoned; today ceremonial wine is fermented by the addition of a simple yeast made from wheat, millet, or beans.

KUDII. In the villages of southern and central Okinawa and sporadically throughout the northern region, the lineage *kaminchu—munchu-gami* (sib *kami*), *kudii* or *kudingwa* (meaning undetermined)—participate with the *nuru*'s group, *nuru chikusai*, in the performance of community rites. These women usually outnumber the *nuru chikusai*, but their role is decidedly a secondary one, that of giving representation to the lineages. In villages where they do not participate it is said that communal rites are not their concern, but elsewhere they are customarily invited and regarded as guests of the *nuru*. Significantly, their participation is most common in those areas where lineage organization is strong, particularly in southern Okinawa.

In addition to the *kaminchu* and religious officials described above, the *nuru chikusai* has an entourage of older women who, while not *kaminchu*, participate in a spectator-servant capacity during the major ritual activities. Formerly, village officials were expected to pray with the *nuru chikusai* on the occasion of important ceremonies; the extent to which these officials comply with this practice today affords another index to the strength of local religion. In most villages, their participation is now limited to one or two of the major ceremonies that are accompanied by festivals in which the entire community takes part.

There also may be found a number of *shiidu* (*shiduu*) or male *kaminchu* whose titles are taken from place names within the community, as for example the Tubaru *shiidu* in Nago; their functions, however, in no way differ from those of the other male *kaminchu*. A number of the lesser *shiidu* below the *ufu shiidu* tend to be of the same lineage as the *nuru*, but no consistent pattern for this could be determined aside from the fact that the newer lineages are without any representation in the *nuru chikusai*. However, I have the impression that most of the ceremonial servants— *utchi-gami* and all *shiidu* below the *ufu shiidu*—do not pre-date the creation of the *nuru* office and appear to be closely associated with her; the *niigami* and *niitchu*, on the other hand, could be likened to the *kudii* of the lineages. In the southern islands of the Ryukyus, Miyako and Yaeyama, an older system, without the *nuru* and great number of ceremonial servants, seems to prevail; there, the chief priestess for the founding lineage (who may be likened to the *niigami* on Okinawa) also functions as the chief priestess of the village.

Ritual Sites

Any place of worship or prayer may be called *ugwanju* (lit., "honorable prayer place"), but those *ugwanju* used for communal rites are fairly fixed in type, so that a rather consistent pattern exists from village to village. Collectively, all sites for community rites are described as *mura ugwanju* or *shima ugwanju*, but more commonly they are called *takidaki* (the several or many *utaki*). In the latter case, more than one *utaki* may be implied, but customarily the term serves to designate all places of import to community religion. I shall enumerate below the major village *ugwanju* and consider their significance with reference to the community.

UTAKI. The *utaki*, or sacred grove, constitutes the most sacrosanct site for community rites. It usually consists of little more than a heavy clump of trees and underbrush with a small clearing at its center; here, a large rock and small censer will be found. The stone is said to represent *ibi* or *ibi ganashii mee*, which is the *kami* name (*kaminaa*) for the founding *kami* or ancestor of the village, suggesting the Japanese 'ujigami' or 'ubusunna gami' (village tutelary deity). Sometimes a three-stone hearth, symbolizing the *fii nu kang*, may be found here, but this *kami* is not the object of worship here as many have assumed. When present, it serves as an intermediary between the supplicants and the *kami* of the *utaki*. The sacred nature of the *utaki* is attested to by the deportment of the *kaminchu:* their voices are low and respectful; solemnity prevails. The gay singing and drinking indulged in at other places never occur. The *utaki* was formerly taboo to all males, including the *shiidu*, throughout the year, and out of bounds for most females during a greater part of the year. These prohibitions have been greatly relaxed or totally ignored in recent years; but the cutting of brush for firewood is not permissible, and it is still believed that *kami-daari* will strike an offender. Rites within the *utaki* are generally conducted in secret. An *utaki*, as previously noted, is spoken of as *shijidakasang* (high in *shiji*); significantly, the founding ancestor or *kami* is believed to be female, despite the fact that the lineages and sibs trace their descent through the male line. A check of land records showed the *utaki* to be owned by the community or its founding lineage. Where more than one *utaki* exists within a given community, they are usually owned by or associated with different lineages; however, one will always be regarded as senior—that associated with the lineage of the *niigami*—and it must be stressed that the *utaki* seldom has any connection with the *nuru*'s lineage.

KAMI ASHAGI. The major site for public ritual is the *kami ashagi* (meaning undetermined), a low thatched roof supported by stone or log pillars and open on all sides. The *kami ashagi* may be found within the house lot of *nundunchi* or in the heart of the village at the edge of the clearing where village meetings are held. Here the public rites are held following the more secluded rites within the *utaki*. The floor of *kami ashagi* is of dirt and bare except for a large log, *tamutugi* (lit., "sleeve log," but meaning "*kami* assistant's log"), on which the female *kaminchu* sit during the ceremonies. The festive mood within the *kami ashagi* contrasts markedly with that in the *utaki*; after prayers and the drinking of ceremonial wine, dancing and singing to the accompaniment of a drum take place. The villagers may gather about the *ashagi* and witness this performance, and it is believed that the *kami* join in the merrymaking.

NUNDUNCHI. The shrine-residence for the *nuru* serves as the initial and terminal point for rites conducted by the *nuru chikusai* in behalf of the community. The importance of *nundunchi* derives from the presence of the *nuru* and the memorial tablets enshrining her predecessors. It is believed that the latter have become *kami* and that their *chiji* is that of the present *nuru*, who, therefore, possesses a personal *kami*, *nuru-gami*, providing her with a direct link to the spirit world. The other members of the *nuru-chikusai* do not possess personal *kami* but make their contact with the spirit world through the *fii nu kang* of their household hearths in the manner of ordinary people.[15] The ancestral tablets, *iifee*, memorializing the former *nuru* are preserved on a special shrine shelf apart from those of the other ancestors of *nundunchi*. On the occasion of all village ceremonies, the *nuru* and her group pray here first and then again at the conclusion of the ceremony. Although present practice permits the *nuru* to marry and enter another house, after death her memorial tablet is kept in *nundunchi* together with those of her predecessors, not in her husband's house. Similarly, her coffin enters the tomb of her brother's lineage if her husband happens to be a member of a different kin group. Her sacred parapher-nalia—white robes, beads, jewel (*mitama*, 'magatama'), hairpin, etc.—are permanently stored at *nundunchi*, so that a *nuru* residing elsewhere must return there to dress for ceremonies. While restrictions on her movement have been considerably relaxed in the past fifty years, belief in her spiritual bondage to *nundunchi* remains steadfast among the older generations.

TUNCHI-YAA. In many villages there is a small shrine structure housing a three-stone hearth which serves as a communal hearth in that its *fii nu kang* functions as an intermediary between the village and the higher *kami* by observing and reporting on village events. This *tunchi-yaa* sup-posedly represents the former residence site of an *aji* or a *jituu* (the Shuri-appointed gentry official), and in the past it was the *nuru*'s function to pray here for the welfare of this official. The *nuru*'s function in the spiritual world paralleled that of the government official in secular life.

When an important ceremonial event is impending, the higher *kami* are invited to attend through a notification delivered at *tunchi-yaa*; this is called *san nichi takabi* or *yu nichi takabi* (three- or four-day prayer; *takabi* derives from the verb *takabiyung*, to make higher, and *utakabi* means "prayer to the *kami*"). Frequently, ceremonial wine is fermented at *tunchi-yaa* three days in advance of a ceremony, thereby serving as notice of a forthcoming rite. In some villages, two or more *tunchi-yaa* may be found; in such cases these are located within the yards of the founding houses of the various lineages or in close proximity to these house lots. The hearth in this case represents that of a lineage founder and serves to link the kin group with this ancestor, who has become a *kami*. Lineage *tunchi-yaa*, except for that of the founding lineage of the community, may or may not be included in the *nuru*'s tour of ritual sites; generally they are included where lineage organization and activity are strong.

NIIYAA. The founding house of the community does not always constitute a focal point of worship insofar as the *nuru* and her group are concerned, for in some villages ritual functions at *niiyaa* may be largely confined to the *niigami* alone. In many communities, however, *niiyaa* constitutes a major ritual site for the *nuru chikusai*.[16] In the front yard of *niiyaa*, usually on the left side, there is a small shrine, similar to *tunchi-yaa*, housing a hearth for the *fii nu kang*, which again serves to link the house (and lineage) with the founding ancestral *kami*. Villagers regard it as a sacred site by virtue of its antiquity and association with the village founder. Although no direct blood tie may be claimed, all village houses are felt to be spiritual descendants of *niiyaa*, and frequently the *niigami* may be asked to pray there on behalf of a village family. The fact that the function of presiding at house construction rites is usually reserved for the *niigami* would seem to be related to this sentiment.

MISCELLANEOUS. There is a variety of types of ritual sites for community rites of lesser importance than those described above; however, their existence is by no means universal. In most villages, the public wells receive a yearly visit from the *nuru chikusai*, and if the ruins of an old castle lie within the territory of a village, the *nuru chikusai* regularly pray there. In seaside villages, prayers are offered on the beach to the sea *kami*; in some places the communal fish weir also serves as a ritual site, and in one community an old salt-making flat has become a place of worship. A number of villages reserve a site, usually on high ground, exclusively for rain-making rites. Additional types and many individual occurrences might be enumerated here; I have merely cited a few examples to indicate their nature. The *utaki, kami ashagi*, and *nundunchi* constitute the focal points for communal rites in virtually all communities, and all other sites tend to be of peripheral or secondary importance in any universal pattern.

Annual Rites

The Chinese lunar calendar is used exclusively in reckoning all ritual events, which are often timed to occur on propitious days. In the past, dates for the major nationally observed rites were determined by Shuri and performed throughout the nation simultaneously, but the lack of any central coordinating agency in this century has produced numerous local variations in timing. Moreover, there have apparently always been a number of ceremonies which are only regionally or locally observed and have never been subject to governmental regulation. It is a rare occurrence, therefore, when the annual cycles of two villages completely agree; but the range of their differences tends to be very slight, for the majority of community rites pertain to the agricultural cycle and the major grain crops—rice, wheat, and millet.

No single village follows all of the annual rites considered below; indeed, many of these rites, as Shimabukuro[17] has shown, are limited to a single community. Furthermore, the content of a single ceremonial event may vary extensively from village to village, and I shall not be concerned with the detailed minutiae of ritual performance. Rather than attempting exhaustive coverage of these rites, I have tried to show that in their function there is a consistent orientation toward the welfare of the people and their basic livelihood. It was stated before that most rites may be arbitrarily categorized as asking or thanking rites and that the former are conceived to be of greater importance than the latter; this is particularly true in the community, where far more elaborate ritual concentration attends the asking ceremonies. Thanking rites, especially those following harvests, are marked by a more festive atmosphere and are observed by the entire community.

With reference to the identification of the various annual rites (or virtually all Okinawan rites for that matter), some clarification of names is necessary. The vagueness which one encounters in determining the titles for the various *kami* obtains for ceremonies as well; it might be said with but slight exaggeration that most ceremonies are without a definite or universally applied name. In fact, it is possible in the course of several interview sessions with a single informant to obtain several "names" for the same ceremonial event; therefore, I have selected those most commonly employed.

FIRST MONTH. The first three weeks in this month are marked by an almost continual round of ceremonial activities, but these mainly involve the household and lineage, with only a few pertaining to the community proper. On the first day of the new year, the *nuru chikusai* arise early to visit all major ritual sites, where brief prayers are offered to the *kami* with a request to provide the people with good crops and health during the new year. This is called *hachi ugwang* (first prayers) or *soogwachi gwantang* (New Year's Day rite).

On that same day, or in some villages on the second day of the new year, the *nuru chikusai* and *kudii* make a tour of all public wells in the village to perform *hachi ubii nadii* (first sacred-water stroking). At this time, fresh water is drawn from each well, and, while praying to the water *kami*, the *kaminchu* dab water on their foreheads in token of respect to that *kami*. There is some feeling that this act not only does honor to the *kami* but also has a lustral effect for the *kaminchu*.

On the second or third day of the new year the *nuru* plays hostess to all the lineage *kudii* at *nundunchi*, where they pray to the shrine shelf of former *nuru*. In some villages, the male heads of the founding houses of the various lineages accompany the *kudii* on this occasion.

Many communities observe a taboo on entering the forested or hilltop areas of the village during the first nineteen days of the new year. At that time, all villagers are forbidden to enter these areas or to collect firewood there. It is believed that many *kami* descend to the mountains at this time of year and that any activity there, particularly cutting wood near an *utaki*, would be offensive to them. Formerly, all paths leading into the wooded area were blocked by a taboo rope, *hijainna*. On the twentieth day of the new year, the *nuru* performs *yama-birachi* (opening the mountain), thus lifting the taboo.

SECOND MONTH. During the second month, often around the fifteenth, *muji nu fuu ugwang* (prayer for wheat ears) takes place. At this time, the *nuru* and her associates visit the major sites of community ritual and ask the *kami* to provide a good wheat harvest in the following month. Greater emphasis is placed on this rite than the harvest rites which follow in the third month.

THIRD MONTH. After harvesting the wheat, *muji nu shirigafuu nu umachii* (thanksgiving ceremony for wheat) is performed by the *nuru chikusai* and *kudii*. Three days before this event, they prepare ceremonial wine from wheat, a few beans or peas, and a little sugar, which ferment into a mild alcoholic beverage by ceremony time.

FOURTH MONTH. On a propitious day near the fifteenth of the month, ceremonies are conducted to rid the fields of insects and pernicious weeds. These rites are known as *abushi-baree* (cleaning the ridges, referring to the small ridges which serve to divide the fields) or *mushi-baree* (insect eradication). Prior to this day, the small ridges which border each plot and serve as boundary markers are cleared of all weeds. On the day of the ceremony, a general work taboo on farming and fishing activities is observed by all families. The *nuru chikusai* first prays at the major *ugwanju* and then proceeds to the beach at the time of an ebb tide. There, insects collected from the fields are placed on small boats fashioned from pandanus leaves, which are carried out to sea by the receding tide. Inland, the *nuru* and her group may visit the various stone lions guarding the paths leading to the village; these lions are called *keeshi* (that which sends away). Prayers are offered with the request to keep all insects and misfortune away from the village.

FIFTH MONTH. On the fourth day of this month the Chinese dragon boat races, *haarii* or *haari-buni*, are held; these are said to have been introduced about four hundred years ago by the Chinese residents of Kume in Naha. In the towns, the various wards compete in canoe races; in the country villages, two or more neighboring villages headed by the same *nuru* are pitted against one another. Although prayers are offered to *ruugu* or to the sea *kami*, this event is not recognized as of great religious importance, and in most communities the *kaminchu* do not wear their white robes. In Itoman, the *nuru* stated that the fierce competition engendered by the races often culminated in fighting in the past and that her prayers sought the *kami*'s aid in assuaging any bitterness.

During the latter half of this month, a propitious day is selected for offering a few ears of the new and as yet unripe rice to the *kami* with requests for a good harvest in the following month. This ceremony, *nni nu fuu ugwang* (prayer for rice ears), where rice is a major crop, is considered the most important of the year. All village *kami* are begged to ask *ting nu kami*, the heaven *kami*, to provide a bountiful harvest. Formerly, in advance of this ceremony many *nuru* went to pray at the twin wells Ukinju Hainju in Tamagusuku, close to Miifudaa, where the first rice is believed to have been planted.

SIXTH MONTH. Harvest rites for rice and millet reaped during the latter part of this month are called *umachii* (the ceremony), *nni nu shirigafuu nu umachii* (rice-thanksgiving rites), or *aa nu shirigafuu nu umachii* (millet-thanksgiving rites). The first day of this observance is exclusively religious, consisting of solemn prayers of thanksgiving and the offering to the *kami* of the first fruits, *hachi mujukui*, usually harvested from the *nuru*'s fields. Several days prior to the event, a rice wine is prepared from the new grain by the *nuru* and her group; this is then offered to the *kami* at all ritual sites while the village *kaminchu* and all *kudii* exchange drinks with the *nuru*. The second day is marked by a more secular celebration in which the entire community participates. Formerly, a number of taboos were set by the *nuru*; during the third and fourth months, prior to the sprouting of the ears, it was forbidden to cut any small sprouting plant in the belief that this action would adversely affect growth of the grain. After the ears had formed, a taboo was imposed on loud noises, singing, or the playing of the samisen or drum for fear that this noise would jar loose the heading grain. For one to two weeks before the harvest, two general work taboos, *yama-dumi* (mountains or fields closed) and *un-dumi* (sea closed), were enforced. By the former taboo all were enjoined from entering the fields for any purpose until harvesting commenced. By the latter taboo fishermen were required to remain on land and women were not permitted to enter or touch the sea for any purpose—washing, bathing, gathering shellfish, or whatever. On completion of the thanking rites, the *nuru* lifted all taboos, harvesting officially commenced, and a happy atmosphere prevailed if the harvest was bountiful. Today these taboos are but haphazardly observed if they are observed at all. The early taboo on cutting young sprouting plants continues to be observed out of individual preference, not because of any community-enforced rule, while the taboo on loud noises has disappeared save as an indivudual sentiment in a few of the more isolated communities. *Yama-dumi* and *un-dumi* are now largely ignored by all except the *kaminchu*. One *nuru* rationalized, "In the past there was no food from outside [imports], and people were more conscientious in observing these rules."

The first day of the harvest celebration, then, is devoted to purely religious observations conducted by the *kaminchu*; the second day is given over to celebrations in which the entire community participates. This day formerly served to mark the lifting of all taboos and offered a release from tensions engendered during the last weeks prior to the harvest, when an early typhoon or severe rainstorm might eradicate the efforts of months. In the past, all non-*yaadui* villages, as well as Naha and Shuri, held great tug-of-war contests on the second day of the harvest ceremonies, but since the war, only a few communities have maintained this tradition. Shortages of rice straw and the considerable expense entailed in making these great ropes were said to be the reasons for limiting this observance, but in the past few years, the tug-of-war has gained increasing popularity. Two large ropes fashioned from rice straw, contributed by the households of the community, are linked through large loops at one end and secured by a log. One rope is regarded as female, the other male. For this event, a moiety division of the community into *iri* (west) and *agari* (east) or *shimu* (lower) and *wii* (upper) may be recognized; generally, *shimu* or *agari* are considered female and pull on the female rope, while *wii* or *iri* represent the male rope. Some say that if the female side wins it is believed that the next year's harvest will be bountiful. Today, where this contest still prevails, the festive aspects clearly outweigh the religious; in effect, harvest observances are becoming mere celebrations rather than solemn religious occasions. Moreover, the very fact that the priestesses themselves place greater emphasis on the asking rites tends to support this trend. Although Japanese agricultural specialists have introduced new varieties of fast-maturing rice which now permit double cropping, little or no attention is accorded the second rice harvest in village ritual life.

SEVENTH MONTH. In the seaside villages of northern Okinawa, sporadically in central Okinawa, rarely in southern Okinawa, one of the major ritual events of the year relates to the sea and is called *unjami machii* (sea-*kami* rite). Closely associated (in time) with this ceremony is another called *shinugu* (hide or hidden); Shimabukuro states[18] that the two are related and that their procedure is essentially the same. In my opinion, however, the two are distinct; in Ada, for example, *shinugu* and *unjami* occur in alternate years. Moreover, their ritual content and orientation differ considerably; *unjami* focuses exclusively on the sea and seems designed to produce a greater supply of fish and to ensure the safety of all who work at sea, while *shinugu* shows no connection with the supply of fish and might best be described as a rite of intensification. In a number of villages in northern Okinawa, the high point of *shinugu* is the appearance of masked ritualists—youth of the village and not *kaminchu*—who visit the households of the community. Nakamura[19] has indicated *shinugu*'s similarity to the masked 'namahage' rites occurring in scattered areas of rural Japan at the new year and to those of Miyako and Yaeyama in the southern Ryukyus. While I am reluctant to accept his contention that these may represent survivals of earlier secret ritual societies, it does seem to corroborate statements and evidence gathered in the southern Ryukyus that the New Year period formerly followed the rice and millet harvests and occurred during the summer months. In the town of Itoman, *shinugu* is now performed in the eighth month and is without any masked ritual; but the ritual period lasts for three days (formerly nine), during which time the unity of the community is reaffirmed by all households. Formerly, in Itoman all households made rice wine three days before this ceremony, the exact amount being determined by the number of males in the household. On the day of *shinugu*, each house poured its contribution into a giant tub, which was offered by the *kaminchu* with prayers to *ibi*, the *kami* of the *utaki*; afterwards the contents were consumed in a community celebration. On this day, young men who had attained their thirteenth, fifteenth, or seventeenth year (not an even-numbered year) were permitted to assume an adult male hairdo. On the following day, a great rope-pulling contest was—and still is—performed with a rope nearly two hundred meters in length and approximately two feet in diameter. The entire rite is without any reference to the sea or sea *kami*, and in parts of northern Okinawa the conclusion of *shinugu* is followed by the weeding and preparation of the rice fields for the next crop.

In contrast to *shinugu*, *unjami machii* underscores the community's dependence on the sea and culminates in the presentation of an offering to the sea *kami*. In Nago, a wild boar (now a rat) used to be thrown into the sea; in Tema, the priestesses throw their ritual headdresses into the community fish weir; and on Kudaka Island, the *kaminchu* and all villagers eat raw fish on the beach. In some villages of northern Okinawa, boat races follow the conclusion of this ceremony.

EIGHTH MONTH. During this month and occasionally in the second month, or whenever pestilence or contagion was rampant in the village, *shimagusarashii* or *shimagusarasaa* (village impairment or village decay) was formerly performed.[20] While the *nuru* and her group prayed at the major ritual sites of the village and at the places of entrance where the stone lions are situated, the men made *hijainna* (taboo ropes) and killed a small pig (occasionally a goat, cow, or horse). The *hijainna* were strung across all paths leading into the village and around all places of worship. Leaves of the *mbashi* plant (*Alocasia cucullata* Schott and *A. macrorrhiza* Schott)[21] were dipped in the animal's blood and affixed to the gate of each house, and the meat was distributed to all houses in the village. In each household, *sang* was fashioned and hung in the four corners of the house and above the pigpen. Bones and sometimes small strips of animal flesh were fastened to the *hijainna* in the belief that the ghosts (*majimung*) or evil spirits (*yanamung*) that cause sickness would be appeased by the sacrifice and would not enter the community.

On the night of the fifteenth, coinciding with the full moon, the young men perform a dance, *shiishi mooyee* (lion dance), with a lion mask. This ceremony begins and ends at the *kami ashagi* after visits to all households in the village. Although the old people believe that the visit of the lion mask will enhance the household's prosperity and health, the ceremony is largely without religious overtones and does not concern the *kaminchu*.

NINTH MONTH. During the latter part of this month, the seed beds for the new rice crop are sown, and in most villages religious observances relating to this event are performed by individual households. In the past, and still today in a few scattered areas, this activity was preceded by *tantui nu umachii*, a ceremonial sowing of the paddy (usually the *nuru*'s). After prayers at all village *ugwanju* for a successful sowing operation, the *nuru chikusai* proceeds to the fields, where the *nuru* casts the first seeds, whereupon all villagers can commence their sowing.

TENTH MONTH. On a propitious day of the tenth lunar month, a ceremony called *fii-geeshi nu ugwang* (prayer to send away fire) is performed. This rite is usually accompanied or closely followed by *miji nu shirigafuu* (thanksgiving for water). In the former rite, there are prayers at *tunchi-yaa* and all household hearths, thanking the *fii nu kang* for its warmth and protection during the year. Rites for the water *kami* are conducted at the village wells and on the beach, with thanks for its protection from fire during the previous year. As a rule, all households which have suffered damage from fire during the past year must contribute to the expense of this ceremony. In Itoman, full-scale houses were formerly erected on the beach and then ignited, with prayers to the *kami* of the tide (by inference, the *kami* of wells, sea, tide, rain, etc., are one and the same) to keep fire away from the village houses. The expense of constructing these buildings was borne by all houses which had been damaged by fire in the previous year, but in recent years the town government has not permitted the *suudee* to collect this exorbitant fine.

ELEVENTH MONTH. No community ceremonies occur during this month.

TWELFTH MONTH. A propitious date during the latter half of this month is selected for the performance of *ufu shirigafuu* (great thanksgiving); on this occasion, the *nuru* and her associates pay their last respects of the year at all ritual sites of significance in the annual cycle, thanking the *kami* for their help during the past year. The *nuru* apparently do not consider this an important ceremony, as some do not wear their white robes for this event. The Itoman *nuru* specifically stated that she believed this to be a rather new observance, but in other communities this occasion serves to mark the beginning of the taboo on the mountain area, *yama-dumi*, which lasts until *yama-birachi* (opening the mountain) on the twentieth of the following month.

In virtually all cases, the priestesses whom I interviewed stated that the major ritual events were those of the second, third, fifth, sixth, and seventh months, relating to the wheat and rice (or millet) crops and to the sea *kami*. The village *kami* are always notified by the *nuru* three or four days in advance of forthcoming ritual events in a ceremony called *utakabi* or *san nichi* (three-day) *takabi*. Usually, this also provides the occasion for making wine, fermented by the addition of yeast to the crop of the season. The major thanking rites tend to be followed by a day of celebration in which the entire community participates. In the case of asking rites, the succeeding day is given over to *kaminchu ashibii* (*kaminchu* play or party). At this time, the *nuru chikusai* and *kudii* gather at the *kami ashagi* or *nundunchi* for several hours of drinking and dancing, in which the *kami* are thought to participate. Formerly, on the occasion of *utakabi* the *nuru* and her female associates went into retreat, *yugumui*, usually within the *utaki* or *kami ashagi*, until the time of ceremony, so as to ensure their freedom from pollution. In recent years, this retreat has been reduced to a single night or has been disregarded altogether.

Special Rites

In addition to the annual rites described above, there are a number of special rites performed by the *nuru* or *niigami* for the benefit of individuals or their households. Most communities, as previously noted, employ the *niigami* for praying at house-construction rites, although in some villages, particularly where the *niigami* died during the war, this function has been assumed by the *nuru*. For boat-launching rites, on the other hand, the builder or owner engages the services of the *nuru*; and in communities where fishing or shipping figures importantly, the boat owners or co-operative annually request the *nuru* to pray at all the *ugwanju* for their boats. When an individual departs on a trip requiring travel at sea, a *kaminchu* (in this case no set practice is followed, hence a *nuru, niigami,* or *kudii*) is engaged to perform *tabi ugwang* (travel prayer). She may also be asked to pray for one who is ill, although the *nuru* may not enter a house of sickness but will pray at public ritual sites. I recorded one instance of a *nuru*'s praying for a young man who was studying for high school entrance exams. Virtually any matter deemed important to the individual's health, welfare, property, or livelihood may occasion the need for the *nuru*'s, *niigami*'s, or *kudii*'s services in prayer. It is in this sphere that the functions of the *kaminchu* overlap those of the *yuta*; yet people clearly make the distinction that while both the *yuta* and *kaminchu* may pray for one's benefit, only the former possesses the power of discerning the causes of misfortune. Hence, in any instance of protracted misfortune, the services of the *kaminchu* are readily dispensed with and those of one or more *yuta* engaged.

Community Religion and Change

I have sought to present the community religion as it existed during the lifetime of the oldest living generation and as it still exists in a few isolated rural areas. The folk-community of the past, which formed a self-contained, self-sustaining unit, is rapidly undergoing transformation into a rural settlement fully integrated into the national state. Concomitant with this development, community religion has experienced progressive deterioration; an eventual outcome of complete disintegration seems inevitable.

What regularities emerge in this change now occurring in the community religion? I found that rites relating to the chief livelihood of the people—agriculture or the sea—have consistently exhibited the greater tendency to survive, particularly where they are closely tied to community celebrations with a strong entertainment feature; increasingly, the latter seems to be displacing the religious feature in emphasis. This would appear to be in accordance with our own experience, as for example in the May Day observances, in which the entertainment aspect has wholly displaced all religious significance. The more isolated areas, particularly those which escaped war damage, have preserved a greater degree of conservatism in religious matters; however, I cannot satisfactorily explain why fishing communities consistently exhibit a greater strength of religious belief and action than farming communities. The fisherfolk, who do not differ significantly in education or participation in national life from the farming population, recognize this difference and ascribe their greater preservation of community religion to the fact that their livelihood is a more dangerous one. It might be noted that women generally occupy a higher status in fishing villages and play a larger role in community affairs, which might in part account for this greater emphasis. Moreover, the fact that the general population looks down upon fishermen may serve to strengthen community bonds within fishing settlements. A question worth considering is whether this greater conservatism in religious matters is unique to Okinawan fishing communities vis-à-vis farming villages or whether it occurs in other cultures as well.

The community religion has an inherent structural weakness in that *kaminchu* offices are retained by specific households and specific kin statuses within those households. As a consequence of the war, when entire families were wiped out, many villages are without eligible replacements for deceased *kaminchu*. I consistently found that the male *kaminchu* are restive in their role as ceremonial servants and are increasingly inclined to withdraw from all participation; yet their loss, while discouraging to the women, has not been seriously damaging, for their contribution to ceremonial life was small even in the past. The crucial roles are played by the *nuru* and *niigami*, and their loss is always destructive. In two cases in which *nuru* have become Christians, all community rites have ceased to be performed through lack of this ritual leader. In another case, an aged, infirm *nuru* is no longer capable of performing her duties, and the *niigami* family has died out; consequently, communal ritual life has languished.

VII

KIN GROUP RELIGION

Introduction

Okinawan society is segmented into extended families organized on a patrilineal principle for worship of common ancestors. The largest aggregate of households recognizing a common blood tie is termed *munchu* in the case of commoners, *uji* or *uji munchu*[1] in the case of the upper classes. All Okinawans hold membership within one of these groups, which may range in size from several to more than a thousand households. Generally, the largest *munchu* are to be found among the commoners of southern Okinawa and among the upper classes who were formerly congregated in Shuri. In the past, members of a *munchu* were restricted to a specific area or region; in recent decades, member households have sometimes scattered widely, although in many places the old spatial concentration still persists. The main function of the extended kin group in Okinawan society has been a ritual one; despite extensive social changes which have transpired since the advent of Japanese annexation, this group has successfully preserved its ritual integrity.

Organization

PARENT HOUSE–BRANCH HOUSE. The underlying principle of the family system is to maintain the family's continuity through an unbroken succession in the male line so that descendant generations will be provided to perform rites for the ancestors. Whenever the extinction of a house threatens, adoption must be resorted to, for it is believed that the ancestors will not only suffer through a lack of prayers but in their despondency will also cause trouble for others. Family leadership devolves to the eldest son, who succeeds to the family wealth, property, and ancestral tablets, which he holds in trust for his eventual successor. Patrilocal residence obtains for the first son, and younger sons are required to establish neolocal residence upon marriage. The establishment of a neolocal residence does not, however, ultimately lead to a severance of all ties with the parental house; instead, ritual obligations of the branch house to the parent house serve to bind the two in a lasting relationship. With the passage of time, the branch house in turn becomes a parent house to branch houses established by its younger sons, and so by this process the network of relationships in the common-descent group constantly ramifies.

A parent house is designated *muutu-yaa* (origin house) with reference to its branch houses (*wakari-yaa*; sometimes, *tachi-yaa*), although it in turn may be a branch of a still older parent house. The process of establishing a new house is referred to as *yaa wakaiing* (breaking off a house) or *yaa tachung* (establishing a house). The founding house of a common-descent group organized on these principles is *ufu muutu* (great origin) or *suu muutu* (head origin) to all of its descendant houses. When the founding house happens to be the founding house for the community as well, it is called *niiyaa* or *kuni muutu* by the villagers, as we have seen. All descendant houses are united under the founding house for ritual action on behalf of common ancestors and for ritual promotion of the common welfare. Each of the member houses bears a ritual obligation toward the founding house similar to that which obtains between a parent house and its branch houses.

SIB AND LINEAGE. The largest aggregate of households recognizing a common blood tie and sharing a common ritual life is the patri-sib, *munchu* or *uji munchu*. There are several distinctions between the *munchu* of the former lower classes and the *uji* (or *uji munchu*) of the upper class. The lower-class *munchu* forms a common burial group and possesses a single permanent tomb used by all members, but the members of an upper-class *uji* usually bury individually on a household basis. The commoner sib (*munchu*) is rarely limited to a single community, whereas, prior to this century, the majority of the upper-class *uji* were located in Shuri and adjacent Naha, although at present their households tend to be more widely scattered than those of the commoners. Both types, however, are organized on a patrilineal principle, and the tomb of the ancestral founder, together with the founding house, constitute focal points of ritual activity. Each sib looks upon its *ufu muutu* as directly descended from the founding ancestor.

The sib is segmented into lineages, for which a variety of terms—*hara, firugi, ichimung,* and *fichi*—may be applied. Generally, the term *hara*[2] enjoys the widest frequency of application. Among commoners, the *hara* within a given *munchu* tend to be spatially restricted to a group of villages in one locality. One of these villages is regarded as the place of origin for the group and the place of residence for the first ancestor; the founding house is located in that community.

The lineage containing the founding house of the sib is regarded as the senior lineage and designated *chatchi-bara* (first-son line or lineage) in contrast to the junior lineages, which may be referred to as *jinan-bara* (second-son lineage), *sannan-bara* (third-son lineage), etc., suggesting their order of creation. For example, the senior or parent *hara* of Hanja Munchu is located in the village of Teruya; the *jinan-bara* is in the neighboring village of Kanegusuku, while the *sannan-bara* resides in Kakazu. The terms second son, third son, etc., do not imply brothers who established branch lineages but rather indicate the segmentation order in time. Where segmentation occurred at a fairly remote date, the parent house in the senior lineage may be unknown to the members of a branch lineage; in such cases, ritual obligations are made directly to the *ufu muutu*, or founding house.

The founding house of a junior lineage is *muutu-yaa* to all of its descendant houses but is designated by them as *naka muutu* (middle origin) with reference to its intermediary position. Although in a large *munchu* there may exist lineages within lineages, the term *naka muutu* is not applied to more than one house of an extended family group residing in a given village. Should a branch lineage from a branch lineage be established in another community, then its founding house will also be termed *naka muutu*; there appears to be no specific term designating a branch of a branch lineage. The members of a branch lineage residing in a separate community may speak of themselves as a *naka munchu* (middle *munchu*); this term implies a branch lineage as a separate residential unit, in contrast to *hara*, which designates a lineage without implying any territorial integrity. In a large, widely scattered sib, the various local lineages may be distinguished simply by community name. For example, a *naka muutu* of So Uji and several descendant houses reside in the *yaadui* settlement of Kitazato; the male head of the *naka muutu* stated that his house was a branch house from still another *naka muutu* located elsewhere, and he referred to it as "a way down *naka muutu*." Other members of So Uji refer to their relatives in Kitazato as the Kitazato-bara. The major lines of any sib are determined with respect to the main or founding line, irrespective of size; only lineages established by younger sons born into the main founding line are considered main descent groups.

Even after the upper classes were resettled in Shuri in the late fifteenth century,[3] each upper-class *uji* (*uji munchu*) continued to recognize a certain village as its place of origin and ancestral home. In that village the first ancestor's tomb was located, and yearly pilgrimages were made to the site. When the new Japanese government curtailed the state pensions which subsidized a goodly segment of the upper classes, there was a mass exodus from Shuri (the capital was also moved to Naha) in search of employment. Many migrated to the rural areas at this time and founded new *yaadui* villages. Higa relates[4] that in 1879 virtually all of the seventy houses of his *uji* (Raku Uji) were located in Shuri but that by 1890 the greater portion of these had scattered into all parts of Okinawa. In some instances, however, a whole lineage would move in a body to establish a new community.

The gentry and nobility were organized into a class system of nine ranks and eighteen grades, and some *uji* included virtually the whole range of grades and ranks. For example, in Shō Uji, which contained the royal family, there were many lineages encompassing the whole of the upper-class ranks. According to Okinawan practice, the first son inherited the rank of his father. Younger sons dropped one rank, but no one of upper-class birth fell below the lowest rank of gentry to become a commoner. Theoretically, positions in the bureaucracy were attained on the basis of achievement in the examination system. Old informants stated that all households within the *uji* were regarded as equal when it came to participating and having a voice in the *uji*'s affairs, but because the head of the founding house often had the highest hereditary rank, the membership tended to defer to his wishes. This deference appears to have been mitigated somewhat by the presence of other men who had attained high government positions on the basis of personal ability and whose words therefore often carried greater weight.

HOUSE NAMES, SURNAMES, PERSONAL NAMES. Within the rural community of commoner origin there is some tendency for lineages to be spatially restricted; hence the not uncommon equation of the term *haru* (field or neighborhood) with lineage. This spatial alignment of a lineage's households within the community has resulted from the practice of branch houses being established in close proximity to their parent house. The system of household names, *yaa n naa*, tends to identify a house with a particular lineage and/or to denote its parent house. In Kanegusuku, for example, the household Naka Ufu Iri (Middle Great West) long ago branched off from Ufu Iri (Great West), and over a period of some several generations a number of younger sons have left Naka Ufu Iri to establish branch houses nearby. Directly descendant from it are Mee Naka Ufu Iri (Front Middle Great West), Agari Naka Ufu Iri (East Middle Great West), Fee Naka Ufu Iri (South Middle Great West), Sannan Naka Ufu Iri (Third-Son Middle Great West), Yunan Naka Ufu Iri (Fourth-Son Middle Great West), Mii Naka Ufu Iri (New Middle Great West), and Tuku Naka Ufu Iri (Tuku Middle Great West). The first three *yaa n naa* indicate their geographical position with regard to their parent house, but all include the name of the parent house, Naka Ufu Iri, as part of their *yaa n naa*. Sometimes, the first branch house of a parent house may take the *yaa n naa* of its parent and simply add the diminutive suffix *gwa*; later, when other branch houses appear, this may be changed, perhaps by prefixing the word *jinan* (second-son) to the *yaa n naa* of the parent house.

Until the Japanese forced the adoption of family names, the *yaa n naa* alone denoted the various houses and identified their families. In the old kingdom, the farmers were not permitted to change their village residence, and younger sons usually built in close proximity to their parent house; consequently, in a relatively stable community it is still a comparatively easy matter to determine the network of relationships within the lineages on the basis of the *yaa n naa*. In most villages, the *yaa n naa* still remain better known than the new family names. The adoption of a family name seems to have been largely a matter of individual choice, although occasionally an entire lineage adopted the same name. These new family names are always common Okinawan place names, although in recent decades the practice has developed of giving these a Japanese pronunciation.[5]

Each upper-class *uji* possesses a single-character name read in the Chinese fashion ('on'); these names were assigned by the government at the suggestion of China when a genealogical records office was created in 1689 and were used thereafter as surnames. In addition, all male members of an *uji* shared the same initial character (*nanui-gashira*) in their personal names. All male members of Bu Uji, for example, had the same surname, Bu, and the same initial character, Ki, in their personal names; thus, Bu Kie, Bu Kizo, Bu Kizen, Bu Kiyo would all be male members of Bu Uji. This system of naming was designated *toonaa* or *karanaa* (Chinese name) to distinguish it from the system of using purely Okinawan names. With the advent of Japanese control, the use of *uji* names as surnames was abandoned;[6] however, the common *nanui-gashira* or initial character in personal names is still retained by males of upper-class descent.

Among the upper classes there was a second surname, usually an Okinawan place name. It was common practice for younger sons on establishing a branch house to adopt a different name from that of their father or to do so in two or three generations after establishment of a branch house. Often, these names were taken from the name of the place where the founder of the new line served as administrator for the government. But in some cases an entire lineage would retain the name of its founder; so, with respect to the Okinawan surname, no consistent practice was followed, unlike the case of the *toonaa*. Frequently, in recognition of meritorious service, the government would award a fictitious governorship, with or without pension, to an official; in most cases the name of this area would be adopted as the family name. As a result, there tend to be a number of Okinawan surnames within the upper-class *uji*; sometimes these are borne by an entire lineage, at other times not. After the Japanese assumed control, these were retained as the legal surnames. As these names are usually common place names, they do not serve to distinguish the former upper-class person from the former commoner.

Both classes possessed purely Okinawan personal names which were determined by kinship relation. It was a fast rule that fathers and sons did not share the same personal name, but the first son usually received his father's father's name. Until the grandson reached the age of fifteen or so, he and his grandfather were differentiated by the addition of the diminutive suffix *gwa* to the grandson's name. No consistent practice seems to have been followed for the younger sons; frequently, the second son was given the name of his mother's father, and the third son that of the paternal grandfather's brother, but others followed the male side exclusively and gave the names of grandfather's brothers to all younger sons. The first daughter received the name of her paternal grandmother or that of her maternal grandmother; again, a lack of consistency prevents establishment of any rule.[7] This system of naming still prevails in many rural villages but has been generally discontinued among urban peoples.

KIN GROUP AND MARRIAGE. The Okinawan sib and lineage are agamous and appear to have been so for a considerable period of time. In the past, village endogamy was an unvarying rule, but within the community the young people were free to select mates irrespective of lineage affiliation. There seems to have been some preference for marriage within the kin group (this pertains only to commoners), although marriage to father's brother's daughter was frowned upon. Formerly, the practice of a bride price existed among the commoners, but it is said that this was not paid when the marriage was between two members of the same lineage or sib. There was, therefore, some sentiment among the poorer families (and the Okinawan farmer was tragically impoverished) for marrying kin; as one old informant put it, "We hated to see the money leave the family." In Kanegusuku I found that 50 per cent of the marriages represented cases of intermarriage within the lineage. In the old village, the distinctions among kinsmen, kindred, and neighbor were somewhat tangled for ego, and as might be anticipated—despite the existence of patri-sibs and patri-lineages—kinship terminology was of the bilateral type.

In marriage, class lines were virtually those of caste. Marriage between *yukatchu* and *hakusoo* was extremely rare and continued to be so until well into this century. Among the upper classes, community endogamy as a marriage rule was nonexistent; moreover, a bride price was not demanded by upper-class families, and marrying outside the kin group appears to have been the commonly preferred practice.[8] At present, urban dwellers show no preference for kin over non-kin marriages.[9] In the rural areas, marriage within the community still prevails in perhaps a majority of cases, and the tendency for kin group marriage may still be discerned, though it is less frequent than in the past. Although the Japanese exhorted the rural people to avoid inbreeding, the net result seems to have been merely to make them sensitive and somewhat reluctant to discuss the subject, rather than to turn them from the practice.

A woman is a member of her father's sib before marriage and her husband's thereafter; however, in actual practice she always retains a ritual tie to her father's or eldest brother's house. If her natal house is nearby after marriage, she may pray regularly at its ancestral shrine; if not, she prays there at least once each year. After death, she is usually buried in her husband's tomb, but if divorced or remarried, in that of her first son or brother. The ritual life of every *munchu* or *uji*, however, depends to a great degree on its female priestesses; these women must always serve in their natal sib, never in that of the husband. In her later years, a woman may be inclined to take a more active interest in her brother's sib than in that of her husband; she may voluntarily assist the *kudii* in ceremonial activities, joining the informal entourage which often accompanies the priestesses in the performance of their duties. Sometimes she may actually become a *kudii* in her natal kin group. The dual kin group affiliation which women often maintain throughout their lives is without significance for their offspring, who are exclusively aligned with the kin group of the husband. In many cases, of course, mother and father are kinsmen.

EXTINCTION OF A HOUSE. The extinction of a member house is a matter of concern for the entire kin group, and to the utmost of its powers the group will try to avoid this eventuality. If a man is without male heirs he is obliged to adopt a son in order to perpetuate his house, but the adopted son must be a member of the same sib. Son-in-law adoption is not resorted to by Okinawans unless the daughter's husband is of the same sib, for it is believed that a family cannot be maintained through the female line for even a single generation. The adopted individual must also be in the son generation, and the Japanese procedure of sometimes adopting a younger brother is not practiced. The ideal candidate for adoption is an elder brother's younger son, with second choice going to a younger brother's younger son. If neither of these is available, then a younger son in a close ascendant house will be adopted, since, ideally, adopted sons from ascendant houses are said to be preferred to those from descendant houses. The adopted son enjoys all the privileges and prerogatives of a natural son and inherits the family property and ancestral tablets.

If a house becomes extinct (and many were exterminated during the war), the lineage is not telescoped; instead, the ancestral tablets are taken by the *muutu-yaa*, the closest ascendant house, or by a descendant house. They are retained by the house until such time as one of its younger sons establishes a branch house. This person then takes the ancestral tablets of the extinct house, adopts its *yaa n naa*, and prays to the tablets as if they were those of his own father, grandfather, etc. In effect, although several generations may have passed, this person will have been adopted by the extinct house.

As a rule, a first son is never eligible for adoption, for it is his duty to inherit the ancestral tablets of his father and to pray for the father's spirit. One notable exception to this principle may occur should the founding house of a *munchu* or *uji* be threatened with extinction, in which case the first son of the closest descendant house (i.e., the senior branch house) may be adopted into the founding house. In this case, the second son in the branch house succeeds to the position of the first son. I found three instances of this practice, but I have also heard shamans advising against it on the grounds that ancestral entanglement would result.

A basic principle of the Okinawan ancestral system holds that no individual, particularly no male, should die without descendants to pray for his spirit. If a younger son dies before marriage and the establishment of a branch house, his memorial tablet is retained in his father's house until another younger son establishes a branch house. Then, the memorial tablet is taken to the new house to be prayed to as its founder. A child who dies before reaching the age of seven is thought to be unfilial and is not accorded this treatment. The feeling also exists that the small child is in a sense prehuman; passing the age of seven, therefore, serves to designate the individual as a social being. Hence, deceased male children of eight years and above ultimately become the posthumous founders of branch houses.

A woman's memorial tablet, as noted above, is kept in the house of her husband or first son; but when a woman dies before marriage, her tablet remains in her natal house. There is no concept of a woman's founding a house.[10] In principle as well as in practice, virtually every male succeeds to the headship of his father's house or founds a branch house.

As a consequence of the battle for Okinawa in World War II, many houses were extinguished, and in virtually every village one encounters empty house lots, each with a very small, box-like, shrine structure at its center, representing the ancestral shrine of the extinct family. Close relatives in the lineage periodically pray and make offerings at this site; if there are no living relatives in the community, unrelated neighbors will tend it in the belief that untended spirits of the dead pose a potential threat to the living. Ultimately, however, a new house will be established there by some male relative according to the process described above, and in time all of the temporarily extinct houses will be revived. In this manner, the integrity of the kin group is preserved.

GENEALOGIES. Until recent decades, commoner *munchu* were without written genealogies; however, within the local lineage the actual descent pattern was well known or could be easily traced, as each house preserved close ritual ties with its parent house and all of its immediate branch houses. Exact relationships in the sib tend to be less well known, particularly in a large organization; often the founding house of an old branch lineage may be unsure of its immediate parent house in the parent lineage. In all events, however, the possession of a common tomb and common ancestor serves to bind together the membership of a large sib in a feeling of close kinship.

All of the upper-class *uji* have possessed accurate genealogies (*chiiji*) dating back at least to the time of the establishment of a government genealogical records office in 1689, and many are able (with what degree of accuracy I am not certain) to trace back their ancestry several hundred years. Bu Uji, for example, has genealogical records tracing its ancestry as far back as the early fourteenth century. After the establishment of the government office, each entry in a genealogy was stamped and authenticated by that office. In a very large *uji*, each of the lineages and often each house also possesses records tracing its position in the larger sib.

In present practice, females are sometimes not recorded in a genealogy; however, I noted in examining a number of genealogies that this laxity in recording females has occurred only for the last five or six generations. Prior to that, females as well as males were recorded, which suggests that there has been an increasing stress on the male line in Okinawan culture. Higa suggests[11] that when the *aji* began their move to Shuri in the late fifteenth century, many of their relatives may have been left behind in the rural areas and hence were not accorded upper-class status. So far as I was able to determine, none of the *uji* recognizes any affinity with commoners residing in the rural districts of its ancestral founders, but it is to be noted that many rural *munchu* of commoner descent claim that their first ancestor was an *aji*. Moreover, the founder's tomb in a commoner *munchu* is called *ajishii*, *ajishii-baka*, or *aji-baka*[12]; although I am uncertain as to the exact etymology of *ajishii*, some old informants expressed the belief that *aji* refers to the former lord of the *majiri* and that *shii* may represent an old word for bones or tomb. While these interpretations should be regarded as speculation, the existence of a founder's tomb called *aji-baka* among the commoners raises the possibility that the ancient villages may have been clan communities and the *aji* clan chiefs.

KIN GROUP DIVISION AND AMALGAMATION. When a *munchu* becomes large or its houses widely scattered, the more isolated lineages may construct temporary tombs for the interment of the corpse until bone washing takes place; thereafter, the bones are transported to the common tomb for permanent burial. In time, if interaction is infrequent, there may be a tendency for these isolated elements to function as independent *munchu*, and eventually the temporary tomb may be used for permanent burial as well. However, the ties to the parent kin group are not completely severed; rather, the case becomes analogous to that among members of an upper-class *uji* in which each house or lineage possesses its own tomb. The distant tomb of the *munchu*'s first ancestor and the founding house continues to be visited, though less frequently, for the purpose of prayers and ritual offerings. No matter how great the distance, some degree of ritual interaction is preserved, and I have recorded instances in which *munchu* segments residing in South America or Hawaii have regularly sent money for tomb maintenance and ritual activities.[13]

Occasionally, two small, unrelated *munchu* may combine to form a larger organization. Where this has occurred, the instigation for this action may usually be traced to a *yuta* who has "heard" from the ancestors that the two groups were once related; in such cases, economic necessity may have encouraged the two small kin groups to amalgamate for construction of a large tomb which could not be afforded separately. In these cases, both groups are small, live in the same village, and have probably intermarried over a long period of time, so that a real kinship already exists on the female side. I did not find a single case of a lineage segment within a large *munchu* breaking off and establishing a new *munchu* through combination with an unrelated kin group; however, Watanabe records[14] one case in which a very small kin group related only through marriage to a large *munchu* was incorporated into the larger group. This combination of unrelated kin groups is a very rare occurrence and appears to be the result of a shaman's advice and/or a last resort taken when small size threatens survival.

ADMINISTRATION. The great size which the Okinawan kin group frequently attains necessitates some machinery for effective handling of its administrative affairs—collecting fees, tomb maintenance, and ritual events. The eldest male in the founding house (*suu muutu*) functions as the titular head, *munchu-gashira*, of the group; but in most cases his position is purely nominal. Actual administration may be entrusted to an appointed chief, *wii* (head or superior), who may come from any one of the member houses. He is aided by one or more administrative assistants, *peeku* (the number depending on the organization's size), and a treasurer, *jingamii*. These men are appointed and advised by an informal council of *munchu* elders. While any male household head is welcome to attend these meetings, in actual practice only men in the middle and late years of life show much interest in these matters. Offices are generally conferred on men of recognized ability, without stipulation as to length of term, and, except for the *munchu-gashira*, no position is retained on a hereditary basis.

Ritual matters are controlled by the *kudii* (the *munchu* or *uji* priestesses), who bear the responsibility of praying for the welfare of the group. Significantly, the *kudii* are oriented in this function primarily toward the *kami* and remote ancestors who have attained *kami* status. They are assisted by several women called *atai* (lot or turn) or *saji* (receiver), who are selected each year from among the older women. Frequently, their selection is determined by lots, as the outcome is thought to be influenced by the *kami*; in other groups, they are appointed in rotation from among the member households. It is their function to collect ritual offerings or money from the various households and to assist the *kudii* in ceremonial preparations. None of these positions is inherited, as they are in the community hierarchy.

A few sibs own common property whose products or rental income are used to finance tomb maintenance and ritual expenditures, but in the majority of cases all financing is done by means of levies against the membership. At least four types of levy exist, and their amounts are determined by the administrative officers in consultation with the elders. The most common tax, *usakati* ('sake' fee), is used, as the name suggests, for purchasing the wine and other offerings used in ritual. This may be levied yearly, quarterly, or prior to each major ritual event. All adult members, male and female, are required to pay the amount stipulated as *usakati*. Another tax, *kibui* (lit., "smoke," but implying a "house"), is assessed yearly on each household; this is used for general administrative expenditures and miscellaneous expenses of the *kudii*. Whenever the necessity for a special expenditure arises—for example, for tomb repair or reconstruction—a special tax, *nmari* (from *nmariing*, meaning "to bear") is imposed on all members regardless of age. Lastly, tomb maintenance and repair periodically necessitate a *munchu*-corvée *buu* (share), which requires that each member household supply one able-bodied adult, male or female, for each day of work. After the war, when most tombs were in ruins, this procedure enabled many *munchu* collectively to reconstruct their common tomb.

Tomb

Much has been written of the large tombs, *haka* or *paka*, which are ubiquitous on the Okinawan scene; it is estimated that there are currently 35,000 of these on the island. Three basic tomb styles exist. Most notable are the large, house-size, omega- or horseshoe-shaped tombs modeled on those of Fukien Province, China. Less impressive but more common are the smaller, gable-roofed tombs generally associated with the upper classes. Lastly, there are many tombs which have been dug or carved out of hillsides and which are marked by a stone front and small door; this type is frequently very old.

The ancestral founder's tomb—*ajishii*, *ajishii-baka*, or *aji-baka*—constitutes one of the major points of homage in *uji* and *munchu* worship. This tomb is usually rather small and is often dug into a hillside; it is not used for burial, being frequented only as a ritual site. In an upper-class *uji*, the *ajishii* is located in the rural area where the ancestors who moved to Shuri some four hundred years ago first resided. Bu Uji has its *ajishii* in the village of Teruya, where their ancestor had ruled as *aji*; at the present time, no members of this *uji* reside in that village, but the site is visited annually by the entire membership. In the case of commoner *munchu*, the *ajishii* is found in the village where its senior lineage resides.

Among the upper classes, each family possesses its own tomb, and there is no common burial; however, the tomb of the lineage founder and often that of the first ancestor in Shuri constitute secondary places of homage after the *ajishii*. Most upper-class tombs are located in the greater Naha-Shuri area; only in the period since Japanese annexation, when many upper-class families left Shuri, have they begun to construct tombs elsewhere.

Commoner *munchu* follow the practice of burying in a common tomb, and these tombs are usually located close to the *ajishii* in the village of the first lineage. Commoner tombs, which are sometimes of great size, are often constructed with two separate chambers, each with its own entrances. The right chamber, *shiruhirashii* (probably, bone-drying place), functions as a temporary tomb where the casket is deposited after the funeral. When a period of from one to three years has elapsed, bone washing takes place. The cleaned bones are then placed in an urn, *jiishigaami*, which is stored in the left-hand chamber, *tooshii*, for permanent burial. The bones remain in these urns for three or four generations, or until such time as no living person shall have known the deceased; then the contents are dumped in a pit located at the rear of the chamber. Ultimately, the bones of all members are thus mingled together; as the membership of some *munchu* includes several thousand persons, and as these tombs have been used for many generations, a single tomb may contain the bones of thousands.

Those who have brought distinction to the *munchu* may be placed directly in the *tooshii*; this is considered the highest honor a *munchu* can bestow on a member. A *nuru*, for example, should be accorded this respect, as may an old *kudii* who has served for many years.[15] Some *munchu* may accord this treatment to all who attained great age, usually the eighty-eighth year. Conversely, feeling often runs high against those who have brought public disgrace upon the group; cases of suicide are sometimes denied burial in the common tomb, and their bodies may be turned over to the Buddhist priest for cremation. Children dying before their seventh year are considered unfilial and may not receive tomb burial; sometimes they are placed under a small mound of rocks near the common tomb, or they may be secreted in a coral outcropping along the beach. Those who have committed a violent crime or who have died from violence are believed possessed by ghosts (*majimung*) or malevolent spirits (*yanamung*); hence, their spirits would be unwelcome among the ancestors, and they are sometimes refused interment. In any event, such problems are taken to the shaman to determine the cause and suggest remedial action. It is extremely rare for a childless Okinawan to adopt a non-kinsman, but when this is done, the adopted son does not realize membership in the *munchu* and is returned to his *munchu* of birth for burial. I have recorded instances in which this action was delayed as long as three or four generations, yet it is felt that ultimately the bones should be returned.

When the membership of a *munchu* is widely scattered, members distant from the main tomb may construct a temporary tomb, *kai-baka*, but, after bone washing, the bone jars are transported to the common tomb for final interment. Informants who had resided in Micronesia, Hawaii, and South America stated that Okinawans in those areas have constructed *kai-baka* but that in most cases the urns are ultimately brought to Okinawa for final burial.

Funerals, as will be shown, are not of direct concern to the sib, but are a matter for the household, close relatives, friends, and neighbors. Occasionally, when the deceased has served the group by playing an active role in its affairs, a small amount of money may be sent as an obituary gift to the bereaved family, but otherwise the event receives little attention. Nonetheless, anticipation of common burial serves to unite the members of a *munchu* in a lasting bond. From the older people especially, one hears frequent expressions of pride in the size and beauty of their tomb, and most Okinawans seem to exhibit a marked concern about the appearance and upkeep of their final resting place.

Kudii

Within the *munchu* and *uji* there are female priestesses (and infrequently male priests) who perform ritual functions on behalf of the group. These women are called *kudii, ukudii,* or *kudingwa* and are sometimes described as *munchu-gami* or *munchu kaminchu*. All *kudii* are differentiated as *uminai kudii* (sister *kudii*) or *umikii kudii* (brother *kudii*), in accordance with a belief that wherever there is worship there must be sibling *kaminchu* (*kami choodee*). Although the *kudii* who are *umikii kudii* wear their white robes in the male fashion, there is no distinction in function between the two groups. An effort does seem to be made as far as possible to maintain an even ratio of *uminai* and *umikii kudii*.

In a large *munchu* or *uji* having many *kudii* (perhaps a dozen or more), the *kudii* may have special ritual functions. All kin groups, as part of their ritual life, pray to the former national sites of worship, and this task is always delegated to the *kudii*. Some of the large sibs may have a special *kudii* to pray to the former castle site of Hokuzan or the northern kingdom; she is designated the Nakijin *kudii* (after the castle's name) and periodically undertakes pilgrimages in behalf of the group to this site. Similarly, there may be a Shuri *kudii* (or a Chuzan *kudii*) and a Nanzan *kudii*, who are entrusted with rites honoring those areas. On major ritual occasions, all *kudii* pray together. Frequently, the oldest *kudii* acts informally as the head of the group, even though her *kami* rank may be below that of some of the others.

There is no fixed number of *kudii* for the *munchu* or *uji*, although there should be a minimum of at least two. Unlike the *kaminchu* of the community, the *kudii* does not inherit her office, and she may "appear" from any member house, with the proviso that she serve only in the kin group of her natal house. It is believed that the *kami* determine the number of *kudii* by giving "notification" to those who are destined for this role. The notification usually progresses into *taari*, as in the case of the shaman. Although community priestesses may experience *kami-daari* prior to taking office, it is by no means a universal occurrence among them; but for the *kudii*, some form of *taari* usually precedes their taking office. Viewed collectively, the *kudii* tend to display far more disturbed personal histories than do the *kaminchu* of the community; in this respect, they differ very little from the *yuta*, and not infrequently *yuta* will be found serving as *kudii* in their kin group.

When a new *kudii* is thought to have appeared, a few older women visit one or more shamans or fortunetellers to determine whether the prospect has *saadaka nmari*. If so, the new *kudii* visits the founding house (*suu muutu*) and prays at the shrine of the founder. A meeting or series of meetings is then called, at which the prospective *kudii* speaks before the assembled *kudii* and *munchu* elders. At this time, she tells of her experiences—what she has seen and heard, where she has visited for prayer—and identifies her *chiji*. Usually, the *chiji* is that of a former *kudii* now deceased, which the new *kudii* claims to have inherited from her predecessor, but she may claim a heretofore unrecognized *chiji*, a forgotten (or nearly forgotten) ancestral spirit whose ritual neglect has caused trouble for the kin group. She may also engage in some verbal sparring with established *kudii* over her qualifications to join their ranks. The whole matter may be debated for many months, depending on her assertiveness and the degree of her recovery from *taari*. Ultimately, she usually succeeds in overcoming all opposition, for the additional *kudii* is viewed as lending strength to the ritual efforts of the group, especially if she fills a vacant office.

Some *kudii* said that they would not enter office in an even-numbered year of life, but I did not find this to be universally true. The *kudii*'s installation usually takes place at the time of a regular ceremony conducted by the other *kudii* and is generally a very simple affair. Thereafter, she regards the anniversaries of her installation as birthdates marking her rebirth as a *kami* person. The position is retained for life, as in the case of community *kaminchu* and shamans.

On major ceremonial occasions, the *kudii* dress in white robes identical to those worn by the female *kaminchu* in the community. In rural villages of commoner origin, the *kudii* often represent their *munchu* or lineage segment in communal rites; consequently, the kin group, through its *kudii*, participates in all of the major agricultural rites of the community. The *kudii* of the *munchu* are not formally affiliated with communal ritual activity but participate on invitation from the *nuru*. In most communities, this is virtually automatic, but in some villages they are not asked. The major rites presided over by the *kudii* are those of the agricultural cycle, occurring in the second, third, fifth, and sixth lunar months. Formerly, the urban *kudii* visited certain major ritual sites in Shuri and Naha on those dates, and at present these rites are still observed at the founding house of the *uji*.

Much the same general restrictions as apply to the community *kaminchu* regarding the avoidance of pollution also apply to the *kudii* as well; they are, therefore, *kaminchu* in the fullest sense. This is particularly evident in the matter of tomb rites, in that they do not pray at the tomb in any official capacity. A *kudii* may attend a tomb ceremony as an ordinary member but not while wearing her white robes of office. Restrictions on attending funerals, visiting houses of sickness, or assisting at a birth are far less severe than those applying to the *nuru*, but *kudii* do nonetheless seek to avoid contamination as far as possible, particularly at ceremonial times. In her official capacity, the *kudii* prays only to the *kami* and to those older ancestral spirits who are regarded as *kami*; she does not pray to the spirits of the recent dead, which is the function of the deceased's close relatives. In several sibs which lost all of their *kudii* during the war, their function had been temporarily assumed by the *saji* or *atai*. These women do not wear the white robes of a *kudii* and are not regarded as *kaminchu*.

The white robes of the *kudii* and any sacred paraphernalia possessed by the kin group are usually stored in the *suu muutu*, but when the kin group is widely scattered, the *kudii*'s robes may be kept at the founding house of the local lineage. These are stored in the first room (on the right-hand side), where there is a small shrine shelf for the first ancestor apart from the ancestral shrine in the second, or middle, room of the house. The *kudii* pray here before and after all ceremonies conducted for the kin group or community. Many *munchu*, particularly in southern Okinawa, keep a small box, called *binshii*, in the founding house and occasionally in a *naka muutu*. A *binshii*, as noted above, is a container for carrying incense, grain, and wine used as ceremonial offerings; whenever the *kudii* perform a ceremony, the *binshii* are taken with them. Generally, each lineage within the community has one *binshii*, and when the various *ugwanju* are visited for communal rites, the *binshii* are placed before the *kaminchu* during the prayer.

In the front yard of the *suu muutu* (and sometimes of an old *naka muutu*), on the right-hand side, there may be found a small shrine structure for the worship of the first ancestor and old ancestors who have become *kami*;[16] this shrine is called *tunchi-yaa* (occasionally *mee ashagi*). Inside *tunchi-yaa* there are one or (usually) two three-stone hearths, depicting the *fii nu kang*, and two shrine shelves above, one for the first ancestor and the other for other ancestors who have become *kami*. These *kami* are prayed to through the *fii nu kang*, which here again serves as an intermediary between man and the *kami*. The *kudii* alone are believed possessed of the power to pray through to the first ancestor, while ordinary members may reach only the lesser ancestral *kami*. If the *suu muutu* should happen to be the founding house of the community, this shrine may be regarded as a community shrine as well and may be used by anyone for the purpose of prayer.

When the founding house of the lineage or sib happens also to be the *niiyaa*, or founding house of the community, the *niigami* and *niitchu* of the community reside there. If the house is *ufu muutu* for the *munchu*, the the *niitchu* will also be the *munchu-gashira*, or titular head of the sib. The *niigami* usually participates in her *munchu*'s rites together with the *kudii*, but her ritual duties at *niiyaa* pertain largely to her function as a community *kaminchu* rather than as a *munchu* priestess.

Annual Rites

Kin group rites may be divided into two classes: those focusing on the tomb and ancestral tablets and oriented toward the ancestral spirits, and those directed toward the *kami* and ancestral *kami* and conducted for the welfare of the membership. Only the latter class of rites involves the *kudii* in their official capacity, whereas the former are the responsibility of the entire membership. Generally, rites performed by the *kudii* are conducted without any sizable participation on the part of the membership. As in the case of the community, all ritual events are determined according to the lunar calendar.

The *kudii* are expected to pray at the *suu muutu* on the first and fifteenth of each month, but in a very large sib with many *kudii* these observances may be confined to the *naka muutu* for those *kudii* in distant areas. At these times, they will pray at the shrine shelf for the first ancestor within the house and/or at *tunchi-yaa*. Hearth rites within the founding house are conducted by the senior female member, as in the case of all houses, and are not the direct concern of the *kudii*.

In many villages, as noted above, it is the function of the *kudii* to give representation to their kin group in all communal rites conducted by the *nuru* and her associates. Before and after these events the *kudii* pray at the founding house of their respective lineages.

During the first few days of the new year, each branch house must visit its parent house (*muutu-yaa*) for prayer at the ancestral shrine. In the same period, visits are made to the local *naka muutu*, and each house is expected to send a representative to the *suu muutu*. At this time, *kudii* go there for prayer to the ancestral founder; they are also expected to visit *nundunchi* in their community for prayers with the *nuru*.

The major *munchu* or *uji* ceremony of the year occurs on a propitious day during the twelve-day period between the twenty-second day of the second month and the third day of the third month. This event is called *ushiimii* ('sei mei' in Japanese; 'ching ming' in Chinese). It was noted in Chapter V that this ceremony was first observed by the king in 1768, suggesting even more recent adoption by the commoner. Among the upper classes, each family visits its tomb and sometimes that of its lineage founder for a day of prayers and feasting in the tomb yard. During the same period they journey to the tomb of the *uji* founder; this event is called *kami ushiimii*, and all members are expected to attend. In the case of the commoner *munchu*, for which the common tomb and that of the first ancestor stand adjacent, the two events are simply combined. Those *shiimii* observances which I witnessed in 1954, 1956, 1957, and 1960 appeared to be wholly unorganized, with family groups arriving and departing throughout the entire day. Each family brought food, drink, and incense, which were offered with prayers at the tomb door; afterwards, feasting and considerable drinking (on the part of males and older females) followed. Presumably, those attending should deport themselves well and pass their time discussing the dead and their achievements; but in practice the event is more like a picnic, and most of the visitors spend their time gossiping and renewing ties with distant kin, who often have not been seen since the previous year. As the turnout usually approximates 100 per cent, with the entire family including children attending, this event serves the function of an annual rite of intensification.

During the thirteenth, fourteenth, fifteenth, and sometimes sixteenth days of the seventh month, the great Buddhist festival for the dead, *ubung* ('o bon'), takes place. A week prior to this event, on the seventh (referred to by the Japanese name 'tanabata') of the month, families individually visit the tomb, asking their relatives to return for *ubung*. The ritual events marking this period are largely confined to observances at the household ancestral shrine and are generally limited to members of the household, but each branch house is expected to visit its parent house and *ufu muutu* or local *naka muutu*. Distant lineages follow the expedient practice of sending one or two representatives to the *ufu muutu*.

In the eighth lunar month, some *kudii* pray to the former sites of national worship, particularly the castle sites of the early kingdoms. Yearly on this occasion, they do *utuushi* (worship from afar) to these places, but periodically—every seventh, ninth, or thirteenth year (no consistent practice is followed)—they make a pilgrimage there, praying at the major *ugwanju*. In a rural village, there may or may not be a fixed site for doing *utuushi*, but in Naha and Shuri two sites have been traditionally used by all *munchu* and *uji* for this purpose. Sachi Hijaa, near Tomari Port in Naha, is the traditional site for *utuushi* to Nakijin, former capital of the northern kingdom, while Bing Utaki, in Shuri, is used to pray to the east, specifically the Chinen and Tamagusuku districts and Kudaka Island, containing the mythical first settlement sites. These events correspond to Nakijin *nubui* and *agari mai*, formerly observed by the national priestesses in the state religious hierarchy.

Special Rites

Whenever a tomb is rebuilt or repaired, religious rites and celebration follow completion of the task. In the religious observance preceding the celebration, representatives from each household are expected to pray and burn incense at the tomb door. The *kudii* do not wear their white robes or participate in an official capacity at this time, and at one tomb-reconstruction ceremony which I attended at Itoman in 1953, a *yuta* member of the *munchu* first prayed at the tomb door on behalf of the group. Anniversaries of tomb repair or reconstruction are observed thereafter on the third, seventh, thirteenth, twenty-fifth, and thirty-third years commemorating that date; these dates are the same as those observed by the family for a deceased member. There is some sentiment, although not always put into practice, that the tomb should be repaired after the observance of the thirty-third year; usually, the surface is cleaned and new mortar applied at this time.

A *kudii* may be engaged by individual members or households of the *munchu* to pray on their behalf. Sometimes when an individual reaches his bad-luck year (*nmari-dushi*), a *kudii*, either the oldest one or one of high *saa*, may be summoned to pray with the individual at the household hearth. Prior to a long trip across the sea (to Japan or the southern islands of the Ryukyus for example), the *kudii* may be asked to pray at the family hearth with the traveler. I have also recorded instances of the *kudii* being asked to pray at the family pigpen to recover a lost *mabui*. At a time of sickness in the house, the *kudii* may be asked to pray at the places of prayer in the village for the individual's recovery. These practices are not universally followed; sometimes a *nuru* or *niigami* may be asked to pray for one who is about to travel or who is sick; or, instead, a *yuta* may be hired to perform these functions. Much depends on the specific circumstances and individual choice rather than on any fixed principle.

Change

It is not uncommon at the present time to hear young people voice disbelief in, if not actual disgust with, the old religion; but few are critical of the *munchu* (or *uji*) system and its obviously religious basis. Some state that the *munchu* meetings and observances seem boring and that they are loath to participate actively in its affairs; but, when pressed, they readily acknowledge that they will no doubt become increasingly concerned with the *munchu* as they grow older and "begin to think about such things." It is to be noted that the Okinawan family system, though differing somewhat from the Japanese in that it preserves a more extensive degree of organization, did not conflict with the Japanese sentiments and law which recognized the family as the cornerstone of society. Moreover, the Okinawan family system, like that of Japan, accords a primacy of interest to the male line. In their structural relationship, the Okinawan *muutu-yaa* and *wakari-yaa* differ only slightly from the Japanese 'honke' and 'bunke'; likewise, the *suu muutu* bears appreciable resemblance to the Japanese 'sō honke.' In both cases, an ancestral system with a ritual focus on the memorial tablets derives from common Buddhist origins. In this instance, the effect of the Japanese annexation did not promote conflict between the old and the new, as both were compatible if not identical. To no small degree, this factor has contributed to the continued vigor of the common-descent group.

By freeing the peasant from his serflike status, the Japanese set off an extensive population movement which often served to make interaction between the members of the kin group difficult; sometimes, as a consequence of this scattering, there occurred a segmentation in the kin group and occasionally a realignment of kin group ties. The complete disruption of all normal life which occurred during the battle for Okinawa in World War II served to further accelerate these developments, and it is to be expected that the current breakdown of the folk-community will further hasten the process. The net result, I anticipate, will be that the extended kin groups will become smaller in size.

In the first decade following World War II, the number of *kudii* was substantially less than in the prewar period, as many were killed during the fighting; but by the second decade it was apparent that their ranks were being replenished. Some informants confidently predict that successors will "appear" for all unfilled positions. Among the upper-class *uji*, which tend to have a more educated membership than the commoner *munchu*, there are some that are wholly without any *kudii*. The leader of one *uji* proudly remarked, "Our members are too well educated to believe in women like that." In this particular case, there is currently one woman within that *uji* who claims to be a *kudii*, but the top male leaders have refused to accord her recognition. This has caused considerable dissension among the members of the lineage to which the woman belongs, and there has been some talk of breaking off and forming a new *uji*, but most members are said to be reluctant to take this step. Probably, therefore, the *uji* leaders will ultimately achieve success in their avowed aim of functioning without *kudii*. The effect of dropping the *kudii* will, of course, be a complete transfer of all kin group affairs into male hands. While this prospect is thus far limited to a few upper-class *uji*, it seems likely that in time the trend will take hold among the commoners of the rural areas as well.

VIII

HOUSEHOLD RELIGION

Introduction

The average Okinawan household contains approximately five members, but an examination of the household registers ('koseki') indicates a range of from one to occasionally more than a dozen persons. The basic unit within the household is the nuclear family, consisting of husband, wife, and their offspring; however, a *muutu-yaa*, or parent house, may contain two or more nuclear families representing successive generations linked through the first-son line. According to government records, there appear to be only relatively slight differences in average size between urban and rural households.

The Okinawan house lot is invariably surrounded by a wall or hedge which often attains the height of a man; the common materials for wall construction are stone, woven bamboo, and, recently, wood. Access to the interior is gained through a single gate, which is partially blocked by a screen (*himpung*) affording privacy from the public view, but as the house lots abut and houses are close together, loud conversation or quarreling may be easily heard by neighbors. The house tends to be centrally located within the lot, and so far as possible it faces in a southerly direction to gain full advantage of the sun, for light, and the cool prevailing breeze in summer. Today, virtually all houses are patterned on the Japanese style, with raised floors and sliding walls in place of doors and windows; roofs are of thatch or tile. The number of rooms is relatively proportionate to the family's wealth. For nearly a decade after the war, many people lived in temporary shacks, but today these have nearly disappeared, save in the urban slums and among the poorest farm families. Generally, the average farm house has two main rooms of approximately equal size across the front, with possibly one or two small, narrow, storage or sleeping rooms in back. The first room on the right-hand side is considered the best room, and guests are usually received there. Along the back wall of this room is a decorative alcove *utuku*, which also functions as a place of prayer. In the second room, which might be likened to a living room, the Buddhist ancestral shrine, *buchidang* or *gujiiring*, is situated against the back wall facing the gate. The kitchen is invariably placed on the extreme left, and often, in accordance with traditional practice, it may have a separate roof and virtually constitute a separate building. It has a dirt floor. The cooking site is located against the back wall. The simplest hearth, still found in some rural dwellings, consists of three elongate stones set upright, forming a triangular base that affords support for a cooking pot. More commonly, a newer style of fireplace fashioned from brick or concrete, with two or three holes on top into which flanged caldrons may be fitted, has replaced the simpler hearth or stands beside it. In urban dwellings, the oil stove has become increasingly common.

In the back of the house lot, behind the house, the pigpen and privy are situated. On the left-hand side of the house or slightly to the front there may be a storage shed for farm tools and grain, and perhaps a stall for a horse or cow. Most houses do not have a private well, and usually there is a large stone or concrete catchment for rain water. Since 1960, many farm villages have received water systems with taps in or near each house. Still, very few houses possess a bath, and in the rural areas they are virtually nonexistent.

Formerly, class rank determined house style. Early accounts relate that farm families lived in simple one-room dwellings with thatched roof, woven bamboo walls, and a dirt floor covered by mats. Upper-class homes were far more sumptuous, but unfortunately the total destruction of Shuri during the war left no remnants of these. Household interiors seem decidedly bare to a Westerner; the bedding is stored away each morning on arising, and, aside from an occasional low table, the interior is devoid of any furnishings. Footgear is not worn in the house, and the inmates spend most of their time seated on the floor, which is covered with mats. Generally, the floors are fairly clean, but the ceilings may be soot-blackened by years of smoke which has filtered throughout the house from a chimneyless kitchen. Except in the homes of the well-to-do and better educated, interior walls are often plastered with colored pictures cut from Japanese and American magazines. Aside from the frame and roof, which are of stout construction, the house is rather fragile and ill-suited to withstand the ravages of a damp climate, the ever-present termites, and the unrestrained mayhem committed by small children; except for the newest houses, the general impression given is one of advanced deterioration.

As the house is small and living quarters generally cramped, little privacy is afforded the individual. Occasionally, in larger houses, the eldest student or a newly married couple may enjoy the luxury of a private room; otherwise, all of the family activities—sleeping, eating, and work— take place within the same walls. While the American may find these living conditions oppressive, the Okinawan seems to draw satisfaction from them. From birth, the individual enjoys close physical proximity to the other members of his family; those who must live alone are pitied.

The family-household is the basic social unit in the community and greater society; the individual is always subsumed within this context, which constitutes his point of reference in the social system. Even births are not recorded separately as in our society. Instead, each individual is entered in a single record ('koseki') for his household; in that document, all pertinent data relating to birth date, birth order, marriage, military service, highly infectious disease (leprosy, tuberculosis), and death are entered. When an individual moves alone to another place of residence, a copy of his family record accompanies him; only by establishing a separate branch house does the individual acquire a separate record (on marriage, a woman is entered in the 'koseki' of her husband's house). Okinawan custom and law (and this obtained equally for prewar Japanese law) have recognized the family as the cornerstone of society, and the institutionalized relationships within the household tend to carry over and form the basic patterns for interaction in the larger society. Within the community, political representation is accorded on a household basis, not to each individual; thus, each family, regardless of size, has but one voice in communal affairs. The traditional relationship of the governing to the governed was patterned after that of parents to their offspring, and the former ruler was referred to as *ufu shuu mee* (great father). In brief, the family has represented a microcosm for the greater society of which it is a part.

In rural areas, the household forms the basic production unit, with its membership functioning cooperatively, working family lands in maintenance of the house. Under the former system of communal land tenure and rotation, each house periodically received new plots in accordance with its size. Although a system of private property now obtains under which the first son inherits the bulk of the family property, it remains, in effect, the property of the household, over which he merely exercises a stewardship. Although practices are changing and some rural-urban differences are now apparent, the common pooling of all family income is still practiced by many families. Among urban dwellers, younger people (particularly younger sons) with salaried employment outside the family appear increasingly disinclined to turn over their paychecks, and separate purses are appearing.

Lastly, the household constitutes a ritual unit. Thus far I have considered the household only as subsumed within the context of state, community, and common-descent-group ritual activity, but of itself it possesses a whole sphere of rites oriented toward the ancestors and the well-being of its membership. It is with this aspect of Okinawan religion that we shall be concerned in this chapter.

Family Relationships

Today, the Okinawan kinship system contains a sizable admixture of Japanese terms which are gradually displacing the Okinawan; yet, among older people, and in deference to them, the native system has continued in use. Regional differences in pronunciation and in terminology may be found, and there were formerly marked class differences in terminology; but throughout the island the basic structuring of the kinship system exhibits a uniformity.

The outstanding feature of the Okinawan system is that it affords little recognition to the strong patrilineal emphasis in social structure; essentially, there is no distinction between father's relatives and mother's relatives. Bilateral terminology, however, is expectable, as Murdock has shown, in a unilinear society with nonexogamous kin groups, since "endogamous unions prevent the expected spatial and social alignment of kinsmen."[1] A second feature of the system is that it strongly emphasizes relative generations and relative ages within generations, but kin terms as a form of address are only applied to those above ego's generation and to those older than ego within his generation. These terms are carried over into relationships within the greater society and may be used as a polite form of address for nonrelatives as well. For generations below ego and for those younger than ego in the same generation, kin terms are used solely for reference, not address; instead, the individuals are addressed by name. While the system largely focuses on the nuclear family, with a number of terms for the various statuses, one of its most impressive aspects is the marked proliferation of terms for siblings; however, virtually all of these are terms of reference indicating relative age, and only the eldest brother and eldest sister are singled out with special terms of address. Among in-laws in the sibling generation, only eldest brother's wife is accorded a special term of address. In the parent generation, there are special terms of address for aunt and uncle which do not distinguish maternal from paternal kin, but the relative age of parent's siblings may also be distinguished by special terms of reference. In the grandparent generation, the terms of address for grandparents are extended to their siblings, but the relative ages of grandparent's siblings are also distinguished in reference. While this differentiation of the relative ages of siblings in both the parent and grandparent generations may be applied bilaterally, there is a tendency to confine it to males in the patrilineal line; consequently, while "big grandfather" may mean either paternal or maternal grandfather's elder brother, in practice it tends to imply the former.

The consistent terminological stress on the relative age of siblings within each generation reflects the fact that there exists a graded system of responsibility within the family system. As has been noted, the basic principle underlying the family system is continuity—a continuity of descendant generations to pray and make offerings to the progenitors of the house. The pivotal position (as Glacken[2] termed it) within the house is occupied by the first son, who inherits the headship of the house. Birth order figures importantly, because in the event of the eldest son's early demise, the second son succeeds to his position. The chief responsibilities of the eldest son include maintaining the wealth and property of the house, providing descendants to ensure its survival, and caring for his parents in their old age. Sisters and younger brothers who eventually leave the house are generally absolved from these responsibilities, for their primary responsibilities lie with their families of procreation; but while residing in their father's house they are expected to work cooperatively for the common welfare. The eldest daughter, particularly, makes an important contribution by assuming a large share of the child-rearing burden from her mother, and, significantly, she may be addressed among the former lower classes with the kin term "little mother" by her siblings.

The wife plays a crucial role in the house by sharing her husband's responsibilities toward the house and providing him with heirs which will ensure its continuity. If her husband dies before their eldest son is grown, she functions as temporary household head until he can assume the responsibility. One of her major functions relates to domestic ritual, which is wholly her domain, or will be on the death of her husband's mother. As in the case of kin group religion, there is a dual focus in domestic religion: that which is oriented toward the ancestors of the house, and that which concerns the *kami*. Both aspects are her charge and are conducted under her direction or by her exclusively.

In the final analysis, the maintenance and continuity of the house are placed over the interests and welfare of any individual member thereof. Children, particularly males, are very much desired and greatly pampered; in fact, the ancestors and *kami* are often requested to provide many children. Nonetheless, infanticide, the sale of young women and girls into prostitution, and the occasional sale of younger sons to the fishermen have been resorted to when a family is in dire circumstances. Similarly, the aged are venerated and indulged, but legends are related of severe famine in the old days which made it necessary to carry the weakest of the aged beyond the edge of the village and leave them to die there of exposure and hunger.[3] These actions are abhorrent to the Okinawan, but when the survival of the house is seriously threatened, all members must be prepared to sacrifice themselves for the sake of the collectivity, and those least important to its survival are sacrificed first.

The matter of incest within the family has relevance to this subject and deserves some consideration here. During the course of my stay on Okinawa, several cases of father-daughter incest were reported in the newspapers, indicating that it was not an unheard-of occurrence. Mother-son incest, on the other hand, was unreported, and I did not encounter any cases or stories of it in the course of field research; in any event, the subject appears to be one that arouses disgust. In marked contrast to this attitude, there is the recurrent theme of incestuous relationships between brother and sister, a topic which appears to fascinate older Okinawans. This may be merely an elaboration of the myth of sibling creator deities set within other contexts, but I have been told by several old women that in the old days brother could marry sister. Haring[4] claims actual reports of contemporary brother-sister marriage on Amami Oshima, north of Okinawa, although he could not verify any of these himself. I have found no instances of this occurring within the lifetime of any of my informants, but the same theme may be found throughout all of the island groups of the southern and central Ryukyus (Okinawa, Miyako, Yaeyama). It was indicated previously that Okinawan society once contained a number of paired offices occupied by siblings: at the head of the state were the *chifijing* and the ruler, directly below them were the *chikasa* and younger brother(s) of the ruler, and in the village there are the *niigami* and *niitchu*. In other instances, the pairing was merely symbolic, as in the case of the *nuru* and the Shuri-appointed official, or among the *kudii* of the *munchu*. In the household, there is no symbolic pairing of the husband and wife as *umikii-gami* and *uminai-gami*. This in turn raises the question of a sister's ritual function in her brother's household. At present, this function is limited to visits for prayer at the ancestral shrine on two or three annual occasions; however, many informants in the fishing community of Itoman related that until recently it was a sister's duty to pray for the safety of a brother away at sea, and it is to be re-emphasized that a woman becomes a *kudii* in her brother's, not her husband's, sib.

Focal Points of Domestic Ritual

ANCESTRAL SHRINE. Within every household there are two main foci for ritual activity: the ancestral shrine, located in the living quarters, and the kitchen hearth. The former enshrines the ancestral spirits of the household—ascendant generations in the eldest son line, their wives, unmarried daughters of the house, and sons who died before attaining their seventh year. The kitchen hearth symbolizes the *fii nu kang*, which is believed to link the household to the higher *kami*.

The ancestral shrine, *buchidang* or *gujiiring*, consists of three sections, usually recessed within an alcove at a height of about one meter above the floor. Uppermost are the memorial tablets, *iifee* or *tootoomee*, which are hung on two levels. The upper level contains the tablets of male ancestors, while the lower level is reserved for female ancestors. Below the tablets may be found one or more steps or shelves (*tana*) where offerings may be placed; censers, flower vases, and wine or tea cups commonly stand there. Beneath this section there is usually a small box or drawer which may be used for keeping the family genealogy or other valuable heirlooms, such as a letter of appointment or commendation which an ancestor may have received from the government. In most homes, the altar and tablets are not screened from public view.

The ancestral shrine is obviously patterned on the Japanese Buddhist model. The very terms which apply to it show this origin: *futuki*, 'hotoke' (ancestor); *buchidang*, 'butsudan,' or *gujiiring*, 'goreizen' (altar); *iifee*, 'ihai' (memorial tablet). While the outward trappings of Buddhism have been acquired, many aspects of Buddhist belief are wholly lacking. Thus, as noted before, the Okinawan seems unaware of the Buddhist attitude toward animal flesh, and offerings of meat on ceremonial occasions are not at all uncommon. Similarly, though the system of ancestral worship accords a relatively low position to women, on Okinawa this is offset by the fact that the senior female member of the household takes charge of all domestic ritual, including that for the ancestral shrine. It is the woman who watches the calendar and announces forthcoming rites. It is she who prepares the ceremonial offerings and places them on the altar; and not infrequently, especially in the case of minor observances, she alone prays there. Even in those rites which demand the full participation of the household, the woman plays a dominant role; the Buddhist ancestral shrine provides no exception to traditional Okinawan practice, which confers ritual superiority on women.

HEARTH. All members of the family may pray at the ancestral shrine and participate in ritual there, but rites at the hearth are conducted exclusively by the senior female member of the house. Males do not ordinarily pray at the hearth. As the hearth *kami*, *fii nu kang*, is believed to be female, it might be presumed that the hearth represents the female principle and the ancestral shrine the male principle in the house; such, however, does not seem to be the case. The two represent the dual ritual orientation of a household toward the ancestral spirits and the *kami*; the hearth essentially provides the principal means of access to the *kami*. As noted above, it is the function of the *fii nu kang* to observe the family's activities, to report on these to the higher *kami*, and to serve as a messenger carrying requests and announcements to the higher *kami* from the family.

The traditional three-stone hearth has been previously described; kitchens lacking it contain a shallow box with three small stones set in a deep layer of ashes to represent it. This box may be placed in back of an oven or beside an oil stove. It is believed that the *fii nu kang* resides in the hearth, and the three stones which serve as its symbol are called *umichimung* (lit., "honorable three things").

Older Okinawans readily assert that the *fii nu kang* is of greater importance than the ancestral shrine. They point out that a house may exist without ancestral tablets but not without a hearth and hearth rites. Although the major function of the hearth in domestic ritual relates to the *fii nu kang* and its link between the house and the *kami*, in addition to this the hearth symbolizes, even to a greater degree than the ancestral shrine, the continuity of the house through time. When a branch house is established, ashes from the parent hearth may be scattered on the new hearth; or if the family moves, ashes are carried to the new hearth from the old. Both actions are thought to ensure continuation of the original hearth. The woman in charge of household ritual prays at the hearth on the first and fifteenth of each month and on virtually all other ritual occasions, save on the occasion of a few rites dedicated exclusively to the ancestors.

SECONDARY RITUAL SITES. The decorative alcove, *utuku* ('tokonoma'), is usually located in the first room on the right-hand side, where guests are received; in poor homes consisting of a single room, it may be located to the right of the ancestral shrine on the back wall facing the gate. Decorative scrolls are usually hung here, together with talismans purchased from the Buddhist priest and believed to give protection from misfortune. It is commonly said that the house *kami* resides in the *utuku*, although there is no unanimity on this point; but in a new house without an ancestral shrine, its importance as a ritual site is second only to that of the hearth. The *utuku* also appears in Japan ('tokonoma'), but Japanese scholarly opinion is divided as to its origin or real significance in the house; however, on Yonaguni Island, at the extreme southwestern end of the Ryukyus, I found that each of the older people possessed a small shrine box similar to the *binshii* described in the previous chapter, which was kept on the *utuku*. These were said to represent the individual's personal *kami*; whether this may indicate an earlier function of the *utuku* or merely an aberrant practice was impossible to determine.

In most upper-class homes (rural commoners do not follow this practice) there may be found an altar to the left of the ancestral shrine for the worship of one of two deities: Kwannung ('Kwannon,' the Buddhist goddess of mercy, in Sanskrit 'avalokitesvara') and Kwanting ('Kuan ti,' the Chinese god of war). No consistent pattern emerges within an *uji* or the lineages thereof as to the distribution of these; so far as I was able to determine, each house made its own decision in choosing to enshrine either or both of these deities. The approximate time of introduction, the reasons for adoption, or the exact function which these have for domestic ritual remains unknown despite intensive efforts at investigation. It was frequently said that every upper-class *muutu-yaa* must have a shrine for at least one of these deities, for which annual ceremonies are held, and apparently branch houses come for prayer on these occasions. One old woman stated that it was the function of the *kudii* to officiate at these rites, but I was unable to find agreement on this from any *kudii*. At the present time, these shrines are not considered of major importance to domestic ritual except for the annual observances.

Outside the house but within the house lot there are several lesser ritual sites where prayers and incense are offered on major ceremonial occasions and which may have a specific ritual function. The pigpen has figured importantly in birth rites and those relating to the recovery of a lost *mabui*. There also exists a rather hazy belief that a pig can discern the presence of malevolent spirits and consequently may indicate their presence to the family. Two other minor places of ritual import are the *yashichi nu gufungshi* ('feng shui' of the house lot) and the *kaa nu gufungshi* ('feng shui' of the well), relating to the *kami* of the house lot and of the well respectively. Both these locations are carefully selected by a *sanjinsoo* when a new house is constructed; the former is usually located on the right side of the house lot and may be marked by a small censer before a large stone; offerings are made here to the *kami* of the house lot. The *kami* of the twelve directions (same as the twelve calendrical signs) may also be prayed to here. Beside the well, if the house possesses one, may be found a small censer for periodical offerings to the well *kami*. Occasionally, the gate may serve as a place of prayer, as there is believed to be a gate *kami* which might halt the entrance of malevolent spirits into the house lot.

Prayer at these sites, however, occurs far less regularly than at the major ritual sites within the household.

Annual Rites

Most of the ceremonies relating to the agricultural cycle which were related in Chapter VI are also observed by the household with prayers and offerings at the hearth and ancestral shrine. Of particular importance in the rural household is the offering of the first fruits to the *kami* and ancestors before they are consumed by the family. Old urban informants relate that in the past the major agricultural rites were also observed by urban households, as these were important to national religious life; however, in recent decades urban households have abandoned such observances. I shall not enumerate them again except to note those major agricultural rites occurring in the second, third, fifth, and sixth lunar months.

The character of ritual offerings depends largely on the import of the event. At a minimum, incense must be offered on any ritual occasion. For biweekly offerings to the hearth, as well as for minor memorial observances at the ancestral shrine, food prepared for the morning meal is first offered to the spirits and then consumed by the family. Important occasions necessitate the preparation of special foods and the inclusion of liquor, but these too are afterwards consumed by the family and guests, nothing being wasted. Although there are few specific stipulations regarding the time of prayer, most people feel that it is best to pray early in the morning after arising, "when the mind is clear."

On the first and fifteenth of each (lunar) month, the woman in charge of household ritual prays to the *fii nu kang*, and many also make a token offering to the ancestral tablets at the same time; precedence, however, is given to the former. Although these dates must be regularly observed, there are few restrictions on praying whenever the need for making a request to the *kami* or ancestors arises. When the housewife conducts the biweekly rites, the *kami* are merely thanked for their help and requested to render further aid to the family. As a general rule, the *kami* and ancestors must be informed of all major events that transpire within the household.

FIRST MONTH. As noted in Chapter VI, the first twenty days of the new year are an almost continual round of ceremonial activities accompanied by considerable interaction with relatives, friends, and neighbors.

On New Year's Day in the rural areas, the family arises early to do *hachi-baru*, a ritual tour of all the scattered fields owned by the household; at each, a few products may be picked, and these are offered to the ancestral shrine. In some houses the housewife draws the first water of the new year from the well and performs *hachi ubii nadii* (first-water stroking) to the well *kami*. Other families, particularly those recently established, may visit their *muutu-yaa* to perform this ceremony. All places of prayer within the house and house lot are prayed to on this day.

During the first three days of the new year, each family maintains an open house, serving food and drink to all visitors; the men are engaged in an almost continual round of visiting at this time. The women remain at home, preparing food and serving guests; there is a feeling that it is bad luck for a nonrelated woman to visit the house during this period, which also serves to keep them home. Visits are made on the first day to one's *muutu-yaa* and to the *suu muutu* or *naka muutu* if they are near. Later, the homes of friends and neighbors are visited. As a rule, a main house does not visit its branch houses, for the mere act of visiting another house is considered an act of respect; hence, the initiative lies with the junior house, as with an employee rather than an employer. A woman usually takes her children, and sometimes her husband, to visit her parents, (or elder brother's) house during this period; she prays to her parents' ancestral shrine, but her husband does not join her.

The seventh day of the new year is called *nanka nu suku* (end of the seventh); at this time, all New Year's decorations are removed from about the house and ancestral shrine. Paper offerings on the ancestral shrine are doused with *saki* ('awamori') and burnt while prayers are said.

On the thirteenth, upper-class households enshrining Kwanting may prepare offerings and pray at the shrine. This rite is called *juusanya* (thirteenth night); it may be repeated on the same date in the third, fifth, or ninth month. In some cases, branch houses may visit their parent house to observe this event; this apparently pertains to the newer branches, not to those which have been established for some time and have branches of their own.

The fourteenth day is known as *soogwachigwa* (little New Year); at this time, offerings are presented to the *fii nu kang* and ancestors, with requests for a good harvest in the forthcoming months; in the urban areas, this date may pass unnoticed.

On the sixteenth day, observances are held for any member of the house who has died in the past year. Food offerings are placed on the ancestral shrine, and paper lanterns may be hung at the tomb. This observance is called *miisa* or *miigusoo* (lit., "new future life"; 'shingosho'), but frequently it is described as a New Year celebration for the dead.

Juuhachiya (eighteenth night) may be observed in upper-class houses having a shrine for Kwannung. It is similar to the rites for Kwanting on the thirteenth. This ceremony may be repeated on the same date in the third, fifth, or ninth month, and, as in the case of the rites for Kwanting, the particular date of observance seems to be arbitrarily selected.

Hachika soogwachi (twentieth New Year's) marks the formal end of all observances for the New Year period. At this time, ancestral spirits and *kami* who are believed to have visited for these events return to their permanent abode. Prayers are offered to the hearth and ancestral shrine. In the rural areas, this event falls on the same day as *yama-birachi* (opening the mountains), when the taboo on entering the wooded area, particularly that around the *utaki*, is lifted.

Sometime during the early weeks of the new year, the woman in charge of household ritual visits the shaman or fortuneteller for *hachi unchi* (first fortune). At this time, the fortune of each member of the household is determined and recommendations made for their course of action throughout the year.

SECOND MONTH. The major ritual event for the household occurs at the time of the vernal equinox, *nchabi*. Prayers and offerings are made to the ancestral shrine, hearth, and places of worship in the yard.

From the twenty-second of this month until the third of the following month, the period of *shiimii* (described in the previous chapter) occurs; during this time, households visit their tombs for prayers and offerings to the ancestors.

THIRD MONTH. On the third day of this month, *sangwachi ashibii* (third-month party or play) takes place. At this time, women of all ages should visit the sea and touch the water. Failing to do this, it is said, will result in their being seduced by a snake (in the guise of a handsome man) and bearing snakes. Virtually all women of all ages regard the belief as probably superstition but state that the observance provides an excellent opportunity for an outing or picnic. This day annually brings thousands of women from both the rural and urban areas to the beaches; inclement weather serves only to postpone the event until the first pleasant day. Most housewives pack a picnic lunch at this time and take all the children to spend the afternoon wading in the water. In the country areas, the women pass their time collecting shellfish.

The wheat harvest takes place during this month, and after the grain is harvested the first fruits are offered to the ancestors and *kami*.

FOURTH MONTH. Aside from the regular biweekly rites to the hearth on the first and fifteenth, no major household rites occur during this month.

FIFTH MONTH. The summer solstice, *kaatchii*, during this month, is marked by observances at the major ritual sites within the house and yard.

SIXTH MONTH. The major ritual event of this month coincides with the rice or millet harvest ceremonies and celebrations observed by the village. The first fruits are offered to the ancestors and *kami*, and in many areas sheaves of the new rice are hung in the *utuku*.

SEVENTH MONTH. On the seventh day, sugar cane is placed on the ancestral shrine and invitations are extended to the ancestral spirits to return for *ubung*, which is held in the following week. The long stalks of cane are said to be used as walking sticks by the ancestors on their return; this constitutes the only instance of the use of sugar cane in Okinawan ritual. The ceremony is always referred to by the Japanese name, 'tanabata.'

On the thirteenth begins the great Buddhist festival for the dead, *ubung* ('obon'), which lasts until the fifteenth or sixteenth. Tombs are visited for welcoming and escorting the ancestors back to their homes, and throughout the remainder of this period food offerings are made to the ancestral shrine at each meal. A considerable interaction among relatives takes place at this time: branch houses visit their parent house, married women return to their parents' houses, and all houses of the sib are expected to send a representative to their *suu muutu* or local *naka muutu*. Very little work is attended to during these three days; most shops and businesses close, and farming operations come to a complete halt. Virtually the whole time is spent visiting and feasting; the intensity of ritual and social activities is surpassed only by that of the New Year period.

EIGHTH MONTH. The autumnal equinox, *nchabii*, falls in this month, and, as during the spring equinox, prayers and incense are offered at the ritual sites in the house and yard.

Offerings are made to the moon *kami* on the night of the fifteenth, *hachi gwachi juuguya* (eighth-month fifteenth night), coinciding with the appearance of the full moon. This appears to be the only instance so far as I could determine when the moon is an object of ritual, but little significance is attached to this rite. On the same evening, the youth of the village perform *shiishi mooyee* (lion dance), with masked dancers visiting every household.

NINTH MONTH. On the ninth day, urban families, particularly those of upper-class origin, pray to the ancestral shrine for those who are away. Supposedly, *saki* flavored by the addition of chrysanthemum petals is offered to the ancestors and drunk at this time, and the term *chikuzaki* (chrysanthemum wine, 'kiku sake') is applied to this ceremony. This rite also appears to be a recent adoption from Japan and of minor importance.

Near the end of this month or early in the following month, depending on the area, the rice beds are seeded; before sowing, the woman charged with household ritual matters prays to the *fii nu kang* and ancestors, asking for a bountiful harvest.

TENTH MONTH. No rites are performed within the house this month except for the biweekly rites at the hearth.

ELEVENTH MONTH. The winter solstice, *tunjii*, occurs during this month; prayers and incense are offered to the major ritual sites within the house and yard. A special dish, *tunjii juushii*, consisting of fried taro and pork, is offered to the ancestors, a clear instance of the use of flesh in contrast to Buddhist tenets. The *kami* and ancestors are asked at this time to provide good crops in the following year.

On the seventh day, all blacksmiths conduct *fuuchi nu yuuwee* (bellows rites). On this day, the blacksmith and his assistants gather at the forge to pray and offer liquor to the *fuuchi nu kami* (bellows *kami*), patron *kami* of the blacksmith. After this rite, the neighborhood is invited into the shop for drink and food.

TWELFTH MONTH. On the eighth day, housewives make *kaasa muchi*, a heavy cake made from pounded glutinous rice and wrapped in a leaf from the wild ginger plant, which imparts a pleasant flavor to the otherwise bland contents. This is first offered to the ancestral shrine and then consumed by all members of the family. According to traditional belief, this cake will give great strength to those who eat it, sufficient, it is said, to combat *uni* (ogres, 'oni'). While nearly every household eats this confection on this day, offering it to the ancestors does not appear to derive from any religious motivation but rather from a desire to share a pleasant treat with them.

On the twenty-fourth, in accordance with Chinese belief, the *fii nu kang* departs for heaven to report on the family's activities throughout the past year. In the few houses which still retain masks of this *kami*, fat or oil may be spread over the mouth of the mask in the belief that only good things will be said of the family by the *kami*. At this time, the woman prays at the hearth and offers food for the departing *kami*'s journey; it is believed that the *fii nu kang* returns on the fourth of the following month, but no rites are conducted in recognition of the return.

On the last night of the year, *tushi nu yuruu*, prayers of thanks are offered to the ancestors for their assistance and protection during the past year.

Rites of Passage

Within the memory of the oldest living generation, rites of passage have been conducted primarily by the household, with the participation of close relatives and neighbors, but in recent years such rites have been reduced in number and simplified. These changes were partially determined by economic necessity as an aftermath of the war, which impoverished everyone; but, in addition, there has occurred a decided change in many traditional practices as a result of Japanese influence. Moreover, as a result of this influence, a number of wholly new and different rites have been incorporated into the life cycle.

BIRTH AND CHILDHOOD. During pregnancy, the mother attempts to avoid potentially dangerous situations; she should particularly not attend funerals, visit a tomb, or enter a house where there has been a birth or death. It is said that exposure to these situations might result in the loss of the child's *mabui*. The father is also expected to be careful at this time, but his activities are less restricted than those of the mother.

Birth usually takes place in the house, with a midwife and/or a few older women assisting. The afterbirth is usually buried in the yard behind the house, and a small bush is planted atop it so that no one can trample on the spot. The umbilical cord is dried and then carefully wrapped;

supposedly, it is kept throughout life and then buried with the individual, but frequently it may be lost or destroyed long before. The soiled mats and clothing may be taken to the beach for washing, or, inland, they may be washed in salted water; in either case, the presence of salt in the water is thought to purify and remove pollution. Formerly, the mother and child were subjected to purification by roasting before a continuous fire in a windowless room for a period of seven to ten days, but this practice was discontinued, even in the more remote areas, during the 1930's. In some areas, the child is given its first bath in the sea, but in Kanegusuku it is deemed important that the child be first washed in water from Kanegusuku Hijaa, the major well of the community; water from the same well is used to wash a corpse. The birth is announced as soon as possible to the hearth and ancestral tablets, with a request to safeguard the child's health.

Six days after birth, the first formal ceremony, *mansang* (full birth), is held. At this time, a name may be selected for the infant, and divination may be employed to determine if the selection has been suitable. Formerly, if the birth occurred while the mother was away from home, a neuter name was given to a male child, as it was believed that a male was more susceptible to attack than a female child away from the protecting spirits of the parent household. On this day, the child may be introduced to the ancestors and hearth and then carried outdoors for the first time. In the yard, the child is taken to all the ritual sites—pigpen, well, gate, and shrine for yard *kami*. The greatest importance, however, attaches to the child's introduction at the hearth to the *fii nu kang* (and, by inference, to all higher *kami*); unless this is done, a child's chance for survival is considered poor. When a child is born out of wedlock, the mother always attempts to take it to the father's house for prayers at his hearth. The mere fact that a man permits this act is taken by all as a recognition of paternity; consequently, where ill-feeling or perhaps some doubt exists, this request may be refused. Stories were recounted of anxious mothers awaiting the opportunity to enter the house and perform this simple rite. In most cases, however, permission is granted, for if the child dies, then, according to belief, its ghost will plague the house and cause misfortune.

Prayers are offered at the hearth and ancestral shrine on the occasion of the child's first journey beyond the house lot. In Itoman, the child should be taken 100 days after birth to visit the *nuru*, who asks her *kami* (*nuru-gami*) to protect the child. On the first anniversary of birth, prayers of thanks are offered to the ancestors for having helped the child through the most difficult year; usually, a small party is given to celebrate the the occasion. Larger celebrations are held for the first son than for other children.

After the first year, actual birthdates pass virtually unnoticed; instead, each individual marks his birth on the first day of the year bearing the animal sign of his birth year. All people, consequently, observe their first birth-year day (*mee tushibii*) during one of the first twelve days of the new year and consider themselves one year older from that day. Prior to the war, residents of Naha and Shuri observed this day with a visit to one of five Buddhist temples, each of which contained images of some of the twelve animal signs. Frequently, older people repeated the visit on the second occurrence of their birth-year day, which was called *atu tushibii*. To this extent, then, each urban resident had a vague association with a Buddhist temple, which was held throughout life. Frequently, however, in the case of children and men, the duty of praying there fell to the mother or wife of the house. Four of these temples were destroyed by the war, and these events are now marked by prayers to the ancestral shrine. In the country areas, less importance is attached to observing *tushibii*, and the responsibility falls upon the housewife to pray on behalf of her husband and children.

It was noted in Chapter III that the recurrence of one's birth year (*nmari-dushi*) every twelve years renders one more susceptible to misfortune; hence, the thirteenth, twenty-fifth, thirty-seventh, forty-ninth, sixty-first, seventy-third, and eighty-fifth years of life are regarded as dangerous. In addition, the first, seventh, and nineteenth years are also considered dangerous. During these periods, the individual should avoid any major action such as marrying, traveling, building a new house, etc., which, it is believed, would probably end in failure. Those who have completed their *nmari-dushi* celebrate that event on the occurrence of their *mee tushibii* in the following year. At this time, they pray to the ancestors and thank them for their assistance. Some people, particularly in the rural areas, hold parties during their *nmari-dushi* in the belief that conviviality will help to dispel possible misfortune. But in most cases the individual prays to the ancestral shrine at the beginning of the *nmari-dushi*, asking the ancestors for their protection, and the woman in charge of domestic ritual prays for this person at the hearth, requesting assistance from the *kami*. These years are regarded as periods of crisis, when extreme circumspection must attend all action; their passing is said to be marked by a feeling of relief.

As a result of the introduction of universal education, most children are given a party to celebrate their entering school. This event is announced to the ancestors, usually with a request to make the child a good student. Friends, neighbors, and close relatives are invited to feast and drink with the family.

ADOLESCENCE. Formerly, the back of a girl's hands and wrists were tattooed after her thirteenth year. This event was celebrated by a household party to which neighbors and relatives were invited, and the ancestors and *kami* were informed of the action. In his thirteenth, fifteenth, or seventeenth year, a boy was permitted to cut his hair in the fashion of an adult male, and, as in the case of the girl, a party was held and the event announced to the ancestors and *kami*. Both events served to mark a recognized change of status for the individual; the young man became a member of the *wakamung-gumi* (youth association), while tattooing indicated that the young woman was ready for marriage (a check of the village records showed that marriages as early as the fourteenth year were not uncommon fifty years ago). Today, both rites have completely disappeared: the Japanese government forced the men to cut their queues, and the practice of tattooing was also discouraged. Now the individual's graduation from school (at the completion of nine years of education) has come to replace these earlier observances as an important event in the life cycle. Gaining entrance to high school and to the new university have also become occasions deserving ritual recognition, and the events are announced, with prayers for aid, to the ancestors and hearth.

MARRIAGE. Formerly, in the country areas, once an engagement had been agreed to by both families, the man was permitted to sleep at the woman's house until marriage; during this time the young couple were referred to as *yung nu miitu* (night couple). In most cases, there was a form of bride service, lasting as long as two years, which had to be served by the man in lieu of a bride price. In many cases, there was matrilocal residence until the first child was born. In northern Okinawa, bride service and temporary matrilocal residence still continue to be practiced in a few of the isolated villages. The formal marriage ceremony, *niibichi* (uprooting), usually took place after the couple had been sleeping together for some time. The first rites were held in the man's house, before the ancestral shrine, where the couple prayed and drank from the same cup. Next, the man visited the woman's house and prayed at the hearth, but not before the ancestral shrine; this constituted one of the few instances when a man might pray to the *fii nu kang*. Sometime during the wedding celebration, which often extended over a period of three days, the youth of the village carried the groom to all the major sites of community worship; there, the *kami* were asked to provide the couple with many children. Marriage practices among the upper classes were decidedly different from those for commoners; upper-class women led secluded lives, and the relatively free interaction enjoyed by the youth of a village was unknown to them. Among the upper classes, marriages were arranged. Bride service, bride price, and temporary matrilocal residence were not practiced by them.

Today, marriage rites have become simpler, and long wedding celebrations are rare. Moreover, marriages are rather casually entered into and easily dissolved. In fact, most marriages in the rural areas appear to be recorded (i.e., legalized) at the time the first child is born; thus, the "marriage" may be said to achieve permanence with the birth of the first child, particularly if it is a male. Until that time, separation is easy. When a young couple think of marriage, a *yuta* or *sanjinsoo* is consulted by the parents to determine if they are compatible and to select a propitious date and time for the ceremony. The tide is an important factor; the most suitable time for marriage is when the tide is rising and approaching high tide. The ceremony is held in the man's house. The couple drink and pray before the ancestral tablets as in the past, but at the present time the groom often does not pray before the hearth in the bride's house. In the rural areas, this latter practice may be observed when the couple are from the same village; however, the practice of taking the groom to the major places of worship within the community has vanished.

ESTABLISHING A BRANCH HOUSE. When a younger son marries, he must leave his father's house and establish a new house. He first prays to the ancestral shrine in his father's house, notifying the ancestors of his action and asking for their continued support and protection. His mother then prays to the *fii nu kang*, so that the *kami* will be informed of this step; after this, she takes ashes (not coals) from the hearth and carries them to the new house. She scatters these on the new hearth or places them in a small container next to the stove. The young bride then joins her in praying to the *fii nu kang* of the new hearth, which is regarded as an extension of the old. Thereafter, it is the duty of the young woman to take charge of all ritual matters in the new house.

ADULT LIFE. After marriage and the birth of children, there are few if any sharp discontinuities which serve to denote the altered status of the individual. The Okinawan man does not retire when his eldest son attains maturity; instead, he takes pride in his continued contribution to the family's livelihood. As the senior male of the household, he retains the position of household head until death and does not usually relinquish this position to his son. Similarly, as a woman grows older she may gradually leave the more demanding household chores to her daughter-in-law; but at the same time her interest in and burden of ritual obligations gradually increase with age. The transition from a mature adult at the height of physical powers to an aged person approaching death is a smooth progression, largely without any perceptible points of status change.

The recurrence every twelve years of the *nmari-dushi*, or crisis year, serves to heighten ritual activity periodically for the individual, although frequently action may be undertaken by others on his behalf. After the sixty-first year, the passing of each *nmari-dushi* provides the occasion for more elaborate celebration and prayers of thanks to the ancestors and *kami*.

Attaining the eighty-eighth year of life is regarded as exceedingly fortunate, and on the eighth day of the eighth month individuals who reach that age are given an elaborate party. All members of a house take pleasure in having a member achieve longevity, and a considerable portion of the family's wealth may be expended for this event.

DEATH RITES. Under present laws, when someone dies, the body must be disposed of within twenty-four hours, but in most cases burial takes place within several hours. All funeral preparations are made in the house, and when death occurs in the fields or farther away from home, the body is returned there as expeditiously as possible. Immediately after death, great quantities of incense are ignited and placed on the ancestral shrine; news of the death is imparted to the ancestors, who are told to expect the new arrival. Next, the village mayor is notified, and he in turn conveys the news to all the villagers. Formerly, when a death occurred, all houses in the community extinguished their fires and threw out whatever food was being cooked there, as it was believed that the hearths had been polluted.

A policeman is summoned to determine the cause of death and to fill out the necessary papers, and notifications are sent to all relatives living outside the community.

The body is washed by female relatives and dressed in the deceased's best clothing. Personal possessions are afterwards divided among the members of the family; nothing is thrown away. Relatives, friends, neighbors, and villagers (one representative from each house) soon begin arriving, each bringing a small sum of money as an obituary gift, which the family uses to defray funeral expenses. In the meantime, the men construct a simple box, in which the body is placed in the flexed position; frequently, a keepsake may be enclosed with the body. A couple of women make white paper flowers, which are set in a base of soft clay.

All who visit the house are served tea, candy, and cake; and on arrival each person burns incense and prays for a successful departure of the spirit. Close neighbors endeavor to render as much assistance to the bereaved family as possible. Formerly, a professional wailer, described as "sort of a *yuta*," was called to the house; this woman was able, it is said, to cry for two hours without stopping. Crying and loud wailing noises, especially on the part of the women, are considered desirable, because "the dead person will feel better." Before the war, a *nimbuchaa* was also summoned to the house. He would sit by the gate, continuously ringing his bell and reciting the *nimbuchi* ('nembutsu'). If the family is prosperous, a Buddhist priest may be called, but often his services are dispensed with. It is his first function to prepare the funeral banners giving the name of the deceased and to make two temporary memorial tablets.

Because of its unpleasant association and partly through fear of pollution from it, the funeral palanquin is stored on the outskirts of the community. When the tide begins to recede, it is brought to the yard and the casket placed inside; then the funeral procession forms. At this point, the Buddhist priest begins to pray, punctuating his speech with the ringing of a small bell. Then he steps to the head of the procession, which slowly moves from the house through the village toward the tomb. The priest is followed by one or two old men carrying the funeral banners announcing the name of the deceased. Next, there is a man carrying one of the two temporary memorial tablets (the other is kept on the ancestral shrine until a permanent one is made). Four or more men follow, carrying the palanquin; these men are rarely relatives, usually neighbors. Sometimes, when a great distance must be covered, an extra set of pallbearers is on hand to alternate in carrying the burden. After the palanquin, a woman follows, scattering the paper flowers which were fashioned earlier in the day. Next come the mourners, males first. The female mourners of all ages make an extravagant display of their emotions; they usually appear to be quite incapable of walking and must be supported on each side by a friend or neighbor. The male mourners weep too, but they tend to do so silently with only an occasional sob. Until the war (I have seen prewar motion pictures of a funeral), female mourners completely covered their heads by pulling up the top of the kimono, wrapping a mat, or using a half-closed umbrella. Friends and villagers (one representative from each house) make up the rear of the procession. Except for members of the bereaved family, children are not allowed to attend; so far as I was able to observe, this is virtually the only event from which they are excluded. It is commonly said that they would make too much noise and cause confusion, but a more plausible interpretation (suggested by an informant) would seem to be the parents fear that a child's spirit might be stolen at the tomb. It was noted before that mothers did not like their children to play near a tomb and would always call them away, whereas in the course of other play activities they might nearly demolish a shrine without a word being said to them.

At the tomb, the casket is removed from the palanquin, and if a priest is present, he prays and then hurriedly walks away. All people present squat in prayer, and great quantities of incense are burned. The close relatives step forward one by one, each offering a final prayer of farewell. Then the tomb door is pushed aside, and the pallbearers maneuver to push the casket through the small entrance. At this point, the female mourners begin to shriek, scream, and clutch madly at the casket and pallbearers, as if to drag the body back into this world. Friends forcibly restrain them after this wild outburst, and they are dragged away sobbing incoherently, incapable of speech or walking. On departing from the tomb, the men and women divide and take different routes back to the village, in belief that the dead person's spirit will thus be confused and not likely to follow. Each one returning from a funeral has salt sprinkled on his person before entering the house. At the house where the death occurred, the three stones representing the *fii nu kang* were formerly removed from the house and thrown into the sea and a new hearth made. At present, the three small stones or ashes representing the traditional hearth are thrown out and new ones put in their place. As a rule, the deceased is no longer referred to by name; instead, a kin term or the posthumous name given by the priest is used.

MEMORIAL RITES. When the funeral party leaves the tomb, a number of items are placed at the tomb door for the use of the deceased in the next world. These include sandals, a cane, a miniature paper umbrella, a lantern, food, and drink. In addition, all the funeral paraphernalia—banners, flowers, and memorial tablet—are left in the tomb yard.

After the burial, the deceased's family enters a forty-nine-day mourning period, throughout which offerings of food and drink are served three times daily to the ancestral shrine. Until the closing decade of the last century, a mourner's hut was erected in the tomb yard for the widow of the deceased; she remained there until the mourning period ended. Although this practice has long since fallen into disuse, the forty-nine-day mourning period is still observed. The day after the funeral, the family returns to the tomb to pray and offer food and drink. It is always said that this custom prevents any false burial; a well-known play in the folk-theater dramatizes this occurrence, as do several myths. On the seventh day after death begins a series of seven memorial rites at the tomb similar to that of the second day. These are held on the seventh (*hachi nanka*), fourteenth (*ta nanka*), twenty-first (*mi nanka*), twenty-eighth (*yu nanka*), thirty-fifth (*ichi nanka*), forty-second (*mu nanka*), and forty-ninth (*nana nanka*) days after death. On the occasion of the last *nanka*, the tomb yard is cleaned and all remaining funeral paraphernalia burned. In the house that night the last memorial rite is held at the ancestral shrine. The temporary memorial tablet of white is removed, and the permanent tablet of red is hung with the other *iifee*.

Thereafter, memorial observances are held on the first, third, seventh, thirteenth, twenty-fifth, and thirty-third anniversaries of death. On these occasions, visits are made to the tomb. The observances are similar to the rites held during the forty-nine days of mourning. Yearly anniversaries of the death are simply observed in the house, with offerings of incense and food to the ancestral shrine. After the thirty-third year, the deceased is no longer singled out for special rites but is accorded the same treatment as other ancestors of the family. Lastly, it should be noted that the rites which have been described are those accorded an adult; in the case of children the elaborate memorial observances may be dispensed with altogether and incense alone burned at the ancestral shrine without any visit to the tomb area. In the case of very small children, all rites may be completely dropped, although a memorial tablet is placed on the ancestral shrine.

BONE-WASHING RITES. There is no set date when bone washing takes place, but it usually occurs one to three years after death. In a large commoner *munchu*, bone washing may take place on the occasion of a later funeral to make room for another corpse. The task is not regarded with pleasure, so there is some tendency to put the matter off until sheer necessity (another death) dictates that the operation be performed.

This event is always preceded by announcements at the ancestral shrine and tomb that bone washing will be done. Only the closest relatives of the deceased—wife, husband, son, daughter, brother, sister, mother, father—participate in this task. Once the mortar holding the tomb door is chipped away, the casket is brought into the tomb yard; however, an umbrella is held above the casket to shade the contents and also, it is said, to keep the spirit from escaping. The person closest to the deceased, usually a wife or son, must touch the remains first; then all set about cleaning the bones, using large chopsticks. When decomposition is not complete, a sickle must be used. The participants cry during the operation; the women may sob loudly. After the bones are picked clean of all flesh, they are washed several times in water and lastly in *saki* (Okinawan *saki* differs from Japanese 'sake' in that it has a much greater alcoholic content, frequently running as high as 40 per cent). The cleaned bones are then placed in a funerary urn, in which the feet, legs, and pelvis are entered first, followed by the backbones, arms, and lastly the skull. The urn is then placed in the left chamber of the tomb for permanent interment. The bone jar is set so that the eyes of the skull face the back of the tomb and not the door, because it is believed that the dead person's spirit will be less inclined to think about leaving if it cannot see outside. At the conclusion, prayers of apology are offered to the deceased for having disturbed his bones.

Upon returning to the house, all those who have participated sprinkle their clothes with salt to remove all pollution. Most people do not like to participate in funerals or bone washing on their *tushibii* and will definitely refrain from doing so during their *nmari-dushi* since, as previously noted, it is thought that the individual is weaker and more susceptible to misfortune at such times. At one of the bone-washing ceremonies I attended, many questions were asked about American funerary practices; several people expressed dissatisfaction with the Okinawan method and ventured that the Japanese or American methods of cremation and burial were superior to theirs. In the village of Oku, I was told that young women now sometimes refuse to participate in bone washing, which is tending to become a male function. Most people, I found, do not like this custom and express the hope that it will soon be changed; however, the low incidence of cremation, even in the urban areas, suggests little likelihood of change in the immediate future.

Conclusion

One of the underlying principles of domestic ritual is that the *kami* and ancestors are in league with the family and must be informed of all that transpires. The significance of this partnership cannot be overemphasized; virtually all important household events are announced to the ancestors and *kami*, and whenever difficulties or problems are encountered, their assistance is requested.

A few examples of typical announcements might be cited. When a young man brought home the first paycheck from his first job, his mother immediately placed it on the ancestral shrine as evidence of the son's success and industry. When a family purchased a new plot of farmland, the deed to the property was displayed not only for the ancestors and *fii nu kang* in the household but at all the major places of ritual within the community as well. On graduation from high school, a young man's diploma was presented to the ancestors and then placed at the bottom of the altar with other family papers and heirlooms. This obligation to keep the ancestors and *kami* informed is never discharged, and the family's ties with the spirit world are constantly being renewed. Failure to do this will result not only in a withdrawal of their support but will probably arouse their anger as well, thereby exposing the family to misfortune. Obligations and responsibilities toward the ancestral spirits do not appear to differ appreciably from those toward the *kami*, and the underlying sentiment for fulfilling these obligations seems to derive not so much from a feeling of deep devotion as from an attitude that it must be done or one will suffer the consequences. Furthermore, this does not seem to have resulted from recent acculturative influences; I am rather more inclined to view it as a characteristic of Okinawan religion, wherein the basic orientation toward the spirit world is that of placation and manipulation rather than veneration. I have tried to refrain, therefore, from applying the term "ancestor worship" to Okinawan ancestral rites, for it too strongly connotes adoration and reverence which, while not perhaps wholly lacking, are nonetheless not characteristic either.

Of the Okinawan social institutions we have considered—the state, community, kin group, and family—the last has best preserved its ritual integrity. I attribute this in no small degree to the fact that the Okinawan family system did not differ appreciably from that of Japan and hence was not subjected to ridicule or positive attempts at change. However, in response to recent economic and technological developments, the family system is presently undergoing extensive alteration. A marked feature of present-day life has been the perceptible emergence of that type of individualism characteristic of urban, industrial society. One discernible change in domestic religion has been a general slackening of interest in all ritual matters, particularly those rites conducted at the minor ritual sites of the house and yard. There is some tendency to drop all rites to the *kami* (excluding those for the *fii nu kang*) and to simplify greatly ancestral rites, particularly memorial observances for the dead. A strong qualification should be inserted at this point, however, for in relating what Okinawans do or do not attend to in their ritual action, a distinction between the commonplace and crisis situation must be delineated. I have been referring primarily to a loss or decline in the ordinary (or formerly ordinary) situation. But when misfortune strikes and the counsel or guidance of a *yuta* is sought, an almost frenzied intensification of ritual activity takes place. Lastly, the dominant position of the housewife or senior female of the house in domestic ritual matters remains unchallenged; whatever other changes have been wrought, her status has not been affected in this regard. It may be expected that this feature of family religion will remain unchanged for many years to come.

IX

CONCLUSION

Although the content of Okinawan religion has altered, and religion as an activity area has contracted markedly, it must be emphasized that certain fundamental characteristics and readily recognizable forms have persisted. In Chapter V, an attempt was made to reconstruct the ancient cult and the historical development of the state religion, and in other chapters the major manifestations of change in recent years have been noted. In concluding, I should like to consider some of the basic features of this religious system and the extent to which these have defined or delimited such changes as have evolved. Certain features of the system have proved most resilient, while others have become increasingly dysfunctional. Essentially, I am concerned here with inherent factors which enabled this system to persist, and with attempting to predict its future in light of our understanding of these.

The system of belief, as has been emphasized, is nonabsolutistic and weakly organized, seemingly composed of many disparate elements or concepts, and virtually lacking a central or unifying principle. There is a plethora of spirit entities in the Okinawan universe; everything, in fact, has spirit. The major spirits are the *kami*. Although they are discrete entities—animistic spirits—there is a vagueness regarding their specific identification and function. Thus, for example, there are *kami* called "bellows *kami*" and "privy *kami*," but these are not titles or proper nouns in our sense; rather, the belief is that a spirit called *kami* dwells in the bellows or privy. Despite a certain consensus that the *kami* may once have been human beings, they are largely depersonalized (excepting perhaps the *chiji* of the shaman), with little representation in myth or in art.

There is an absence of color in shrines, religious adornment, and paraphernalia, as well as a lack of graphic representation of the supernatural. The artistic achievements of the Okinawan have been confined to weaving, pottery, lacquer ware, and stone masonry—practical, secular arts. Mythology has been given far less emphasis than historical tradition, and, significantly, the most common myth form is the etiological myth. There appears to be a remarkable lack of imagination evinced with regard to the spirit world, and an utter void in the area of metaphysical speculation or curiosity.

This absence of complexity in the system of belief may account for the unreceptiveness to more sophisticated belief systems, in that there seems to be an unwillingness or inability to digest or assimilate what is intellectually complex. The history of Buddhism in Okinawa provides an illustration of this point. Buddhism was spread through the island by the messianic zeal of Japanese priests and abetted by the anti-Christian policy of the Satsuma government; it found acceptance, I believe, as an efficacious system for handling the troublesome spirits of the dead, but it was assimilated shorn of nearly all philosophical properties.

This vagueness or absence of complexity characterizing the belief system has constituted a survival factor. It has made possible assimilation of foreign traits (as in the cases of Taoist hearth rites and Buddhist ancestral rites), but it has also proved a barrier against sophisticated belief systems alien to Okinawan thinking. An attack upon or loss of any segment of Okinawan belief does not endanger the whole. More importantly, one key aspect of the belief system has withstood refutation: that all serious misfortune stems from supernatural causes. An Okinawan may have learned in school that certain diseases are caused by microorganisms and may be convinced of this, but, should he succumb to disease, he may nonetheless look to the supernatural as the agency inflicting the microorganism upon him.

Essentially, the orientation toward the spirit world is highly pragmatic; spirits are propitiated to achieve specific ends; rarely are the goals ambiguous. Ritual action, therefore, is directed toward specific goals—a good harvest, a safe journey, good health, success in some venture, etc.—or toward avoidance of misfortune, the converse of what is desirable. The Okinawan recognizes a certain reciprocity between himself and the *kami* and ancestors: in return for rites and offerings, they will assist him in attaining his goals. Inattention to ritual matters will incur their displeasure, resulting in a withdrawal of support and possible retaliation; consequently, primary emphasis must be given to maintaining ritual obligations. Except for timing, however, there is a relative absence of compulsiveness in attending to the details of ritual performance; ritual content may be found to vary from village to village and often from house to house within a village. Most rites today are acknowledged to be considerably abbreviated, even when compared to those of the immediate prewar period; yet little anxiety appears to be engendered by this state of affairs. The content and emotional attitude characterizing a ritual performance are not of major importance; the basic concerns are going through the motions of performance and timing, and obtaining the desired effect with the minimum expenditure of effort needed.

Chapter III gave some indication of the variety of ritual types which characterize Okinawan religious action. At the present time, the ritual complex is undergoing modification in that certain rites of importance in the past are being abbreviated, slighted, or even dropped. This religion found expression basically through four major social institutions: the state, community, kin group, and family-household. Each of these institutions preserved a ritual function as a part of organized activities. Rites which were peculiar to the state or community are today either extinct or in decline, whereas those basic to the kin group and family have displayed relatively more vigor. The significant point is that the former have not been slighted or omitted because they were necessarily disvalued but rather because the social institutions which gave them meaning and expression have ceased to function or have grossly altered.

It is in the organization of roles and degree of role differentiation that this religious system exhibits the greatest elaboration and complexity. Thus, in the religious system—characterized by myriads of vague deities and slight metaphysical speculation—there exists a precise organization of roles and functions, down to the level of a *nma-tui* (horse holder) or a *niibu-tui* (ladler). This rigid differentiation of roles surely reflects a basic concern with the ordering of human relationships. Inflexibility in the role structure constitutes a major weakness, for excessive rigidity disallows adaptability to change. Within the community (and formerly the state), not only are the religious roles hereditary, but also a prescribed hieratical gradation of functions and responsibilities precludes an acolyte from taking over. Hence, where key ritual specialists are absent, the entire structure may be rendered dysfunctional. The integration of religious roles with certain social institutions inevitably results in their being highly responsive to any significant changes in the latter; consequently, when the kingdom was dissolved, the national religion soon collapsed; and now as the folk-community is breaking down, community religion verges on extinction.

Ritual responsibility within the group has traditionally been delegated to specialists, and neglect of ritual performance is believed most likely to result in supernatural punishment, first for the specialist and secondarily for the group as a whole. Ascribing primary accountability to a specialist has not only conferred some measure of security upon the layman but also has provided additional motivation for the specialist. To a limited degree, such motivation has contributed to the survival of the system, since rites may continue to be performed where proper functionaries are present, even though the group no longer actively renders support. Again, it does not appear that the services of group ritualists are positively disvalued but rather that the sentiment for group unity which gave them purpose in the past has declined.

At present, the whole of Okinawan society is being restructured, and changes occurring in the major social institutions have served to atrophy the traditional religious functions of those institutions. The old emphases on communalism and familialism are giving way to an emphasis on individualism characteristic of an urban, industrial society. The Forgotten Kingdom of the nineteenth century has been destroyed by incorporation into a larger nation-state, and the isolated folk-community of the past is being transformed into a rural settlement closely aligned with the urban centers and larger national entity. Although changing at a slower pace, the kin group and family are experiencing a weakening of traditional bonds which provided unity in the past, and, inevitably, their ritual functions will also pass. I have observed, however, that even among well-educated, highly acculturated individuals the belief system still has import, particularly in its identification of the supernatural as the primary cause of misfortune. Thus, for the individual, religion minimally retains a functional significance in time of crisis.

It is already apparent in the urban areas that the shaman has assumed some of the functions formerly performed by the community or kin group priestess. Moreover, the shaman continues to be regarded as the ultimate authority in matters relating to misfortune. In addition, her activities (unlike those of the priestesses) bring considerable monetary reward, so that role recruitment remains high. Her unstructured role in society affords a greater adaptability than that enjoyed by the priestess, who is now encumbered by her institutional affiliation. Undoubtedly, the shaman will continue to minister to religious needs in time of crisis.

It seems likely that, despite manifold changes, certain aspects of this religion will persist for some time to come but that there will be a shift in activity focus from the collectivity to the individual. A revitalization of traditional Okinawan religion in response to the emergence of individualism does not appear probable. Rather, through the disintegration of traditional institutions, predominantly individual-oriented rites and specialists will remain.

NOTES

Preface

1. The main island of Okinawa and adjacent neighboring islands include more than 500 communities.
2. Chamberlain, 1893: 280.
3. Allport, 1950: 13.

Chapter I

1. Suda, 1950: 114.
2. *See* Newman and Eng, 1947*a*.
3. Allan H. Smith, 1958.
4. Hattori, 1955*a*.
5. *See* Shimabukuro Zempatsu, 1937: map following 258.
6. Some qualification must be made for television. In the fall of 1961, traditional Okinawan drama was presented almost nightly on television and enjoyed great popularity. It remains to be seen, when live television broadcasts from Japan become available, whether Okinawan drama will persist in this medium.
7. Kyūgakkai, 1959: 196–248.
8. Kanaseki, 1955.
9. Haring, 1952: 11.
10. Kanaseki, 1955.
11. Iha, 1922: 8–9.
12. Williams, 1910: 26.

Chapter II

1. Haring (1949: 855) has this to say: "Generally mistranslated as 'god,' *kami* resembles the South Sea concept of *mana*, which denotes mysterious impersonal supernatural power resident in places, persons, material objects, or ghosts." I am not qualified to comment on the applicability of this interpretation to Japan; but it would not, in my opinion, cover the Okinawan meaning of the term.

2. Shimabukuro Genshichi, 1950a: 138.
3. Spencer, 1931.
4. Torigoe, 1944: 111–133. *Also see* Nakahara Zenchū, in Omachi, ed., 1959: 161–174.
5. Yanagita, ed., 1951: 544.
6. Shimabukuro Genshichi, 1950a: 138.
7. *See* Yanagita, ed., 1947: 125–151.
8. Ibid.
9. Op. cit. 128.
10. Shimabukuro Genshichi, 1950a.
11. The exact time dimension in Shimabukuro's description of community religion is not clear; it appears to vary from remote antiquity to historic present, with no distinction as to what is observation, documentation, and speculation.
12. Shimabukuro Genshichi, op. cit., 146.
13. Shimabukuro Genshichi, 1929: 169.
14. Op. cit., 171.
15. *See* Seki, 1940.

Chapter III

1. Shimabukuro Genshichi, 1950a: 142.
2. Bramsen, 1910.
3. Clement, 1902.
4. Yanagita, ed., 1951: 23.
5. In 1956, while in Yaeyama, I was told that a few "old" priestesses in rural villages still followed this practice in secret.
6. I had earlier thought this rite to be extinct but found that it was held in a village of eastern Shimajiri in 1960. Cole describes a similar rite among the Tinguian.
7. The Okinawan term for flatterer is *andaguchi* (oily mouth).

Chapter IV

1. According to the records of the Social Education Section, Education Division, Government of the Ryukyu Islands, in 1961 there were 5,000 Christian church members, 15,000 members of the Seichō no Ie, 20,000 members of the Sokagakkai, and in all other organized sects approximately 1,000–2,000 members. Mrs. Yuriko Mine, head of this section, regards the Christian figures as reasonably accurate and the others as somewhat inflated. These membership figures were reported by the religious organizations; but even accepting these at face value, the total is only 42,000 for the entire American-held Ryukyus, approximately 5 per cent of the population.
2. The *Ryūkyū Koku Kyū-ki* of 1731 (*see* Iha et al., 1940–41, Vol. 3: 239–251) indicates that the four settlements comprising Naha were without priestesses.
3. Norbeck, 1955: 117.
4. This section on the *yuta* is based on field work conducted during 1960 and 1961; a more detailed analysis of the subject will be presented in my forthcoming monograph, *Yuta, a Socio-Psychological Study of Shamanism.*

5. Harada, 1949: 13.

6. The term *hanji* also applies to the fortunetellers (*sanjinsoo*), but *hanji-gami* is reserved exclusively for the shamans.

7. Miyara (1925) reports a legend given by some Anna Mura residents that they were originally itinerant doll-play performers from Kyoto who were stranded while performing in Okinawa and were then forced into this lowly occupation.

8. The term *nimbuchaa* also has the meaning of "leper" in some areas of Okinawa.

9. Sakima, 1936: 87.

Chapter V

1. Spencer, 1931: 95–97.

2. Shimakura and Majikina, 1952: 22–23.

3. Higaonna, 1950*a*: 101.

4. Tamura, 1927: 74; Higaonna, 1950*a*: 101; Arakaki, 1955: 41.

5. This belief in the priority of Kudaka as the first settlement predominates in southern and central Okinawa, where most of the population is concentrated.

6. Miyagi Shinji, 1954: 237.

7. Yanagita, 1950.

8. Ibid., 179.

9. Doolittle, 1876, Vol. 2: 83; Gamble, 1954: 376.

10. Miyagi Shinji, 1954: 271.

11. Spencer, 1931.

12. Iha, 1922.

13. Ibid., 34.

14. "The frequent expression 'shaman family' (*wu chia*) seems to suggest that the profession was often hereditary. But in Ch'i (northern Shantung) such an expression would have had no meaning, for there every family was a shaman family: 'among the common people the eldest daughter is not allowed to marry. She is called the "shaman child" (*wu-erh*) and is in charge of the family's religous rites. This custom still (i.e., *ca.* A.D. 80) persists.' " (Waley, 1955: 10.)

15. Miyagi Shinji, 1954: 143.

16. Spencer, 1931: 98.

17. Glacken, 1955; Kerr, 1958.

18. Miyagi Shinji, 1954: 71–143.

19. *See* Yanagita, ed., 1947: 125–151.

20. Concerning the protohistoric ruler Pimikwo (*ca.* third century A.D.?), Groot (1948: 31) writes, "From the description given by the Chinese annals, we can derive that Pimikwo was a 'shaman.' She was not married, and devoted herself to the cult of the gods. The people respected her orders as being of divine authority. She lived in a storied palace surrounded by a stockade and guarded by soldiers. She has 1000 attendants. As the medium of communication between the queen and the people, there was only one man, her own brother, who assisted her in government."

21. Sakima, 1926*b*: 53.

22. Ibid., 56–57.

23. Ibid., 58.

24. Ibid., 59.

25. Ibid., 62.

26. Not to be confused with the homonym *chimi*, meaning "sin" ('tsumi').

27. Old Okinawans refer to these by the names of the principal castles: Nachijin-gusuku (Hokuzan), Suigusuku (Chuzan), Ufu Zatugusuku (Nanzan), or Tamagusuku (Nanzan). In the latter case, the Tamagusuku is regarded as older and more sacred.

28. It is significant, I believe, that Shō Hashi came from Sashiki Majiri, adjacent to the Chinen-Kudaka area.

29. In every old village of commoner origin, one kin group is recognized as the oldest and, within that, one house is regarded as the founding house. Usually, this house is referred to as *kuni muutu* (village origin) or as *niiyaa* (root house). The first daughter of this house becomes *niigami*. Higa (1950: 149) contends that the Okinawan village developed from a single kin group hamlet.

30. Miyagi Shinji, 1954: 133.

31. Although passing an examination was mandatory for entrance into the bureaucracy, this alone did not suffice to obtain a job for lower-ranking gentry; the support of a sponsor or patron from the nobility was usually required in addition.

32. In the kingdom, all upper-class houses and the living quarters or shrine-residences of priestesses, village level and above, were given a house name to which was suffixed the word *udung* or *tunchi*. There were three grades of *udung* for the nobility, and two classes of *tunchi* for the gentry; distinctive house styles characterized each. The main shrine-residence for the *chifijing* was called Chifijing Udung; in the villages, the shrine-residence for the *nuru* was and still is referred to as *nundunchi* (*nuru nu tunchi*).

33. Spencer, 1931: 105–106.

34. Miyagi Shinji, 1954: 134–135.

35. Iha, 1922: 32; Miyagi Shinji, 1954: 109.

36. Miyagi Shinji, (1954: 128–129) lists 49 *nuru* in the 136 villages of Kunigami (northern Okinawa), which gives a simple average of 1 *nuru* per 2.7 villages. The *Ryūkyū Koku Kyū-ki* (*see* Iha et al., 1940–41, Vol. 3: 240–251) indicates 99 *nuru* in the 167 villages of Shimajiri (southern Okinawa), which gives a simple average of 1 *nuru* per 1.7 villages. My survey of 120 villages showed that this relatively greater concentration in the southern area still holds true.

37. Iha, 1922: 47–48.

38. Origuchi, in Shimabukuro Genshichi, 1929: 23 (introduction).

39. Kerr, 1958: 104.

40. Iha, 1938: 147–149.

41. *Anganashii* is a contraction of *amu ganashii*, *amu* meaning "mother" and *ganashii* being an extremely polite honorific.

42. In Yaeyama several priestesses related that the period between the summer rice harvest and fall planting was formerly regarded as the new year period and that no festivals were held during the eighth lunar month, which was considered sacred. Among some of the Taiwan aborigines, this same period is still regarded as the new year.

43. I was informed by an Okinawan scholar and by a close relative of the last *chifijing* that, actually, from this date a dowager queen was eligible for the office, and that the office was never given to a married woman.

44. Kerr, 1958: 208.

45. Origuchi, in Shimabukuro Genshichi, 1929: 23 (introduction).

Chapter VI

1. Higa, 1950: 149.

2. Loc. cit.

3. As noted before, the original four communities of Naha did not have an organized hierarchy of priestesses, but the Sobe Ufu Amu officiated at certain rites held there.

4. It is my impression, based on field work in the southern Ryukyus and study of literature on the northern Ryukyus, that the local lineage predates the sib. The Okinawan type of *munchu* organization is not found elsewhere in the Ryukyus, except where migrants have moved in from Okinawa. Moreover, on Okinawa proper it tends to be strongest in the southern and central areas.

5. *See* note 2, Chapter VII, for a definition of *hara*.

6. The term *kumi* is both Japanese and Okinawan and refers to a collectivity of persons, not to a geographic unit per se.

7. The total area of a given village, including all fields and house sites, is subdivided into a number of areas called *haru*. In Kanegusuku, for example, there are a total of eight *haru* today. Often, the *haru* are named with reference to location in the residential area, which constitutes the heart of the village territory. Village houses tend to face in a southerly direction to gain full advantage of the sun for light and the prevailing cool breeze in summer; hence, the fields to the east and west of the house sites are frequently designated *iri-baru* (west *haru*) and *agari-baru* (east *haru*). North of the village (i.e., behind the housing area) is *kushi-baru* (back *haru*); south of the village, in front of the houses, is *mee-baru* (front *haru*). Other *haru* may bear the names of streams or prominent landmarks; a beach area might be referred to as *hama-baru*.

8. *See* Kitahara, 1957, for a study of pseudo-moieties in rural Japan.

9. The highest-ranking administrative position was hereditary, but this man did not reside in the area administered; he occupied an office in the capital.

10. This amounted to somewhat more than $1,000 by current value; it was a staggering amount, far beyond the capacity of a peasant.

11. The exact meaning of these words is unknown to me and my informants. Numerous writers have suggested that *nuru* is cognate to the Japanese 'norito,' a Shinto prayer or ritual. My guess is that it derives from the verb *nuiing* ('noru'), meaning "to ride on" and used figuratively to indicate spirit possession; the *nuru* also rode a horse in making her ceremonial rounds of the villages. As for *kumui*, Origuchi (in Shimabukuro Genshichi, 1929: 20) states that it was an honorific term for someone with an official position.

12. Higa (1950: 152) notes that during the kingdom villagers were moved and new villages established by administrative action.

13. Shimabukuro Genshichi, 1950*a*: 146.

14. No exact translation can be offered for *shiidu*; it generally applies to a male *kaminchu* or to a male having direction over some activity. In Shuri, the leader of the *nimbuchaa*, who was not one himself, was called *shiidu* and was contacted to engage the services of a *nimbuchaa* for a funeral. In rural communities, male *kaminchu* are often designated *shiidu* or *shiidu-gami*; thus, the *niitchu*, as the highest-ranking male *kaminchu*, may be termed *ufu shiidu* (great *shiidu*).

15. This would be at the hearth in their house of birth.

16. This tends to be more common in southern Okinawa and in satellite villages.

17. Shimabukuro Genshichi, 1929.
18. Ibid., 34.
19. Nakamura, 1952.
20. *See* note 7, Chapter III.
21. Tawada (1951: 148) states that *mbashi* provides an effective remedy for staunching a rapid flow of blood.

Chapter VII

1. The exact etymology of *munchu*, which is usually transcribed with the characters for "gate" and "middle," is conjectural. It is commonly said to derive from *mung* (gate) and *tchu* (person or persons); there is no obvious cognate in Japanese or Chinese; the closest approximation appears to be the Korean 'munchung,' transcribed with the same characters. *Uji* seems cognate with the old Japanese term 'uji,' meaning "clan." In practice, either class may employ the term *munchu* when speaking of its kin group.

2. This term has been widely mistranslated as "belly," due to the Okinawan practice of transcribing it with the character for "belly" in Japanese. In this instance, however, the character has been employed solely for its phonetic value rather than for any ideological significance. Properly, *hara* has the meaning of "side" or "line" in Okinawan. Moreover, the Okinawan term for "belly" is *wata*, not the Japanese 'hara,' so the distinction is obvious. Higa (1952: 196) has clarified this misconception, and my informants indicated his interpretation to be correct. Watanabe (Yanagita, ed., 1947: 255) states that *hara* means both "tomb" and *munchu*; in its widest application, *hara* designates only a segment of a *munchu*. Moreover, *hara* and *haka* (tomb) are not synonymous. Sometimes the *haru*, or area name within a village where a main tomb and senior lineage are located, may be taken for the group name and/or tomb name; perhaps this is the source of Watanabe's confusion.

3. *See* pp. 105, 107. Beginning in 1724, the government encouraged impoverished gentry to migrate from Shuri into the rural areas, where they established new farming communities. What percentage of the total upper-class population these emigrants constituted could not be determined.

4. Higa, 1952: 195.

5. E.g., Gusukuma to Shiroma, Arakachi or Arakaki to Shingaki, Yuji to Yogi, etc.

6. An exception exists in the case of descendants of the former ruling Shō family.

7. I do not regard this lack of consistency in naming daughters and younger sons as necessarily reflecting devolution resulting from extensive cultural change.

8. Within the upper-class ranks there was also a preference for hypergamy.

9. This excludes new residents whose principal social contacts may still be in the villages.

10. Some commoner *munchu* claim upper-class origin by virtue of the fact that their first ancestor was the offspring of an upper-class man and a commoner woman. Since these unions could not be legitimized, the child was excluded from membership in the father's *uji* and usually from the mother's *munchu* as well; thus, when this child reached maturity and created a family of his own, he became the founder of a new kin group. I have heard such *munchu* jokingly referred to as *winagu munchu* (female *munchu*); however, the recognized founding ancestor is not the woman but her son.

11. Higa, 1952: 195.

12. Watanabe (Yanagita, ed., 1947: 255) errs in referring to the common tomb as *ajisoi* (sic) *baka*; the *ajishii* in an old *munchu* denotes a small tomb where the founder is believed to be interred.

13. The bones of overseas migrants also have been returned for burial in the kin group tomb.

14. Yanagita, ed., 1947: 255–256.

15. Since a woman is buried in her husband's tomb, the *kudii* and her husband would have to be members of the same kin group for her to be accorded this respect.

16. There is some difference of opinion as to when an ancestor becomes a *kami*. Some believe that this occurs after the thirty-third anniversary of death, when the last memorial rites are held; others hold that it takes place three or four generations after death, when no acquaintances of the deceased are still alive.

Chapter VIII

1. Murdock, 1949: 48.

2. Glacken, 1953: 109.

3. In some villages there was formerly an annual rite, led by the *nuru* and village officials, in which the *kami* of the funeral palanquin was asked to lead the oldest members of the community, by order of age, to their death. Informants said that this was done to relieve the drain on the food supply.

4. Haring, 1952: 26, 85.

GLOSSARY

aa nu shirigafuu nu umachii. Millet-thanksgiving, communal rite held during sixth lunar month.

abushi-baree. Cleaning the ridges (that divide the fields), communal rite of fourth lunar month; alternate name: *mushi-baree.*

agari mai, agai maai. Eastern tour; formerly an annual pilgrimage to the sacred sites on the southeast coast conducted by the state priestesses.

aji, anji, andzu. Formerly a hereditary rank in the nobility; earlier, the feudal lord or chieftain of a *majiri.*

aji nu yuu. Age of the *aji,* the feudal period.

ajishii, ajishii-baka, aji-baka. Tomb of a sib founder.

akamataa. Male snake spirit.

ama-gui. Rain-asking rites.

amami, amami kang ganashii, amami kami nu ganashii mee. Heaven *kami;* more commonly, *ting nu kami.*

Amamiko, Amamiku, Amamikyo, Amamikyu. Name listed in old accounts for the female sibling creator deity.

amanchu. Heaven people, the mythical first settlers of Okinawa.

ama nu yuu. Age of heaven, the age of the *amanchu;* also called *kami nu yuu.*

amichujiing. To purify the body with water.

anganashii. See *ufu amu.*

atai. Lot or turn; a woman appointed to collect ritual funds and to assist the priestesses of a sib.

atu tushibii. Second year-day, the second occurrence of one's birth-year day in the first lunar month, sometimes an occasion for domestic rites.

Bideeting. 'Benten' or 'Benzaiten' in Japanese; 'Sarasvati' in Sanskrit; one of the three *kami* enshrined at Chifijing Udung in Shuri.

bijuru. Divining stone.

binshii. A wooden container for rice grains, incense, and wine used in sib and communal rites.

booji. 'Bozu'; Buddhist priest.

buchidang. 'Butsudan'; household ancestral altar; also called *guriijing.*

chatchi. First son.

chatchi-bara. First-son line, the senior lineage of a patri-sib.

chichung. To hear; in a religious sense, to hear the voice(s) of the spirit(s).

chifijing, chifijing ganashii mee. Chief priestess of the Okinawan kingdom.

chigari. Pollution.

chigarimung. A person or thing that is polluted.

chii. A general term denoting "spirit."

chiiji. 'Keizu'; genealogy.

chiji. The particular *kami* or remote ancestral spirit served by a priestess or shaman; the concept also includes the meaning of being heir to this spirit.

chijiing. To screen off, to fence off, to taboo.

chikasa. Formerly a priestess in the national religious hierarchy who served a younger brother of the ruler. *Chikasa kumui:* polite term for a *chikasa.*

chikuzaki. 'Kiku sake'; chrysanthemum wine, a domestic rite of the ninth lunar month.

chimbee. See *ufu amu.*

chimi. A priestess who provided ritual support for an *aji.*

chinumaki. A garland of leaves worn by priestesses during a ceremony.

chiruunin. Immigrants or sojourners; newcomers to a rural area.

chiitatiyaa. A shaman who specializes in divination.

duu-wachi. Self-recognition; used with reference to a prospective shaman or *kudii* who promptly recognizes a call to office, thereby escaping supernatural punishment (*taari*).

fafuji. See *uya fafuji.*

fichi. Connection; used as a suffix meaning "lineage."

fiidama. Fireball or meteor; usually a malevolent spirit.

fii-geeshi nu ugwang. Prayer to send away fire, communal rite of tenth lunar month.

fii nu kami, fii nu kang. Fire *kami,* hearth deity.

firugi. Splinter; used as a suffix meaning "lineage."

fungshi. Chinese 'feng shui'; wind and water, a key concept of geomantic lore, but commonly conceived of as a *kami.*

funi nu kami. Boat *kami,* patron of the boatbuilder.

futuki. 'Hotoke'; ancestor or ancestral spirit (in the male line).

fuuchi nu kami. Bellows *kami,* patron of the blacksmith.

fuuchi nu yuuwee. Bellows rites, conducted by blacksmith in eleventh lunar month.

fuuru-gami. *Kami* of the pigpen or toilet.

gukuraku. 'Gokuraku'; Buddhist paradise.

guriijing. 'Goreizen'; see *buchidang.*

gwansu chiji. Ancestor *chiji*; see *chiji.*

haarii, haari-buni. Boat race (Chinese dragon boat race), communal rite of the fourth day of the fifth lunar month.

hachi-baru. First field, ceremonial tour of all family land on first day of new year.

hachi gwachi juuguya. Fifteenth night of eighth month, domestic rite for moon *kami.*

hachika soogwachi. Twentieth day of new year, domestic rite marking formal end of New Year season; corresponds to *yama-birachi* in rural areas.

hachi mujukui. First fruits, first-fruits rite.

hachi ubii nadii. First sacred-water stroking, domestic rite performed with first water drawn from well on New Year's Day; see *ubii nadii.*

hachi ugwang. First prayers of new year.

hachi unchi. First fortune, the first fortunetelling rite of the new year for an individual or family.

haka, paka. Tomb.

hakusoo. 'Hyakushō'; commoner.

hama urii. Descent to the beach for purification in salt water.

hanji. An old term signifying the diviner (*sanjinsoo*); now applied to *yuta* as well.

hanshi nu taari. One of the female assistants to the chief priestess of the Okinawan kingdom.

hara. Line or side; used as a suffix meaning "lineage."

haru. Field or area, a local division of a village.

haru yaadui. See *yaadui.*

hijainna. Taboo rope.

ibi, ibi ganashii mee. Spirit of ancestral founder of a village, usually located in the sacred grove (*utaki*); believed to be a female spirit.

ichiining. To curse.

ichijama. Sorcery.

ichijamaa. Sorcerer.

ichi mabui. Live *mabui*, the spirit of a living person; see *mabui*.

ichimung. 'Ichimon'; lineage.

iifee. 'Ihai'; ancestral tablet(s); also *tootoomee*.

ii-gami, ii-gang. See *utchi-gami*.

imi. 'Yume'; dream.

imi-gukuchi. Dreamlike feeling or sensation, hallucination, waking vision.

ishigantuu. A stone with three characters, placed at crossroads and places of entrance to ward off malevolent spirits; sometimes called *keeshi*.

jiinchu. Natives, the original settlers of a village, in contrast to *chiruunin*.

jii nu kami, jiitchi, jiitchi nu kami. Earth *kami*.

jiishigaami. Funerary urn.

jingamii. Treasurer, sib official.

jituu. Steward; formerly the governor of a district (*majiri*).

juuhachiya. Night of the eighteenth, domestic rite in upper-class homes for Kwannung.

Juuninsuu. Council of Ten; formerly a state committee for religious matters.

juusanya. Night of the thirteenth, domestic rite in upper-class homes for Kwanting.

kaa nu gufungshi. *Fungshi* of the well; technically, the geomantic evaluation of a well, but commonly used as another term for well *kami*.

kaa nu kami. *Kami* of the well or spring.

kaasa muchi. *Kaasa* cake, a minor domestic rite of the twelfth lunar month.

kaatchii. Summer solstice, domestic rite of the fifth lunar month.

kai-baka. A temporary tomb used by a segment of the kin group, far removed from the main common tomb.

kakaimung. Attachment or thing caught, a supernaturally imposed sickness or affliction regarded as a sign or notification from the spirit world.

kami. Deity.

kami arabi. *Kami* curse afflicting a group.

kami ashagi. A thatched roof supported by poles or stone pillars and without walls, used as the major site for public rites conducted by the community priestesses.

kami ashibii. *Kami* play, a period of feasting, drinking, and dancing following a major community rite.

kami choodee. *Kami* sibling, the ritual pairing of *kudii* as *uminai* (sister) and *umikii* (brother).

kami-daari. *Kami* curse afflicting an individual; also *taari*.

kami-gutu. *Kami* matters.

kaminaa. *Kami* name, divine name for a *kami* or a high-ranking priestess.

kaminchu. *Kami* person, a religious functionary charged with conducting rites for a group; may also be applied to a shaman.

kaminchu ashibii. *Kaminchu* play or recreation, a private celebration for religious functionaries following a major rite.

kami nu yuu. The age of the *kami*, the beginning of the world; also called *ama nu yuu*, the age of heaven.

kami ushiimii. An annual rite of the second or third lunar month for the founder of a sib; see also *shiimii*.

kamizaki. Ceremonial wine; also *miki*.

kanabui. An inborn capacity enabling certain people to see ghosts.

kaniuchi. A euphemism for *nimbuchaa*.

karanaa. Chinese name (used by upper classes in contrast to their Okinawan names); also called *toonaa*.

karii. Luck.

karii-yanjung. To break luck.

kashira. Head or chief, of village, sib, or age group.

katchimiing. To catch; used to indicate spirit possession.

keeshi. That which sends back; a term applicable to any object that has the power to deny entrance or to repel malevolent spirits, principally applied to the *shiishi* and *ishigantuu*.

kibui. Smoke; a numerical classifier for counting houses; also used with reference to a house tax levied by the sib.

kibui nu amu. Mother of the house (obsolete).

kijimung, kijimunaa. A tree spirit associated with the Indian banyan.

kudii, kudingwa. Sib priestess; sometimes called *munchu-gami* or *munchu kaminchu*.

kumi. Group, a collectivity of persons, as in *wakamung-gumi*.

kuni muutu. Country origin, the founding house of a village; see also *niiyaa*.

Kunkung Ganashii Mee. One of the three *kami* enshrined at Chifijing Udung in Shuri.

kuruu. Blackie, black one; applied to an individual ostracized from all communal activities.

kuyumi. Lunar almanac, a basic reference for a fortuneteller.

Kwannung. 'Kwannon'; Buddhist goddess of mercy.

Kwanting. Chinese god of war, 'Kuan ti.'

mabui. The vital, life-sustaining human spirit; see *ichi mabui, shini mabui*.

mabui-gumi. Replacing a lost or dropped *mabui*.

mabui nugi. Withdrawal of *mabui* from the body (in response to action of an external, supernatural agency).

mabui uti. Dropping the *mabui*, usually from shock or fright.

machigee. Mistakes; in a religious sense, erroneous or improper ritual action.

majimung, majimunaa. Ghost.

majiri. Originally a feudal fief, the domain of an *aji*, but from the end of feudalism (early sixteenth century) until 1907, a government district encompassing a dozen or more villages; equivalent to Japanese 'son.'

mani-gutu. A form of atavism with a negative, disvalued connotation; simulating the action of an ancestor.

mansang. Full birth, a rite of passage held for a child six days after birth; also called *ruku nichi mansang*.

matchii, umatchii. 'Matsuri'; rite, ceremony.

mee ashagi. See *tunchi-yaa*.

mee tushibii. First year-day, the day coinciding with one's birth year during the first twelve days of the new year, regarded as a birthday, an occasion for domestic rites.

Mihira. The three wards of Shuri, capital of the kingdom.

miisa, miigusoo. New Year for the dead, domestic rite on sixteenth day of first lunar month.

miji-gami. Water *kami*.

miji nu shirigafuu. Thanksgiving for water, communal rite of tenth lunar month.

miki. Ceremonial wine; also *kamizaki*.

minnuku. An inedible food offering, used as a lure for malevolent spirits to prevent theft of edible food offerings to the ancestors.

mitama. 'Magatama'; a large, comma-shaped, stone jewel worn by the chief priestess of a village.

Mitunchi. The three shrines—Shun-dunchi, Makang-dunchi, and Jibu-dunchi—in Shuri, presided over by the *ufu su nu mee*.

muji nu fuu ugwang. Prayers for wheat ears, a communal rite of the second lunar month.

muji nu shirigafuu nu umachii. Wheat-thanksgiving ceremony, a communal rite of the third lunar month.

mujukui nu hachi. First-fruits rite.

munchu. Patri-sib; commonly used with reference to a commoner sib, but may be applied to the upper-class *uji* as well.

munchu-gami. See *kudii*.

munchu-gashira. *Munchu* chief, hereditary leader of a patri-sib, the eldest male in the founding house.

munchu kaminchu. See *kudii.*
muni agi. Ridgepole raising, a house-construction rite.
mura. Village, a single community constituting a basic political and religious unit; used interchangeably with *shima.*
mura ugwanju. The ritual sites of a community; also, *shima ugwanju.*
musang. Layman; one lacking knowledge of *kami* matters.
mushi-baree. Insect eradication, communal rite of fourth lunar month; alternate name: *abushi-baree.*
mutariing. To possess, to hold, to carry; used to describe spirit possession.
muutu-yaa. Origin house; any parent house within the patrilineage or patrisib.
naka munchu. Middle *munchu,* a localized lineage which has branched off from a senior lineage in another community.
nanka. Seventh, name for one or all of the seven memorial rites held during a forty-nine-day period after death. These occur on the seventh (*hachi*), fourteenth (*ta*), twenty-first (*mi*), twenty-eighth (*yu*), thirty-fifth (*ichi*), forty-second (*mu*), and forty-ninth (*nana*) days after death.
nanka nu suku. End of the seventh, a domestic rite occasioned by removal of all New Year's decoration on seventh day of new year.
nanui-gashira. Initial-character name; initial Chinese character in personal name shared by all male members of an upper-class patri-sib.
nchabi. Equinox, an occasion for domestic rites in the second and eighth lunar months.
niibichi. Uprooting, marriage.
niibu-tui. Ladler, a male *kaminchu* in the village, charged with serving ceremonial wine to the priestesses during a ritual.
niigami, niigang. Root *kami,* second-ranking community priestess, usually the eldest daughter of the founding house of the community.

niigang-yaa. See *niiyaa.*
Niiree Kanee, Giree Kanee. 'Nirai Kanai'; a name found in early accounts, said to be an island in the eastern seas, the place of origin of the Okinawan people; not a part of current belief.
niitchu. Root person, highest-ranking male *kaminchu* in the village, usually the eldest son of the founding house; alternate name: *ufu shiidu.*
niiyaa. Root house, the founding house of a community, the house of a *niigami;* also *niigang-yaa.*
nimbuchaa. One who recites *nimbuchi;* the Okinawan pariah, charged with bell ringing and reciting the Buddhist invocation at funerals; all were members of the Jōdō sect.
nimbuchi. 'Nembutsu'; the Buddhist invocation.
nma-dima, nma-zaki. Horse fine, horse 'sake'; a fine paid by women who married outside the village in violation of the endogamous rule.
nma n jaa, nnjaa. Horse caretaker; see *nma-tui.*
nma-tui. Horse leader, a male *kaminchu* in the village, charged with leading the horse of the chief priestess; alternate name: *nma n jaa* or *nnjaa.*
nma-zaki. See *nma-dima.*
nmari-dushi. Birth year, one's year of birth reckoned according to the twelve animal signs of the calendar; its recurrence every twelfth year is thought to render one more susceptible to misfortune.
nni nu fuu ugwang. Prayers for rice ears, a communal rite of the fifth lunar month.
nni nu shirigafuu nu umachii. Rice-thanksgiving, a communal rite of the sixth lunar month.
nuiing. To ride, to ride on or in; used to describe spirit possession.
nujifa. An exorcistic rite for leading a lost spirit to the tomb.
nundunchi. Shrine-residence of the *nuru,* chief village priestess.

nuru, nuru kumui. Chief village priestess.

nuru chikusai. Nuru's group, all community *kaminchu* serving the *nuru*; sometimes specifically the female *kaminchu* serving her.

nuru-gami. Personal *kami* spirit of the chief village priestess; usually equated with the spirits of her predecessors.

nuru-ji. *Nuru's* field(s), the hereditary landholdings of the chief priestess of a village; they were not subject to reallocation under the communal land tenure system.

peeku. In the patri-sib, the administrative assistants to the sib chief or head.

ruku nichi mansang. See *mansang.*

ruugu, duugu. 'Ryūgu'; in Okinawan belief, the residence of the sea *kami*, but in China and Japan, a dragon palace located on the bottom of the sea.

saa. The rank or value of an individual's spirit.

saadaka. High *saa.*

saadakachu. High-*saa* person; used with reference to a *kaminchu.*

saadakasang. High *saa.*

saadaka nmari. High-*saa* birth; used with reference to one destined to become a *kaminchu.*

sagai gwansu. See *ugwanbusuku.*

sagung-gami. Searcher *kami*, a male *kaminchu* in the village, charged with collecting ritual offerings or ritual fees from the villagers; see *saji.*

sajakai. See *saji.*

saji. Receiver; in the village, a male *kaminchu* charged with collecting ritual offerings or ritual fees; in the patri-sib, a female elected to this responsibility; also *sajakai.*

saki. A distilled alcoholic beverage averaging from 20 to 40 per cent alcohol; Okinawan *saki* is called 'awamori' in Japanese.

sang. A taboo sign made from a twisted loop of straw or grass.

sangwachi ashibii. Play or outing of the third month, an island-wide observance of the third day of the third lunar month, when all women visit the sea.

sanjinsoo. Fortuneteller.

sannanmung. A young woman selected to chew grain for fermenting ceremonial wine.

san nichi takabi, yu nichi takabi. Three-day notification, four-day notification; a communal rite to notify the *kami* of a forthcoming ceremony.

sheeku nu kami. Carpenter *kami*, patron of the carpenter or woodworker.

shiidu, shiduu. A male leader; in ritual matters a male *kaminchu.*

shii. Spirit; probably the common term for all concepts of spirit.

shiimii. 'Sei mei' (Japanese); 'ching ming' (Chinese); the major sib and family rite of the year, observed at the tombs on a day between the twenty-second day of the second lunar month and the third day of the third lunar month; see also *kami ushiimii*, which occurs during the same period.

shiishi. 'Karashishi'; a pottery or stone lion placed on the roof or at places of entrance to a village for the purpose of warding off malevolent spirits; alternate name: *keeshi.*

shiishi mooyee. Lion dancing, a communal rite of the eighth lunar month performed by the village youth with a large lion mask.

shiji. Spirit power of the *kami*; a vague concept with possible animatistic characteristics; a force perhaps detachable from the *kami*; also used for the spirit in a male line.

shijidakadukuru. High-*shiji* place, a place which harbors great *shiji* power; used with reference to the sacred grove (*utaki*).

shijidakasang. High *shiji*, of high *shiji.*

shijidaka nmari. High-*shiji* birth; used with reference to the higher-ranking female *kaminchu.*

shiji kamiing. To place *shiji* on the head, the act of receiving *shiji*, performed by a *kaminchu* on taking office.

shiji nu kata. *Shiji* line or side, the male line or side.

shiji nu nmaga. *Shiji* grandchild, a grandchild in the male line.

shima. Island, but also commonly used as a term for village; a synonym for *mura*.

shimagusarasaa, shimagusarashii. A communal rite often held during the eighth lunar month or on any occasion of pestilence to rid the community of malevolent spirits believed to be the cause of sickness.

shimanpee. Village parent, an elderly male charged with cleaning village ritual sites under the direction of the chief priestess.

shima ugwanju. See *mura ugwanju*.

shiminchu. Ink person; formerly, a commoner who could read.

Shinerikyo, Shinerikyu, Shineriku. Name listed in old accounts for the male sibling creator deity.

shini mabui. Spirit of a dead person; see *mabui*.

shinugu. A communal ceremony of the seventh or eighth lunar month, usually accompanied by masked rites.

shirashi. Notification.

shirigafuu nu ugwang. Prayers of thanks.

shiruhirashii. Right-hand chamber of a tomb, used for temporary interment prior to bone washing.

soogawachigwa. Little New Year, a domestic rite of the fourteenth day of the first lunar month.

soogwachi gwantang. New Year's Day rite.

suudee. 'Sodai'; a male elected or appointed to the duty of collecting ritual offerings or ritual fees from the villagers; in many areas this office has replaced the hereditary *sagung-gami* and *saji*.

suu-gumi. Father group, the middle-age group in the old village.

suu muutu. Head or chief origin house, the founding house of a patri-sib; alternate name: *ufu muutu*.

taa nu kami. Paddy *kami*.

taari. See *kami-daari*.

tabi ugwang. Travel prayers, a domestic rite to insure a safe return for the journeyer.

tachi-yaa. Branch house; alternate name: *wakari-yaa*.

takidaki. Ritual sites, usually of a community.

tamutugi. A log within the *kami ashagi* on which the higher-ranking priestesses are seated during ritual.

tantui. See *tantui nu umachii*.

tantui nu umachii. Paddy-sowing rite, a communal rite of the ninth lunar month.

tatti ugwang. Prayers of asking or supplication.

teeku-gami, teeku shiidu. Drum *kami* or drum *shiidu*, a male *kaminchu* in the village, charged with care of the ceremonial drum(s).

tiida-gami. Sun *kami*.

tiifichee. Hand holders; formerly, a technique for detecting persons guilty of a crime; all members of the village were herded into a small area and required to find nonrelative partners; those who had difficulty in doing so were considered guilty.

ting nu kami. Heaven *kami*, vaguely regarded as supreme; also *uting nu kami*.

toonaa. Chinese name; see *karanaa*.

tooshii. Left-hand chamber of a tomb, used for permanent interment after bone washing.

tootoomee. Ancestral tablets; also, *iifee*.

tuchi nu ufu yakuu. State diviner, a high politico-religious office in the Okinawan kingdom until the early part of the eighteenth century.

tunchi. A gentry residence or that of a high-ranking priestess; the term was suffixed to the house or shrine name.

tunchi-yaa. Shrine containing a hearth and altars belonging to a community and/or a patri-kin group; alternate name: *mee ashagi*; also *tung* or *tung-yaa*.

tung, tung-yaa. See *tunchi-yaa*.

tunjii. Winter solstice, a domestic rite of the eleventh lunar month.

tushibii. Year-day; technically, any day which has the same animal sign as one's birth year, but used with reference to its first occurrence in the new year (i.e., during the first twelve days), when one is automatically considered a year older irrespective of actual birthdate; see *mee tushibii*.

tushi nu yuruu. New Year's Eve.

ubii. Lustral water.

ubii nadii. Water stroking, placing a few drops of water on the forehead in homage to the well *kami* or water *kami*.

ubuku. Cooked rice used as an offering.

ubung. 'Obon'; Buddhist festival for the dead, held during seventh lunar month, thirteenth through fifteenth or sixteenth day.

uchatoo. Tea used as an offering.

uchiwa shiidu. Fan *shiidu*, a male *kaminchu* in the village, charged with fanning the chief priestess during ceremonies.

udung. Residence of a noble.

ufu amu, ufu ang. Great mother, a priestess in charge of a large population center; also *anganashii, chimbee*.

ufu-gui. Great solicitor, the senior assistant to the chief priestess of the Okinawan kingdom.

Ufu Jimi Nu Mee. One of the three *kami* enshrined at Chifijing Udung in Shuri.

ufu muutu. Great origin, the founding house of a patri-sib; alternate name: *suu muutu*.

ufu niigami. Great *niigami*, the senior *niigami* by hereditary rank in those communities which have two or more *niigami*; alternate name: *waka nuru*.

ufu shiidu. Great *shiidu*, the highest-ranking of the male *kaminchu* in the village; more commonly called *niitchu*.

ufu shirigafuu. Great thanksgiving, a communal rite of the twelfth lunar month.

ufu shuu mee. Great father, the king of Okinawa.

ufu su nu mee. A national priestess in charge of one of the three regions of Okinawa.

ufu suu-gumi. Grandfather group, the village elders.

ugamisaa. A shaman specializing in prayer as a principal means of curing.

ugwanbusuku. Insufficiency of worship (believed to be a common cause of misfortune); also called *sagai gwansu*.

ugwang. Prayer.

ugwanju. Praying place; any site of regular worship.

uji, uji munchu. An upper-class patri-sib.

ukoo. Incense.

ukudii. Honorific for *kudii*.

ukudji. Divination by lots (usually rice grains).

umachii. 'Omatsuri'; ceremony or rite.

umamui. 'Omamori'; protective talisman or amulet.

umeeii. See *utchi-gami*.

umichimung. The three-stone hearth, representing the hearth or fire *kami* (*fii nu kang*).

umiki. Ceremonial rice wine.

umikii-gami. Brother *kami*, the male sibling creator deity; alternate name: *wikii-gami*.

uminai-gami. Sister *kami*, the female sibling creator deity; alternate name: *winagu-gami*.

umui. A religious song; usually recorded as 'omoro' in Japanese 'kana.'

unaraurii. Installation ceremony for the chief village priestess (*nuru*) and, formerly, for any of the national priestesses of higher rank.

unchi. Fortune.

un-dumi. Sea closed, a taboo on fishing or entering the sea.

uni. Demon.

unjami. Sea *kami*.

unjami machii. Sea-*kami* ceremony, a communal rite of the seventh lunar month to increase the fish supply.

uranaisaa. A diviner or shaman specializing in fortunetelling.

uruu-dushi. An intercalary year.

usakati. 'Sake' fee, a ritual tax imposed on the members of a community or sib.

ushiimii. See *shiimii.*

utakabi. An inviting or notifying ceremony for the *kami* performed by the *kaminchu* three or four days in advance of a major rite; also *san nichi takabi.*

utaki. 'Otake'; sacred grove.

utchakaiing. To lean on; also used to indicate spirit possession.

utchi-gami. A female *kaminchu* serving the chief priestess of a village and functioning in the latter's place when she is polluted; sometimes called *ii-gang* or *umeeii.*

utchi nu hanshi. One of the female assistants to the chief priestess of Okinawa.

utuku. 'Tokonoma'; a decorative alcove located in the living room, frequently used as a place of prayer.

utuushi. Worship from afar, praying through to a religious site far distant.

uya fafuji, fafuji. Ancestor(s) (without any connotation of lineality).

wachi jichi. One of the female assistants to the chief priestess of Okinawa.

wakamung-gumi. Youth group, the age group including all unmarried youth of the village; in recent decades superseded by the national 'seinendan.'

waka nuru. See *ufu niigami.*

wakari-yaa, tachi-yaa. 'Bunke'; branch house.

wikii-gami. See *umikii-gami.*

winagu-gami. See *uminai-gami.*

winagu nati. Becoming female; a temporary ceremonial transvestism formerly required of males entering the *utaki.*

winagungwa chiji. Daughter *chiji*; see *chiji.*

yaa. House.

yaadui. Field settlement, a non-nucleated village, usually founded by upper-class settlers; also *haru yaadui.*

yaa nu naa, yaa n naa. 'Yago'; household name.

yaa tachung, yaa wakaiing. To establish a branch house.

yabuu. A healer who sometimes employs prayer or magical formulas.

yagamayaa. Noisy house, an informal meeting place for unmarried youth of the village.

yama-birachi. Opening the mountain, a communal rite of the twentieth day of the first lunar month ending the taboo on entering the mountain areas.

yama-dumi. Mountain closed, a taboo on entering the fields and /or the wooded or mountainous areas.

yanakaji. Malevolent wind (believed capable of causing disease).

yanamung. Malevolent spirit.

yanamung-baree. To exorcise a malevolent spirit.

yashichi-gami. *Kami* of the house lot.

yashichi nu gufungshi. *Fungshi* of the house lot; technically, the geomantic evaluation of a house lot, but commonly interpreted as another name for house-lot *kami.*

yugumui. Seclusion of a priestess (or priestesses) for one or more nights in a shrine or sacred grove prior to a major ceremony.

yukatchu. Good people, the upper classes.

yumi chiji. Daughter-in-law *chiji*; used with reference to a priestess who obtains office by marrying into a household.

yung nu miitu. Night (time) couple; a young, unmarried couple permitted to sleep together in the woman's home, usually during the man's term of bride service.

yuta. Shaman.

BIBLIOGRAPHY

WESTERN SOURCES

Abbreviations

AA   *American Anthropologist*, Menasha, Wisconsin.
AJPA   *American Journal of Physical Anthropology*, Philadelphia.
AJS   *American Journal of Sociology*, Chicago.
BMFJ   *Bulletin de la Maison Franco-Japonaise*, Tokyo.
FEQ   *Far Eastern Quarterly*, Lancaster, Pennsylvania.
JAF   *Journal of American Folklore*, Richmond, Virginia.
JRAI   *Journal of the Royal Anthropological Institute*, London.
MN   *Monumenta Nipponica*, Tokyo.
SIRI   *Scientific Investigations in the Ryukyu Islands*, Pacific Science Board, National
        Research Council, Washington, D.C.
SWJA   *Southwestern Journal of Anthropology*, Santa Fe, New Mexico.
TASJ   *Transactions of the Asiatic Society of Japan*, Tokyo.

Allport, Gordon W.
    1950. *The Individual and His Religion*. New York.
Anonymous
    1879. "The Quarrel between China and Japan." *The Japan Gazette*, November 26.
    1892. "Letter From Riukiu." *The Japan Weekly Mail*, April 23: 563–565.
    1904. *Summary of the Land Adjustment in the Okinawa Prefecture*. Compiled by "The
        Temporarily Organized Okinawa Prefecture Land Adjustment Bureau."
        Tokyo (?).
Aston, W. G.
    1905. *Shinto, The Way of the Gods*. London.
Bennett, Henry B.
    1946. "The Impact of Invasion and Occupation on the Civilians of Okinawa."
        U.S. Naval Institute Proceedings, 72: 263–275.

Bettelheim, B. J.
1850. "Letter Giving an Account of his Residence and Missionary Labors in Lewchew During the Last Three Years." *Chinese Repository* (Canton), 19: 17–49, 57–89.
n.d. *Loochoo Mission 1850–52.* London.
Binkenstein, R.
1943. "Taichū Shōnin." *MN*, Vol. 6: 219–232.
Bramsen, William
1910. "Japanese Chronology and Calendars and Japanese Chronological Tables." *TASJ*, 37: 1–303.
Brinkley, Frank
1883. "The Story of the Riukiu (Loochoo) Complication." *The Chrysanthemum*, 3: 122–153.
Brunton, R. H.
1876. "Notes Taken During a Visit to Okinawa Shima, Loochoo." *TASJ*, 4 (1st Series): 66–77.
Bull, Earl R.
1958. *Okinawa or Ryukyu: The Floating Dragon.* Newark (Ohio).
Burd, William W.
1952. *Karimata—A Village in the Southern Ryukyus.* SIRI Report No. 3.
Cary, Otis
1909. *A History of Christianity in Japan.* 2 vols. London.
Chamberlain, Basil Hall
1893. "Manners and Customs of the Loochooans." *TASJ*, 21 (1st Series): 271–289.
1895a. "Comparisons of the Luchuan and Japanese." *TASJ*, 23 (1st Series): XXXI–XLI.
1895b. "Essay in Aid of a Grammar and Dictionary of the Luchuan Language." *TASJ*, 23 (1st Series), Supplement: 1–272.
1895c. "The Luchu Islands and their Inhabitants." *The Geographical Journal*, 5: 289–319, 446–462, 534–545.
1896. "A Preliminary Notice of the Luchuan Language." *JRAI*, 26: 47–59.
Clark, Charles A.
1932. *The Religion of Old Korea.* New York.
Clement, Ernest W.
1902. "Japanese Calendars." *TASJ*, 30 (1st Series), Pt. 1: 1–82.
Clutterbuck, Walter J.
1910. "The Lu Chu Islands." *Travel and Exploration*, 4, No. 20: 6–88.
Cohen, Yehudi
1958. "Commercialized Prostitution in Okinawa." *Social Forces*, 37: 160–168.
DeGroot, J. J. M.
1910. *The Religion of the Chinese.* New York.
Doolittle, Justus
1876. *Social Life of the Chinese.* 2 vols. New York.
Embree, John F.
1939. *Suye Mura, A Japanese Village.* Chicago.
1941. "Some Social Functions of Religion in Rural Japan." *AJS*, 47, No. 2: 184–189.
Fink, Harold
1947. "The Distribution of Blood Groups in Ryukyus." *AJPA*, 5, No. 2: 159–163.

Ford, Clellan S.
1950. "Occupation Experience on Okinawa." *The Annals of the American Academy of Political and Social Science*, 267: 175–182.

Furness, William H.
1899. "Life in the Luchu Islands." *Bulletin of the Museum of Science and Art* (University of Pennsylvania), 2, No. 1.

Gamble, Sidney
1954. *Ting Hsien, a North China Rural Community.* New York.

Glacken, Clarence J.
1953. *Studies of Okinawan Village Life.* SIRI Report No. 4.
1955. *The Great Loochoo.* Berkeley.

Groot, Gerard
1948. "An Essay on Early Japanese History." *TASJ*, 1 (3rd Series): 24–46.
1951. *The Prehistory of Japan.* New York.

Gubbins, J. H.
1881. "Notes Regarding the Principality of Loochoo." *The Japan Gazette*, August 6, August 8.

Guillemard, F. H. W.
1889. *The Cruise of the Marchesa to Kamchatka and New Guinea with notices of Formosa, Liu Kiu, and Various Islands of the Malay Archipelago.* London.

Hacker, W. R.
1951. "The Kuril and Ryukyu Islands." In Otis W. Freeman, ed., *Geography of the Pacific.* New York.

Haguenauer, M. C.
1929–30. "Melanges Critiques." *BMFJ*, 2, No. 3–4.
1931. "Relations du royaume des Ryukyu avec les pays des mers du sud et la Corée." *BMFJ*, 3, No. 1–2.

Hall, Basil
1818. *Account of a Voyage of Discovery to the West Coast of Corea and the Great Loo Choo Island.* Philadelphia.

Halloran, Alfred L.
1856. *Eight Months Journal.* London.

Haring, Douglas G.
1949. "Japan and the Japanese, 1868–1945." In Ralph Linton, ed., *Most of the World.* New York.
1952. *The Island of Amami Oshima in the Northern Ryukyus.* SIRI Report No. 2.
1953. "The Noro Cult of Amami Oshima: Divine Priestesses of the Ryukyu Islands." *Sociologus*, 2: 108–121.
1954. "Comment on Field Techniques in Ethnology Illustrated by a Survey in the Ryukyu Islands." *SWJA*, 10: 255–267.

Hattori, Shirō
1948. "The Relationship of Japanese to the Ryukyu, Korean, and Altaic Languages." *TASJ*, 1 (3rd Series): 101–133.

Holtom, D. C.
1940. "The Meaning of Kami." *MN*, 3: 1–27, 392–413.

Hsu, Francis
1952. *Religion, Science and Human Crisis.* London.

Karasik, Daniel D.
1948. "Okinawa: A Problem in Administration and Reconstruction." *FEQ*, 7: 254–267.
Kerr, George H.
1958. *Okinawa: The History of an Island People.* Rutland (Vermont).
Kidder, J. Edward
1959. *Japan before Buddhism.* New York.
Komai, T., and G. Fukuoka
1936. "Frequency of Multiple Births Among the Japanese and Related Peoples." *AJPA*, 21: 433–447.
Lanman, Charles
1880. "The Islands of Okinawa." *The International Review*, 8: 18–27.
La Rue, Adrian Jan Pieters
1951. "The Okinawan Classical Songs, an Analytical and Comparative Study." Ph.D. dissertation, Harvard University.
Laufer, Ludwig G.
1953. "Cultural Problems Encountered in the Use of the Cornell Index Among Okinawan Natives." *The American Journal of Psychiatry*, 109: 861–864.
Leavenworth, Charles S.
1905. *The Loochoo Islands.* Shanghai.
Lieban, Richard W.
1955. "The Land System of Kudaka Island." *Sociologus*, 5: 150–156.
1956. "Land and Labor on Kudaka Island." Ph.D. dissertation, Columbia University.
Ling, S. S.
1955. "Bone-washing Burial Customs and Ancestral Bone Worship in Southeast Asia and Around the Pacific." *Academia Sinica Annals*, 2: 175–194.
Maretzki, Thomas W.
1957. "Child Rearing in an Okinawan Community." Ph.D. dissertation, Yale University.
Marett, R. R.
1908. "The Conception of Mana." *Transactions of the Third International Congress for the History of Religions*, Vol. 1. Oxford.
Moloney, James Clarke
1945. "Psychiatric Observations on Okinawa Shima: The Psychology of the Okinawan." *Psychiatry*, 8: 391–399.
1954. *Understanding the Japanese Mind.* New York.
—— and Charles R. Biddle
1945. "A Psychiatric Hospital in Military Government." *Psychiatry*, 8: 400–401.
McLeod, John
1818. *Voyage of His Majesty's Ship Alceste along the Coast of Corea, to the Island of Lewchew, with an account of Her subsequent Shipwreck.* London.
Murdock, George P.
1949. *Social Structure.* New York.
Newman, Marshall T., and Ransom Eng
1947a. "The Ryukyu People, a Biological Appraisal." *AJPA*, 5 (New Series): 391–399.
1947b. "The Ryukyu People, a Cultural Appraisal." *Annual Report, Smithsonian Institution*: 379–406. Washington.

Norbeck, Edward
  1952. "Pollution and Taboo in Contemporary Japan." *SWJA*, 8: 269–285.
  1954. *Takashima, a Japanese Fishing Community.* Salt Lake City.
  1955. "Yakudoshi, a Japanese Complex of Supernatural Beliefs." *SWJA*, 11:
        105–120.

Nuttonson, M. Y.
  1952. *Ecological Crop Geography and Field Practices of the Ryukyu Islands, Natural
        Vegetation of the Ryukyus, and Agro-climatic Analogues in the Northern Hemi-
        sphere.* Washington.

Passin, Herbert
  1955. "Untouchability in the Far East." *MN*, 11: 27–47.

Perry, Matthew C.
  1856. *Expedition of an American Squadron to the China Seas and Japan performed in
        the years 1852, 1853, and 1854.* 2 vols. Washington.

Pitts, F. R., W. P. Lebra, and W. P. Suttles
  1955. *Post-War Okinawa.* SIRI Report No. 8.

Satow, Ernest
  1872. "Notes on Loochoo." *TASJ*, 1 (1st Series): 1–8.

———— and Karl Florenz
  1927. "Ancient Japanese Rituals." *TASJ* Reprints, 2: 5–164.

Schwartz, Henry B.
  1907. *The Loo Choo Islands, A Chapter of Missionary History.* Tokyo.
  1908. *In Togo's Country.* New York.
  1909. "Christian Work in the Liu-Chiu Islands." *The Christian Movement in Japan,*
        7: 204–212. Tokyo.
  1910. "Japan's Oldest Colony." *Japan Magazine,* 1: 84–91.
  1910. "A Wedding in Loo Choo." *Japan Magazine,* 1: 405–408.

Shiratori, Kurakishi
  1936. "The Liu Chiu Words in the Sui-Shu." *Memoirs of the Research Department
        of the Tōyō Bunko,* 8: 1–29. Tokyo.

Simon, Edmund M. H.
  1913. *Beitrage zur Kenntniss der Riukiu-Inseln.* Leipzig.
  1914. "The Introduction of the Sweet Potato into the Far East." *TASJ,* 42 (1st
        Series): 711–726.
  1927. "Der Feuergott der Riu-kiu Inseln." *Deutsche Gesellschaft fur Natur-und
        Volkerkunde Ostasiens, Nachrichten aus der Gesellschaft,* 8: 4–5.

Simon, Gwladys Hughes
  1952. "Some Japanese Beliefs and Home Remedies." *JAF,* 65: 281–293.

Smith, Allan H.
  1952. *Anthropological Investigation in Yaeyama.* SIRI Report No. 1.
  1958. "Dactyloglyphic Characteristics of the Natives of Kabira, Southern Ryukyu
        Islands, and Their Implications for the Ainu Substratum Hypothesis."
        Unpublished paper presented to annual meeting of the American Anthro-
        pological Association, Washington, D.C., November 23, 1958.

Smith, Allan H.
  1960. "The Culture of Kabira, Southern Ryukyu Islands." *Proceedings of the
        American Philosophical Society,* 104: 134–171.

Smith, George
  1853. *Lewchew and the Lewchewans.* London.
  1861. *Ten Weeks in Japan.* London.
Smith, Trude
  1961. "Social Control in a Southern Ryukyuan Village." *Research Studies* (Washington State University), 29: 51–76, 151–174, 175–209.
Spencer, Robert Steward
  1931. "The Noro, or Priestesses of Loo Choo." *TASJ*, 8 (2nd Series): 94–112.
  1937. "Some Materials for the History of Religion." In Genchi Kato, ed., *Commemoration Volume: The 25th Anniversary of the Foundation of the Zaidan Hojin Meiji Seitoku Kinen Gakkai or Meiji Japan Society:* 137–142. Tokyo.
Steiner, Paul E.
  1947. "Okinawa and Its People." *The Scientific Monthly*, 44: 233–241, 306–312.
Taeuber, Irene
  1955. "The Population of the Ryukyu Islands." *Population Index*, 21: 233–263.
Tigner, James L.
  1954. *The Okinawans in Latin America.* SIRI Report No. 7.
United States Army, General Headquarters, Commander-in-Chief, Far East
  1950. *The Ryukyu Islands—Pre-War Population and Employment Census Data for 1940 and 1944.* Tokyo.
United States Civil Administration Ryukyus
  1952–60. *Civil Affairs Activities in the Ryukyu Islands.* 1–8. Naha.
United States Department of the Navy, Office of the Chief of Naval Operations
  1944. *Civil Affairs Handbook: Ryukyu Islands.* Washington.
United States Office of Strategic Services
  1944. *Okinawan Studies*, No. 1, 2, 3. Honolulu.
Waley, Arthur
  1955. *The Nine Songs, a Study of Shamanism in Ancient China.* London.
Weber, Max
  1951. *The Religion of China*, tr. Hans H. Gerth. Glencoe (Illinois).
Weiss, Leonard
  1946. "United States Military Government on Okinawa: Aims and Methods of the Naval Administration in Restoring a Shattered Island Society." *Far Eastern Survey*, July 31: 234–238.
Williams, S. Wells
  1885. "Notices of Fu-sang, and Other Countries Lying East of China, Given in the Antiquarian Researches of Ma Twan-lin." *Journal of the American Oriental Society*, 11: 89–116.
  1910. "A Journal of the Perry Expedition to Japan (1853–1854)." *TASJ*, 37, Pt. 2 (1st Series): 1–259.
Wirth, Albrecht
  1897. "The Aborigines of Formosa and the Liu Kiu Islands." *AA*, 10: 357–370.
Yang, C. K.
  1961. *Religion in Chinese Society.* Berkeley and Los Angeles.

JAPANESE SOURCES

Abbreviations

H	*Hōgen* 方言		[Dialect], Tokyo.
JZ	*Jinruigaku Zasshi* 人類学雑誌		[Journal of Anthropology], Tokyo.
M	*Minzoku* 民族		[Ethnology], Tokyo.
MD	*Minkan Denshō* 民間傳承		[Folklore], Tokyo.
MK	*Minzokugaku Kenkyū* 民族学研究		[Ethnological Studies], Tokyo.
NM	*Nihon Minzokugaku* 日本民俗学		[Japanese Folklore], Tokyo.
R	*Ryūkyū* 琉球		[Ryukyu], Naha.
RC	*Rekishi Chiri* 歴史地理		[History and Geography], Tokyo.

Arakaki Magoichi 新垣孫一
1955. *Ryūkyū hasshō-shi* 琉球発祥史
[History of Ryukyu Origins].
Mawashi.

Harada Toshiaki 原田敏明
1949. "Buraku saishi ni okeru sha-manizumu no keikō" 部落祭祀におけるシャマニズムの傾向
[Shamanistic Tendencies in Village Rites]. *MK*, 14: 7–13.

Hattori Shirō 服部四郎
1955a. "Gengo-nendaigaku sunawachi goi-tōkeigaku no hōhō ni tsu-ite" 「言語年代学」即ち「語彙統計学」の方法について
[On the Method of Glotto-chronology or Lexico-statistics]. *MK*, 19: 100–101.
1955b. "Okinawa hōgen no gengo-nendaigaku-teki kenkyū" 沖縄方言の言語年代学的研究
[A Glotto-chronological Study of Okinawan Dialects]. *MK*, 19: 142–151.

Higa Shunchō 比嘉春潮
1926. "Okinawa hontō no kamika-kushi" 沖縄本島の神隠し
[Spirit Capture on Okinawa]. *M*, 1: 377–378.
1950. "Okinawa no sonraku soshiki" 沖縄の村落組織
[Structure of the Okinawan Rural Community]. *MK*, 15: 149–152.
1952. "Shuri no munchu to saishi" 首里の門中と祭祀
[Religious Rites and the *Munchu* of Shuri]. *MD*, 16: 194–199.
1960. *Okinawa no rekishi* 沖縄の歴史
[Okinawan History]. Naha.

Higaonna Kwanjun
東恩納寛惇

1907-1908. "Kyū-Ryūkyū no kaikyū seido" [The Class System of Old Ryukyu]. *RC*, 9: 369-374, 483-487; 10: 591-594.
舊琉球の階級制度

1918. "Kyū-Ryūkyū no ikai seido" [The Court Rank System of Old Ryukyu]. *RC*, 31: 27-37, 153-158.
舊琉球の位階制度

1925. *Ryūkyū jinmei-kō* [A Study of Ryukyuan Names]. Tokyo.
琉球人名考

1950a. "Okinawa rekishi gaisetsu" [An Outline of Okinawan History]. *MK*, 15: 101-108.
沖縄歴史概説

1950b. *Nantō fudoki* [A Gazetteer of the Southern Islands]. Tokyo.
南島風土記

Iha Fuyū
伊波普猷

1916. *Ko-Ryūkyū* [Old Ryukyu]. Tokyo.
古琉球

1919. *Okinawa josei-shi* [History of Okinawan Women]. Tokyo.
沖縄女性史

1922. *Ko-Ryūkyū no seiji* [The Government of Old Ryukyu]. Tokyo.
古琉球の政治

1938. *Ryūkyū gikyoku jiten* [Dictionary of Ryukyuan Drama]. Tokyo.
琉球戯曲辞典

1942a. *Okinawa-kō* [Okinawan Studies]. Tokyo.
沖縄考

1942b. *Onari-gami no shima* [The Island of Onari-gami]. 2nd ed. Tokyo.
をなり神の島

—— Higaonna Kwanjun, and Yokoyama Shigeru, eds.
伊波普猷・東恩納寛惇 横山重 編

1940-41. *Ryūkyū shiryō sōsho* [Ryukyu Historical Material Series]. 5 vols. Tokyo.
琉球史料叢書

Kanaseki Takeo
金関丈夫

1955. "Yaeyama guntō no kodai bunka" [The Ancient Culture of the Yaeyama Islands]. *MK*, 19: 107-141.
八重郡島の古代文化

Kawamura Tadao
  1942. *Zoku Nampō bunka no tankyū*
        [Sequel to an Investigation of
        the Southern Culture]. Tokyo.

河村只雄
  続南方文化 の 探究

Kinjō Chōei (Kanagusuku Chōei)
  1934. "Shuri-Naha hōgen ni okeru
        shinzoku kankei no go ni tsuite"
        [On the Kinship Terms of the
        Shuri-Naha Dialects]. *H*, 4: 50–
        59.
  1944. *Naha hōgen gaisetsu*
        [An Outline of the Naha Dia-
        lect]. Tokyo.
  1952. "Okinawa," in *Nihon shakai
        minzoku jiten*
        [A Dictionary of Japanese So-
        ciety and Folk Customs]. Vol. I:
        103–112. Tokyo.

金城朝永
  首里那覇方言における親族
  関係の語に就いて

  那覇方言概説

  沖縄
  日本社会民俗辞典

Kitahara Machiko
  1957. "Nihon ni okeru sōbunsei"
        [The Dual System in Japan].
        MK, 21: 207–212.

北原眞智子
  日本における双分制

Kokubu Naoichi
  1957. "Kudaka Shima no san-gatsu
        no matsuri"
        [The Third Month Ceremony
        of Kudaka Island]. *NM*, 4,
        No. 4: 52–63.

国分直一
  久高島の三月の祭

Kyūgakkai rengō Amami Ōshima kyōdō
chōsa iin-kai

[Nine Learned Societies' Amami Oshima
Joint Reserach Committee]
  1959. *Amami: shizen to bunka*
        [Amami: Nature and Culture].
        2 vols. Tokyo.

九学会連合庵美大島共同
調査委員会

  庵美：自然と文化

Mabuchi Tōichi
  1952. "Okinawa to Taiwan"
        [Okinawa and Taiwan]. *MD*,
        16: 394–399.

馬淵東一
  沖縄と台湾

Miyagi Eishō
  1954. "Okinawa Kunigami chihō no
        nōkō girei"
        [Agricultural Rites in the Kuni-
        gami Region, Okinawa]. *NM*,
        2, No. 2: 117–129.

宮城栄昌
  沖縄国頭地方の農料
  儀礼

Miyagi Shinji
1954. *Kodai Okinawa no sugata*
[Aspects of Ancient Okinawa].
Naha.
1956. "Yambaru no mura"
[Yambaru Villages]. *R*, 4: 15–65.

Miyamoto Engen
1952. "Okinawa Kunigami no shinugu matsuri"
[The *Shinugu* Ceremony of Kunigami, Okinawa]. *MD*, 16: 296–
301.

Miyara Tōsō (Miyanaga Masamori)
1925. Okinawa no ningyō shibai
[Puppet Shows of Okinawa].
Tokyo.
1934. *Nantō sōkō*
[Studies on the Southern Islands].
Tokyo.
1950. "Ryūkyūgo gairon"
[An Outline of the Ryukyuan
Languages]. *MK*, 15: 125–135.
1953. "Ryūkyū minzoku to sono
gengo"
[The Ryukyuan People and
Their Language]. *MK*, 18: 369–
379.

Nakahara Zenchū
1950. "Omoro no kenkyū"
[Studies of the *Omoro*]. *MK*,
15: 153–165.

Nakamura Takao
1952. "Namahage oboegaki"
[Notes on *Namahage*]. *MK*, 16:
311–320.

Okuno Hikorokurō
1952. "Nantō mura naihō"
[Inner Law of Villages in the
Southern Islands]. *Hōmu shiryō*
[Judicial Affairs Materials], Vol.
320. Tokyo.

Omachi Tokuzo et al., eds.
1959. *Nihon minzokugaku taikei*
[An Outline of Japanese Folk
Culture]. Vol. 12. Tokyo.

Origuchi Harumi
1950. "Shidō wo chūshin ni"
[On the *Shidō*]. *MK*, 15: 358–359.

宮城真治
古代沖縄の姿

山原の村

宮本演彦
沖縄国頭のシヌグ祭

宮良当壯
沖縄の人形芝居

南島叢考

琉球語概論

琉球民族とその言語

仲原善忠
おもろの研究

中村たかを
なまはげ覚書

奥野彦六郎
南島村内法

大間知篤三 他編
日本民俗学大系

折口春洋
勢頭を中心に

Ōtō Tokihiko
　1940. "Kamado to irori"
　　　　[Oven and Hearth]. *JZ*, 55,
　　　　No. 629: 119–123.
　———— et al., eds.
　1957. *Fūdoki Nihon: Kyūshu-Okinawa-*
　　　　hen
　　　　[A Gazetteer of Japan: Kyushu-
　　　　OkinawaVolume].Vol.1.Tokyo.

Sakima Kōei
　1926*a*. "Ko-Ryūkyū no nyonin seiji"
　　　　[Female Government in Old
　　　　Ryukyu]. *M*, 1: 637–652.
　1926*b*. *Nyonin seiji-kō*
　　　　[A Study of Female Govern-
　　　　ment]. Tokyo.
　1936. *Shima no hanashi*
　　　　[Island Tales]. Tokyo.

Segawa Kiyoko
　1948. "Okinawa no kon'in"
　　　　[Okinawan Marriage]. *MK*, 13:
　　　　285–296.
　1960. "Okinawa no josei"
　　　　[Okinawan Women]. *NM*, 12:
　　　　1–22.

Seki Keigo
　1940. "Hebi muko-iri hanashi no
　　　　bumpu"
　　　　[Distribution of the Serpent-
　　　　Bridegroom Folktale]. *MK*, 6:
　　　　439–472.
　1952. "Okinawa no mura-mura"
　　　　[The Villages of Okinawa].
　　　　MD, 16: 55–64.

Shimabukuro Genshichi
　1929. *Yambaru no dozoku*
　　　　[Local Customs of Yambaru].
　　　　Tokyo.
　1950*a*. "Okinawa no minzoku to shin-
　　　　kō"
　　　　[Religion and Folk Customs in
　　　　Okinawa]. *MK*, 15: 136–148.
　1950*b*. "Kisetsu iri narabi ni yashiki-
　　　　gami"
　　　　[Kami of the Household and
　　　　Seasons]. *MK*, 15: 148.

Shimabukuro Genichirō
　1952. *Okinawa rekishi*
　　　　[Okinawan History]. Naha.

大藤時彦
　かまどといろり

大藤時彦 他論
　風土記日本：九州
　沖縄篇

佐喜眞興英
　古琉球の女人政治

女人政治考

シマの話

瀬川清子
　沖縄の婚姻

沖縄の女性

関敬吾
　蛇智入譚の分布

沖縄の村々

島袋源七
　山原の土俗

沖縄の民俗と信仰

季節入並に屋敷神

島袋源一郎
　沖縄歴史

Shimabukuro Zempatsu, ed.-in-chief
1937. *Nantō ronsō*
[Studies of the Southern Islands].
Naha.

島袋全発 編
南島論叢

Shimakura Ryūji and Majikina Ankō
1952. *Okinawa issennen-shi*
[A Thousand-Year History of
Okinawa]. 4th ed. Naha.

島倉龍治・真境名安興
沖縄一千年史

Suda Akiyoshi
1950. "Jinruigaku kara mita Ryūkyūjin"
[Physical Anthropology of the
Ryukyuans]. *MK*, 15: 109–116.

須田昭義
人類学からみた琉球人

Tamura Hiroshi
1927. *Ryūkyū kyōsan sonraku no kenkyū*
[A Study of Communal Villages
in the Ryukyus]. Tokyo.

田村浩
琉球共産村落之研究

Tawada Shinjun
1951. *Okinawa yakuyō shokubutsu ya-
kukō*
[Medicinal Uses of Okinawan
Pharmaceutical Plants]. Naha.

多和田真淳
沖縄薬用植物薬効

Torigoe Kenzaburō
1940. "Kodai Ryūkyū sonraku ni
okeru miko soshiki"
[The *Miko* System in the Ancient
Ryukyuan Community]. *MK*,
6: 473–497.
1944. *Ryūkyū kodai shakai no kenkyū*
[A Study of Ancient Ryukyuan
Society]. Tokyo.

鳥越憲三郎
古代琉球村落に於ける
巫女組織

琉球古代社会の研究

Uchida Sueko
1907. "Ryūkyūjin no butsuji ni kansuru gishiki"
[Ceremonies Related to the
Buddhism of Ryukyuans]. *JZ*,
22, No. 253: 293–296.

内田寿之子
琉球人の仏事に関する
儀式

Watanabe Masutarō
1940. "Ryūkyū no dōzokudan ni
tsuite"
[On the Ryukyuan Kin Group].
MK, 6: 498–518.

渡辺萬寿太郎
琉球の同族団について

Yanagita Kunio
1950. "Kaijingu-kō"
[Notes on the Sea-*Kami* Palace].
MK, 15: 178–193.

柳田国男
海神宮考

—— ed.
  1947. *Okinawa bunka sōsetsu*
         [Essays on Okinawan Culture].
         Tokyo.
  1951. *Minzokugaku jiten*
         [A Dictionary of Folk Culture].
         Tokyo.
  1955–1956. *Sōgō Nihon minzoku goi*
         [A Comprehensive Japanese Folk
         Culture   Dictionary].   5 vols.
         Tokyo.

Yawata Ichirō
  1950. "Ryūkyū senshigaku ni kansuru
         oboegaki"
         [Some Notes on the Prehistory
         of the Ryukyus]. *MK*, 15: 117–
         124.

Yohena Kōtarō
  1960. *Ryūkyū nōson shakai-shi*
         [History of Ryukyuan Farm
         Village Society]. Naha.

Yonaguni Zenzō
  1953. *Okinawa rekishi nempyō*
         [A Chronology of Okinawan
         History]. Tokyo.

柳田国男 編
沖縄文化叢説

民俗学辞典

綜合日本民俗語彙

八幡一郎
琉球先史学に関する覚書

饒平名浩太郎
琉球農村社会史

与那国善三
沖縄歴史年表

INDEX

Adoption practices, 160–162
Age groups, 127–128
Age reckoning, 48
Ancestors. *See* Spirit concepts, *futuki*

Birth order: and inheritance of rank, 156; and kinship terminology, 180–181
Bone washing. *See* Rites, bone washing
Booji. See Buddhist priest
Buddhism: shallowness of belief in, 66; recency in Okinawan history, 99; spread facilitated by Japanese missionaries, 118; as cult of dead, 119–120
Buddhist altar and tablets, 25, 182–183
Buddhist priest (*booji*), 88–89

Calendar (lunar): and susceptibility to misfortune, 36–37; and ritual practices, 47–49
Chifijing. See State priestesses
Chiji. See Spirit concepts, *chiji*
China: evidence of prehistoric contacts with Okinawa, 10; cultural ties with Okinawa, 11–13; influence on religious policies of kingdom, 117–120
Class. *See* Social class
Community organization: 124–129; ritual moieties, 123; households, 124–126; lineages, 126; neighborhoods, 126; age groups, 127–128; religious, 133–139
Community priestesses:
nuru, secluded life in past, 58; establishment of office, 108–109; chief priestess of community, 134–135
niigami, 135–136; possibly chief priestess in past, 105
Community rites. *See* Rites, community

Community ritual sites: 139–142; *utaki*, 139–140; *kami ashagi*, 140; *nundunchi*, 141; *tunchi-yaa*, 141–142; *niiyaa*, 142; misc., 142
Community social control, 129–133
Cursing, 40

Death rites. *See* Rites, death, memorial
Defilement of sacred place, 34
Disease. *See* Health and supernatural concepts
Divination. *See* Rites, divining and fortunetelling
Dress. *See* Ritual, dress, paraphernalia

Education: Japanese, 9; of shaman, 82

Family, Chapter VIII. *See also* Kin group; Household
Fii nu kang. See Hearth; Spirit concepts, *fii nu kang*
Fire. *See* Hearth
First son: and family leadership, 154; inheritance of father's rank, 156; pivotal position, 180
Food, diet, 4. *See also* Ritual feasting and offerings
Fortuneteller (*sanjinsoo*), 85–88
Futuki. See Spirit concepts, *futuki*

Genealogies: 162–163; government office attesting to accuracy, 118
Geomancy. *See* Rites, geomantic
Ghosts (*majimung*). *See* Spirit concepts, *majimung*

239